THE COLLAPSE OF THE EASTERN MEDITERRANEAN

As a 'Medieval Warm Period' prevailed in western Europe during the tenth and eleventh centuries, the eastern Mediterranean region, from the Nile to the Oxus, was suffering from a series of climatic disasters which led to the decline of some of the most important civilizations and cultural centres of the time. This provocative study argues that many well-documented but apparently disparate events – such as recurrent drought and famine in Egypt, mass migrations in the steppes of central Asia, and the decline in population in urban centres such as Baghdad and Constantinople – are connected and should be understood within the broad context of climate change. Drawing on a wealth of textual and archaeological evidence, Ronnie Ellenblum explores the impact of climatic and ecological change across the eastern Mediterranean in this period and offers a new perspective on why this was a turning point in the history of the Islamic world.

RONNIE ELLENBLUM is professor at the Hebrew University of Jerusalem and a life member of Clare Hall, University of Cambridge. He is the author of the prize-winning *Crusader Castles and Modern Histories* (Cambridge, 2007). His first book, *Frankish Rural Settlement in the Latin Kingdom of Jerusalem* (Cambridge, 1998), has become a standard work for the study of Crusader geographies.

# THE COLLAPSE OF THE EASTERN MEDITERRANEAN

## *Climate Change and the Decline of the East, 950–1072*

RONNIE ELLENBLUM
*The Hebrew University of Jerusalem*

CAMBRIDGE
UNIVERSITY PRESS

CAMBRIDGE UNIVERSITY PRESS
Cambridge, New York, Melbourne, Madrid, Cape Town,
Singapore, São Paulo, Delhi, Mexico City

Cambridge University Press
The Edinburgh Building, Cambridge CB2 8RU, UK

Published in the United States of America by Cambridge University Press, New York

www.cambridge.org
Information on this title: www.cambridge.org/9781107688735



First published 2012
3rd printing 2013
First paperback edition 2013

*A catalogue record for this publication is available from the British Library*

*Library of Congress Cataloguing in Publication Data*
Ellenblum, Ronnie
The collapse of the eastern Mediterranean : climate change and the decline of the East,
950–1072 / Ronnie Ellenblum.
pages cm
Includes bibliographical references.
ISBN 978-1-107-02335-2
1. Islamic Empire. 2. Social change – Mediterranean Region – History – To 1500.
3. Climate and civilization – Middle East – History – To 1500.
4. Climatic changes – Social aspects – Middle East – History – To 1500 5. Mediterranean
climate. 6. Middle East – Climate – History – To 1500. I. Title.
DS38.3.E45 2012
909′.09822401–dc23
2012004204

ISBN 978-1-107-02335-2 Hardback
ISBN 978-1-107-68873-5 Paperback

# Contents

# Maps and figures

MAPS



FIGURES

# Tables

# Acknowledgments

I wish to express my gratitude to the institutions, colleagues and friends who have helped me throughout the years to complete this book. I began working on it while I was a fellow in the Jerusalem Institute for Advanced Studies and completed it while I was a fellow in another abode of Jerusalemite knowledge – the Scholion Interdisciplinary Research Center in Jewish Studies. I would like to thank the fellows of both groups who shared ideas and knowledge with me and especially Gideon Avni, Israel Finkelstein, Gideon Shelach, Sharon Zuckerman, Nily Wazana and Irad Malkin. Generous grants from the Israel Scientific Foundation and the German–Israeli Research Foundation enabled the completion of the work.

Numerous scholars made suggestions, passed on references, pointed out my mistakes and induced me to revise my interpretations. Benjamin Z. Kedar, Ora Limor, Iris Shagrir, Robert Bartlett, Reuven Amitai, Norman Yoffee, Uri Bitan, Miriam Frenkel and Daniela Heller Talmon read the manuscript and commented on it. Other friends and scholars were patient enough to attend conferences and follow the development of the ideas. I would like to thank Peter N. Miller, Miri Rubin, Thomas Madden, Oron Shagrir, Amikam Elad, Alex Yakobson and many others. Yohay Goelle improved my English, Tamar Soffer produced the best possible maps and illustrations from my data, Adi Binnun helped me with the GIS, and Dr Uri Bitan and Dr Leigh Chipman helped me with the Arabic and Shay Eshel helped with the Greek. I owe them thanks.

I believe the thesis presented in this book should apply to the general public and not only to professional Orientalists, and therefore I made several concessions such as not using diacritics in placenames and words that can be Romanized or westernized to make it more accessible. I did use diacritics and Hijri calendars, however, for names of people and in direct transliterations from the Arabic.

The book was written while events similar to the ones therein described were shaking the entire world. Food prices were soaring, hunger prevailed in east Africa, and the Danube and the Black Sea were covered with ice. Kingdoms and realms of the eastern Mediterranean, from Tunisia through Libya to Egypt, and the bureaucracies of the same region, from Syria to Greece, undergo radical changes and are on the verge of collapse. Political and economical transformations are translated into cultural ones: religious fanaticism is leading to radical changes in the school curriculum and is impacting upon the education of future generations. The present volume suggests a common reason that led, a millennium ago, to the economic, cultural and political decline of the eastern Mediterranean. Is it possible to assume that a common reason, possibly a period of similar climatic change, is responsible for the present decline of extensive parts of the eastern Mediterranean? I leave it to readers to decide and find out.

This book is dedicated with love to my wife Lenore and to my children Gali, Yuval and Maya.

PART ONE

# *The collapse of the eastern Mediterranean*

CHAPTER ONE

# Presenting the events

This study relates the story of a series of well-documented climatic disasters that altered the face of the eastern Mediterranean in the mid eleventh century, leading to the physical decline of some of the most important civilizations and cultural centres of the time. The change was manifested in an exceedingly long series of droughts in the Nile Valley – no less than twenty-seven years of insufficient summer rises of the Nile in 125 years – that spread famine and pestilence throughout both Egypt and its neighbouring countries, in widespread droughts that affected the Levant and the eastern Mediterranean coast, and in extremely severe and long periods of freeze that affected the steppes of central Asia, Khurasan, Iran, the Jazira and Armenia. The climatic disasters began in AD 950, were very effective from the late 1020s onwards, attained their most disastrous effects during the mid 1050s, and were abated during the early 1060s (in Iran and Iraq) and the early 1070s (in Egypt and in Asia Minor).

The climatic disasters of 950–1072, however, were limited to the eastern Mediterranean and are not recorded in the western European or Iberian chronicles of the time. On the contrary, if climate is mentioned at all in contemporaneous western or Iberian chronicles, it is in the context of a period of comparative opulence and continuous calm. An imaginary line can be drawn, from Qayrawan in the southwest, through Rome and to the northern

Balkans, to divide the regions that were affected by the climatic disasters from those which were spared and enjoyed the benefits of the mild climate of the 'Medieval Warm Period' or the 'Medieval Optimum', which prevailed in the west.

## A WAVE OF NOMADIZATION AND DISLOCATION

The famines and pestilences that followed in the wake of the droughts and the cold spells led to the decimation of cities and agricultural provinces throughout the region. The cold spells, however, had additional widespread domino effects: they were followed by enormous waves of dislocation and outbound emigration of pastoralists, who left their freeze-stricken summer pastures and winter abodes, conveying violence to the neighbouring, equally drought-stricken provinces in their search for warm places, pastures, fodder and food. The lingering colds left the pastoralists with no other choice but to migrate to warmer regions and to have recourse to plunder for their own food. The domino effect was felt by countries that lay outside the region of the cold spell no less – very often much more – than it was by the countries in which the cold spells and droughts were the most severe.

## COLLAPSE OF BUREAUCRACIES

The climatic disasters were also accompanied by a collapse of bureaucratic and political institutions, which were unable to withstand the sharp decline in the state income, followed by a parallel increase in the expenditure of the state for defence against the nomads and for the supply of food for the starved populations. The economic crises led to the devaluation of currencies that reached, in the case of Byzantium, 27 per cent of the value of the nomisma during the 1050s, or to the failure of states to finance their own armies and administrations. Unpaid soldiers and bureaucrats rebelled against and toppled numerous dynasties, including the ruling dynasties in Baghdad, Constantinople (both of them collapsed in the same year, 1055–6), Cairo and elsewhere. All of these collapses followed years of severe dearth that consumed the reserves and left central government without adequate means even for the needs of the ruling elites themselves.

## THE CREATION OF NOMADIC STATEHOODS

The collapse of the well-established dynasties led, in several cases, to the creation of 'nomadic statehoods' – administrations which were created ad hoc by the victorious nomads, who found themselves in ruling positions. Such an entity is known to have existed in the past, but rarely, if ever before, do we have a detailed description of its creation and characteristics, as we have in the case of the takeover by the nomads of Baghdad, one of the most important cultural centres of the world at the time. The detailed accounts of the 'conquest' of Baghdad by the nomads contain unrivalled amounts of data concerning the development of such an entity.

## THE DECLINE OF URBAN CULTURE

Some of the major cities and urban centres of the region, from Nishapur to Fustat, from Baghdad to Qayrawan and from Ramla to Ani were pillaged and conquered, partially destroyed and virtually deserted. Even cities as big as Constantinople or Rome underwent decline at the same time.

Smaller cities that had flourished uninterrupted since the Roman period now experienced decline or abandonment. Extensive recent excavations show that many of the cities of Palestine, including Tiberias, Caesarea Maritima and Jerusalem were decimated within one decade, between the second half of the 1050s and the mid 1060s.

## DESERTION OF MARGINAL AGRICULTURAL PROVINCES

Populous agricultural regions and hinterlands in eastern Asia Minor and Ifriqiya, in the Jazira and in the Negev declined and were no longer able to sustain the cities; many of them underwent desertification and never recovered. The most obvious examples are the settlements of the Negev and Ifriqiya, two provinces that had flourished since Late Antiquity and had successfully withstood the transition from the Roman and Byzantine regimes to the Early Muslim regime. Both underwent desertification and were abandoned during the climatic disaster of the tenth to eleventh centuries, either because of the violent activities of dislocated pastoralists (as was the case with Ifriqiya) or because of the drying up of the region (as was the case in the Negev).

## DECLINE OF CULTURES

The conquest of Baghdad in 1055 coincides with the end of the period in which eastern Islam reached one of its highest intellectual achievements, known as the 'Shi'a Golden Age' or the 'Renaissance of the tenth and the eleventh centuries'. Well-known institutions of learning and knowledge, public and semi-public libraries and academies were abandoned during this period, and were replaced, during the 1060s, by different types of learning. In some of the cases, where the dispersion of learning institutions or the looting of cultural treasures and libraries are well documented, the decline of the former intellectual centres of learning can be explained by the crisis itself. In tens of other cases, we have no idea about the end and the dispersion of the previous institutions, but the period in which they disappear corresponds to that in which the violent nomadic tribes were most active. The transformation is discerned also in the disappearance of the Jewish academies (*yeshivot*) of the East and the abrupt end of the period of the 'geonim' in Baghdad (and later in Syria too).

## MINORITIES AND THE ISLAMIZATION OF THE LEVANT

Disasters intensify inter-religious strife and lead to the persecution of the undefended minorities: Christian, Zoroastrian and Jewish. Many of them were among the first to emigrate out of the region, leaving their impoverished and weakened communities behind. Christian dioceses ceased to exist, and the Christian population was reduced considerably. In some cases, persecutions were orchestrated by the authorities, probably in an attempt to direct the rage of the hungry mob away from the central administration that was unable to cater to their basic needs. Such persecutions during periods of dearth and hunger led in three separate cases to the looting and destruction of the Church of the Holy Sepulchre, to forced Islamization or to the deflection of destructive powers away from Islamic centres towards Christian ones.

All these events are well documented in contemporary literature and all the significant events were thoroughly studied by modern scholars. Dozens of chronicles written in Arabic, Greek, Syriac, Armenian, Coptic and Persian relate the history of the region at the time and describe the events in detail. The ecological crisis that hit the eastern Mediterranean during the tenth and eleventh centuries was probably the most documented climatic disaster in pre-modern history. The detailed documentation facilitates a comprehensive

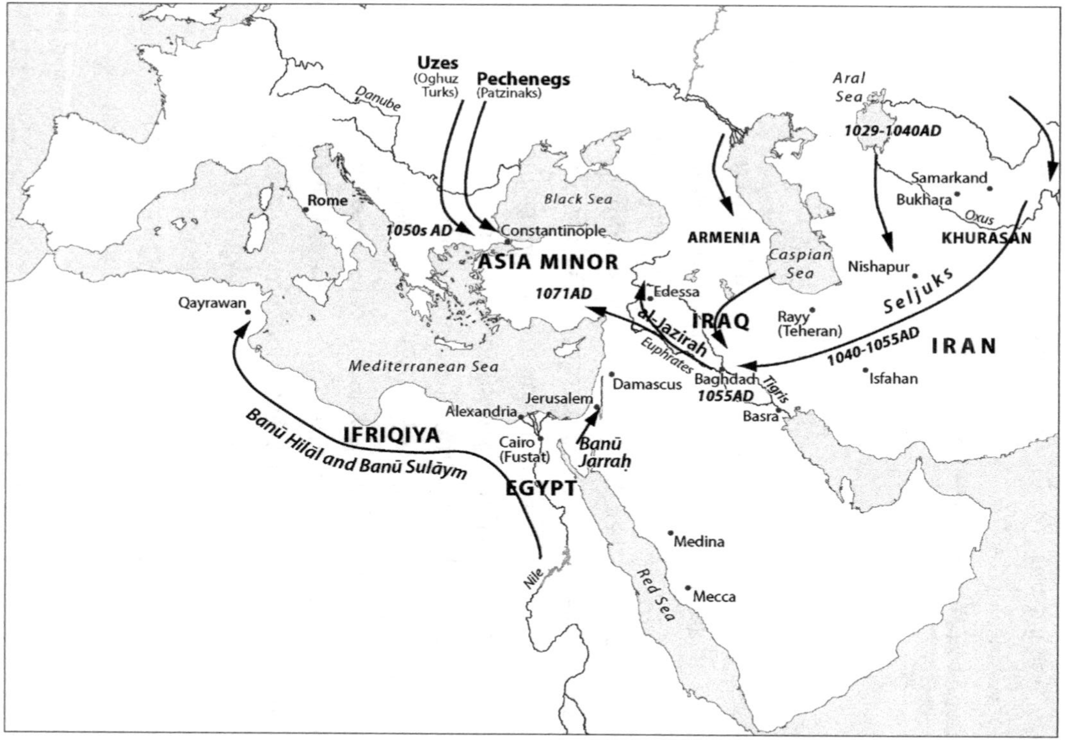


Map 1.1 Nomadizations and dislocations in the eastern Mediterranean in the eleventh century.

reconstruction – sometimes on an annual or even a monthly basis – of this ecological disaster, and it might shed a better light on the evolution of similar, quasi-epic movements of dislocated pastoralists or of the sudden collapse of seemingly stable bureaucracies in the past. The crisis affected the limited (though vast) region of the eastern Mediterranean, and while it persisted for only a comparatively short period, it affected many cultures and was described by chroniclers trained in different intellectual environments. Therefore, the various descriptions of the crisis can be compared to various 'cameras' located at different angles to document a single event and to reflect the different attitudes and interpretations of the different cultural perspectives upon a single disastrous event.

Though all the significant events were properly studied, many of the studies attempted to provide separate political or economical explanations for the events and failed to mention cross-regional and non-political characteristics, while ignoring the concurrence of many of them. Each study explored only a part of a puzzle that is played out on a regional scale. Different and wider levels of analysis and interpretation are required, however. Thus, for example, the studies that refer to the disappearance of the age-old Jewish *yeshivot* of Babylon do not refer to the events in Iran and Mesopotamia at the same time, or to the activities of the Oghuz Turks in these regions, which occurred in that same period. The scholars who dealt with the crumbling of the Macedonian dynasty in Constantinople in 1055 and the rise of the first of the Comneni ignored the destruction of Baghdad and Qayrawan, which occurred almost at the same time, and so on.

The same probably holds true for the simultaneous desertification of Ifriqiya, the Negev and extensive areas in Asia Minor, together with the neglect of aqueducts in Palestine and Rome, or for the possible connection between the sack of libraries in Fustat and Baghdad and the end of the golden age of scientific and philosophical research in the eastern Islamic world and the hunger that prevailed in these centres during those years.

The simultaneity of such events is likely to escape scholarly attention because the events occurred in different countries and were narrated in sources written in various languages. Historians prefer to write histories of regions whose languages they read properly. The abundance and variety of the written sources, and the multiplicity of the languages in which they were written, led to the creation of many fragmentary and separate histories for the various subregions, and to the ignoring of the non-political and non-economic regional characteristics that tie them together. The history of contemporaneous western Europe, on the other hand, a region which is not much bigger than the eastern Mediterranean, is read as a comprehensive narrative referring to a single geographical unit both because of the scarcity of written sources and because many of them were written in Latin only.

Richard Bulliet's recent volume should be mentioned here as a relevant exception. Bulliet tries to explain the decline of a major country (Iran) in the tenth and eleventh centuries by using non-political explanations: 'Iran experienced a significant cold spell in the first half of the tenth century, followed by prolonged climatic cooling in the eleventh and twelfth centuries, [and] the colder weather affected not just Iran, but central Asia, Mesopotamia as far south as Baghdad, Anatolia and Russia.'[1] Bulliet will be quoted extensively in this volume, but he, too, ignores the simultaneous effects of additional waves of nomads on both Asia Minor and the

[1] Richard W. Bulliet, *Cotton, climate, and camels in early Islamic Iran: a moment in world history* (New York: Columbia University Press, 2009), p. 69.

other centres of the region, including Palestine and North Africa, presenting instead only 'his' part of the puzzle.

Attempts to interpret physical and cultural declines in terms of climatic disasters are often discarded as deterministic. Historians prefer long-term social, economic or cultural processes or even short-term political events such as conquests, the rise of new dynasties or the takeover of cities and countries by their rivals as valid interpretations for declines. Even unique disasters, such as earthquakes, are often mentioned as legitimate explanations for the decay and decline of cultures, unlike climate and nature itself.

Natural phenomena such as droughts and cold waves, earthquakes and tsunamis, are ephemeral occurrences indeed. They do have dreadful consequences – increasing mortality, causing hunger and spreading misery – but when rains and mild weather return and when the inherent productivity of the land is restored and the shortage disappears, the extreme climatic events are gradually forgotten.[2] Climatic disasters even as great as the calamity that hit the eastern Mediterranean during the tenth and eleventh centuries are no different. When the extreme events abated and the annual precipitation returned to average, the memory of the disaster faded away. Nine hundred years were needed to rediscover, decipher, assemble and depict a sequence of events that caused so much despair and allegedly altered some of the most established civilizations of the eastern Mediterranean.

The present hypothesis tries to collate the separate stories of droughts and severe cold that hit the eastern Mediterranean and to weigh the cultural and societal characteristics that disappeared during the lingering and repeated disastrous events.

[2] See, for example, Craig J. Richardson, 'How much did droughts matter? Linking rainfall and GDP growth in Zimbabwe', *African Affairs* 106 (424) (2007), 463–78.

CHAPTER TWO

# Deconstructing a 'collapse'

## 'OVERSHOOT AND COLLAPSE' THEORY VERSUS 'RESILIENCE' THEORY

Two theoretical schools attempt to evaluate and reconstruct the effects of ecological disasters on the decline of cultures and civilizations. One school of thought believes that ecological collapses can actually lead to the decline of cultures and civilizations and that they are preceded by 'overshoots' of the environmental resources.[1] The other school denies the validity of the concept of 'collapse' in societal discussions, instead preferring to emphasize cultural, economic and demographic 'resilience'.[2]

The 'collapse' school, whose best-known advocate in the last two decades is Jared Diamond, believes that the past 'overshoots', that is, that erroneous ecological decisions made by the ruling elites led to the overexploitation of vital resources and to the impoverishment of ecosystems that finally resulted in a real collapse that brought civilizations to their very end. Diamond, an ecologist and

[1] Jared M. Diamond, *Collapse: how societies choose to fail or succeed* (New York: Viking, 2005). For an overview of this approach, written by one its leading opponents, see Joseph A. Tainter, 'Archaeology of overshoot and collapse', *Annual Review of Anthropology* 35 (2006), 59–74; see also William R. Catton, *Overshoot: the ecological basis of revolutionary change* (Urbana: University of Illinois Press, 1980).

[2] Norman Yoffee, 'Orienting collapse', in *The collapse of ancient states and civilizations*, ed. Norman Yoffee and George L. Cowgill (Tucson: University of Arizona Press, 1988), pp. 1–19.

ornithologist who taught geography at the University of California, Los Angeles, defines 'collapse' in terms borrowed from Population Ecology. For him, 'collapse' is 'a drastic decrease in human population size and/or political/economic/social complexity, over a considerable area, for an extended time'.[3]

Diamond bases his 'overshoot' theory mainly on a handful of civilizations and communities: Easter Island, Pitcairn Island, Henderson Island, the Anasazi (especially Chaco Canyon), the Maya and Norse Greenland. The validity of these examples for the creation of a comprehensive theory of collapse is controversial. His adversaries claim that four of them are too small and are isolated islander communities. And indeed, the conditions of life in many of these communities are comparable to the life of isolated ecological 'populations' in the biological sense of the word. Biological populations are often bound to a specific ecosystem without the ability to emigrate out of it, to absorb newcomers or to change their identity or religion. Every change has to be met by an equal adaptation to the new equilibrium – or by the eradication of the unadapted 'population'. Tiny and isolated communities of islanders can behave like 'biological populations', but it is doubtful if one can deduce from the uncertain events that preceded their failure on societal collapse in general. Civilizations do not simply 'disappear' or 'collapse'. They are adaptive and flexible and often undergo decay or change. Environmental crises, even disastrous ones, very rarely – if ever – determine the demographic fate of complex civilizations and bring them to extinction

Realizing that collapses are more complex than simple overshoot, Diamond developed a detailed and more nuanced theory to explain the collapse environment: 'The Anasazi and Maya were . . . undone

[3] Diamond, *Collapse*, p. 3.

by water problems'; 'Deforestation was a major factor in all the collapses of past societies described in this book.'

This version of neo-Malthusianism is concerned with local or regional overpopulations that may lead to environmental degradation and to the depletion of the regional resources. The exhaustion of the resources, say the proponents of this approach, may lead to ecological collapses similar to those that occurred in the past, and today's Third World trouble spots are presented as suffering from similar environmental deterioration: 'it's the problems of the ancient Maya, Anasazi, and Easter Islanders playing out in the modern world'.[4]

This attitude became popular simultaneously with a renewed concern over a global overpopulation and over the exhaustion of the resources on a global scale. The partisans of the 'collapse' school present the alleged declines or 'collapses' of ancient civilizations as a pre-figuration of future events. Deforestation, salinization of underground water resources or the siltation of watering canals are often presented as possible explanations of ecological overshoots and collapses, although the very existence of such events can neither be verified nor disproved archaeologically or historically. Similar conjectured hypotheses were developed to explain the decline of the civilization of the Maya,[5] the fate of the third dynasty of Ur,[6] the destiny of the Harrapans civilization and the end of Mycenaean

[4] Ibid., pp. 490, 487 and 516.

[5] For an amassing of unsupported hypotheses concerning the idea of 'civilizational collapse', see Sing C. Chew, *World ecological degradation: accumulation, urbanization, and deforestation, 3000 BC– AD 2000* (Walnut Creek, CA: AltaMira Press, 2001), especially pp. 20–39. For the alleged overshoot of the Maya civilization, see C. W. Cooke, 'Why the Mayan cities of the Peten district, Guatemala, were abandoned', *Journal of the Washington Academy of Sciences* 2.13 (1931), 283–7; William R. Bullard, Jr, 'Maya settlement pattern in northeastern Peten, Guatemala', *American Antiquity* 25.3 (1960), 355–72.

[6] For the 'collapse' of the third dynasty in Ur, see T. Jacobsen and R. M. Adams, 'Salt and silt in ancient Mesopotamian agriculture', *Science* 128 (1958), 1251–8.

Greece, and even that of the Roman Empire itself.[7] Jared Diamond's neo-Malthusian attitudes and his claim that ancient leaderships could have expected future collapses and could have prevented them by making different, and more sustainable, decisions, echo his concerns about the future of the planet itself and about the ability of present leaderships to rationally plan a sustainable future. Elites know, he says, or at least should know, that their erroneous decisions can lead to a catastrophe, but in many unfortunate events they still adhere to their politically, economically, religiously or tribally motivated irrational decisions. For him, the demographic and cultural collapse of the Rapa Nui (Easter Island) is an example of a society that destroyed and deforested itself to death. A combination of a growing population that demanded more resources, he says, and a leadership that had an obsession with building sculptures led to increased pressure on the environment. 'In just a few centuries', he wrote in 1995, 'the people of Easter Island wiped out their forest, drove their plants and animals to extinction, and saw their complex society spiral into chaos and cannibalism. *Are we about to follow their lead?*'[8] Diamond does not hide his educational agenda, which he preaches throughout the book: rational societies should stick to rational ecological decisions, otherwise they will lead the way to their own extinction.

The other school, whose most prominent advocates in the last two decades have been Joseph A. Tainter, Norman Yoffee, Patricia

[7] Chew, *World ecological degradation*, pp. 26–36, 56; J. D. Hughes, *Ecology in ancient civilizations* (Albuquerque: University of New Mexico Press, 1975); J. D. Hughes and J. V. Thirgood, 'Deforestation in ancient Greece and Rome: a cause of collapse', *Ecologist* 12 (1982), 196–208.

[8] Jared M. Diamond, 'Easter's end', *Discover* 9 (1995), 62–9; emphasis the present author.

A. McAnany and Geogre Cowgill,[9] prefer focusing on the abilities of human societies to absorb disturbances rather than on their alleged collapses.[10] A collapse of a civilization, they say, is so rare an occurrence that it should be regarded as no more than a coarse generalization.[11] Proponents of this school see a resemblance between 'collapse' and

> 'A low-resolution digital photograph [which] is fine when small, compact, and viewed at a distance but dissolves into disconnected parts when examined up close . . . Crises exist, political forms are changed, and landscapes are altered, but rarely do societies collapse in an absolute and apocalyptic sense . . . Things can change profoundly, but fundamental elements of a society such as the belief systems and ways of making a living retain their basic structure.[12]

The resilience theory is based on the concept that both ecosystems and cultures have multiple potential equilibria that can change over time and are repeatedly redefined by stabilizing and destabilizing forces. Resilience theory, therefore, emphasizes past experiences of change and accepts the inevitability of both stability and transformation, denying the idea of a total collapse. Neither stability nor transformation is assumed to be the norm; rather, systems are seen as moving between the two in what has been termed an *adaptive cycle*.[13]

[9] Joseph A. Tainter, *The collapse of complex societies* (Cambridge University Press, 1988); Patricia A. McAnany and Norman Yoffee (eds.), *Questioning collapse: human resilience, ecological vulnerability and the aftermath of empire* (Cambridge University Press, 2010).

[10] B. Walker and D. Salt, *Resilience thinking: sustaining ecosystems and people in a changing world* (Washington, DC: Island Press, 2006).

[11] See Shmuel N. Eisenstadt, 'Beyond collapse', in Yoffee and Cowgill (eds.), *Collapse of ancient states and civilizations*, pp. 236–43, especially 242.

[12] Patricia A. McAnany and Norman Yoffee, 'Why we question collapse and study human resilience, ecological vulnerability, and the aftermath of empire', in McAnany and Yoffee (eds.), *Questioning collapse*, pp. 1–17, especially pp. 5 and 10.

[13] For the development of resilience theory, see C. S. Holling, 'Resilience and stability of ecological systems', *Annual Review of Ecology and Systematics* 4 (1973), 1–23;

Many of the test cases presented by the proponents of both schools are not supported by sufficient and adequate historical data and rely to too great an extent on the fragmental nature of archaeological evidence. The test cases of the 'collapse' school refer too often to very small and marginal communities and from their (too often conjectured) fates try to make deductions about the future of complex civilizations. The more convincing 'resilience' theory, on the other hand, attempts to find artificial 'resilience' even in clear cases of societal collapse, like the simultaneous decline of the eastern Mediterranean between the Late Bronze and Iron Age I, the collapse of the civilization of the Maya, or the comparatively abrupt end of the Indus Valley civilization.

Resilience theory, therefore, like its counterpart, echoes biological and ecological theories, although its 'multi-equilibria' concept is more appropriate to the study of complex cultures and civilizations. The proponents of this theory agree, however, that sudden, short-lived and unexplained successions of changes did occur in the past, and that the multi-dimensional abrupt changes, such as the 'collapse' of the eastern Mediterranean between the late Bronze Age and Iron Age I, that lasted for only fifty years (from *c.* 1200 to 1150 BC) and had such strong effects that it is apparent archaeologically almost anywhere in the eastern Mediterranean, can be labelled 'collapse'.[14] The absence of adequate historical documentation, however, prevents us even in such a case from deciding whether the disaster was the result of an overshoot, or whether it was induced

C. S. Holling and Lance H. Gunderson, 'Resilience and adaptive cycles', in *Panarchy: understanding transformations in human and natural systems*, ed. Lance H. Gunderson and C. S. Holling (Washington, DC: Island Press, 2002), pp. 25–62; Charles L. Redman and Ann P. Kinzig, 'Resilience of past landscapes: resilience theory, society, and the *longue durée*', *Conservation Ecology* 7.1 (2003), 14; Charles L. Redman, 'Resilience theory in archaeology', *American Anthropologist* 107.1 (2005), 70–7.

[14] Harvey Weiss, 'The decline of Late Bronze Age civilization as a possible response to climatic change', *Climatic Change* 4.2 (1982), 173–98.

by an ecological disaster similar to that which occurred in the eleventh century AD. Similarly, it is hard to decide if this abrupt and enormous change is a real 'collapse' or if the continuing traits that are discernible in the cultures that followed this event are important enough to bring it as an example of the resilience of earlier civilizations.

Despite the diametrically opposed approaches of the two schools, they both succeed in diminishing the psychological effect of the term 'collapse' and in positioning it in a conceivable rather than a catastrophic framework.

The 'overshoot and collapse' approach does this by positioning the idea of the collapse within the limits of rational thinking. Collapse can be avoided if rational and sustainable decisions are taken. Awareness of the effects of ecological decisions and political pressure that promotes sustainability can prevent collapses in the future.

The resilience theory is using tools borrowed from the French School of the *Annales* and ideas that were taken from theories of the '*longue durée*' and actually extend them to cross-civilizational dimensions.[15] The alleged 'collapses', according this theory, are no more than temporary fluctuations, though very discernible ones, in the long-term developments of economies, societies and cultures. The fate of civilizations is not determined by momentous disasters, even if such disasters are conceived of as being catastrophic or as deterministically important at the time of their occurrence.

The 'resilience school' is right in claiming that the very popular term 'collapse' should be handled cautiously, or at least should be clearly defined. Heaping this term on historical events about which we do not know anything for sure, or applying it to any serious political, economical or demographic fluctuation, can easily lead to

[15] See Fernand Braudel, 'Histoire et sciences sociales: la longue durée', *Annales: Histoire, Sciences Sociales* 13.4 (1958), 725–53.

the vulgarization of the reading of history itself. Civilizations do not simply disappear, and collapses, if they exist at all, occur very rarely. The proponents of this school are also right in claiming that many of the natural disasters are ephemeral occurrences which, sooner than later, are brought to conclusion. When the disaster is over, the survivors tend to return to the way of life with which they were acquainted before the beginning of the disaster.

The 'collapse school', on the other hand, is right in claiming that major changes that simultaneously affect important characteristics of civilizations do occur, and if the change is big and long enough and if it leaves durable imprints on the affected society, then it can rightly be labelled 'collapse'.

## HISTORICAL ANALYSIS OF A CLIMATIC DISASTER

The thesis presented in the present volume is that societal collapses do exist, but they are not as terminal as the proponents of the 'collapse' theory believe them to be. Even when the catastrophes are powerful enough to cause societal transformations, they are no more than ephemeral and short-lived events. Drought can linger on for many years and be followed by hunger, pestilence and mass death; but when rain and mild weather return and when the inherent productivity of the land is restored, the calamity is soon forgotten and people return to their mundane habits, as ever before.

There are, however, irreversible changes and persisting effects that evolve during crises and outlive their ephemeral causes, forever altering some of the cultural, ethnic and economic characteristics of the societies that were hit by the disasters. Only a detailed study based on detailed historical documentation can decipher the intricate chain of acts and effects and reconstruct the domino effects that lead to simultaneous destructions, abandonments and transformations of cultures and communities.

The unprecedented quantity of detailed descriptions relating the events of the tenth and eleventh centuries enables such an analytical assessment of a real historical disaster, and the distinction between real structural changes resulting from the unexpected ecological events and ephemeral occurrences that disappear once the disaster is over.

Climatic and ecological disasters, like any other historical events, are transformed and developed over space and time. Therefore, the geographical or ethnic complexity of the region in which they occur and the legacy of the civilizations that live in it should be taken into consideration when the history, geography and cultural effects of a disaster are assessed.

The droughts and cold spells of the tenth and eleventh centuries were not continuous, and were 'interrupted' by long intervals of mild weather and more abundant crops. Some of the intervals were long enough for the memory of earlier periods of dearth to fade away. Contemporary chroniclers were not even aware of the extended and regional nature of the disaster, describing it, like modern scholarship, as a series of sporadic and unrelated events that brought misery to specific regions and affecting mainly the lives of their own co-religionists.

A fragmental nature and long intervals between periods of crisis and periods of calm characterize climatic crises. If droughts and famines last uninterruptedly for decades, then they will lead to the abandonment and total desertification of the region, and their lingering effects will be all the more destructive if a region as vast as the eastern Mediterranean is affected. The disastrous nature of the crisis of the eleventh century, however, was not the result of an uninterrupted period of stable dearth but the result of: (a) many repetitive events in an accumulative short period of time (approximately 120 years); (b) too short 'intervals' of calm weather between the consecutive years of famine; (c) the escalating magnitude of each of the separate events.

The ancient bureaucracies and empires of the Mediterranean knew how to deal with food crises, developing tools and practices in order to reduce the disastrous effects of the famines. The hoarding of surpluses and their efficient distribution during periods of dearth were well known in Pharaonic times and were also well practiced in Mesopotamia, Iran, Rome and Byzantium, regions which relied on past experiences for avoiding hunger in the future. Administrators of all periods, however, could prepare themselves only for catastrophes on the scale experienced in the past while providing adequate answers to questions such as 'How much grain is consumed in a year?', 'The surplus of how many average years is enough to prevent hunger in one year of famine?', 'For how many years of famine should the country prepare itself?', or 'What is the perfect distribution of granaries, and which granaries should be opened first?' The answers were not trivial and also depended on the grain's 'shelf life' and on the allocation of budgets for granaries and for administrators who planned only for an unforeseen future, but all the answers depended exclusively on the experience of the past.

The biblical story that presents Joseph as the perfect administrator also provides mythological answers to some of these questions: (a) administrators should be prepared for the worst possible imminent crises; (b) the surplus that can be hoarded in one year of plenitude is estimated as sufficient for the needs of a year of dearth; and (c) the 'shelf life' of the hoarded grain is as long as seven years.

The seven-year-long biblical famine was a very rare occurrence, so rare that another was not recorded in Egypt until the second half of the eleventh century. It is possible, therefore, to assume that the compiler of the Bible had information about a similar disaster and used it as an exemplum and warning for future administrations. The rarity of the biblical disaster, however, caused this example to be forgotten and the increase in the population, together with the high cost of constructing additional granaries, led the future administration to abandon the biblical example. Medieval Egyptian sources provide us with the data that was relevant at the time: during the famine of 1055–6, Egypt needed to import 400,000 irdabbs (approximately 32,000 tons) to prevent hunger. During the vizierate of al-Afḍal (487/1094–515/1121), less than fifty years after the 'big calamity' – a seven-year-long famine – and following a decade of abundance, the Egyptian state granaries contained only 1 million irdabbs, or 80,000 tons, of grain, a quantity sufficient to cater only for two and a half years of similar famine.[16]

The effects of climatic disasters on the population and the prospects of governments to survive are dependent not only on their efficiency during the crisis but also on the intensity, length and rhythm of calamities that preceded the actual event (during which the reserves were consumed), on the productivity of the land during the intervals of rainy seasons, and on the efficiency of the government in storing the surplus during these intervals. In the

[16] Tāj al-Dīn Muḥammad Ibn ʿAlī Ibn Muyassar, *al-Muntaqā min akhbār miṣr (Choix de passages de la Chronique d'Égypte d'Ibn Muyassar)*, ed. Ayman Fuʾād Sayyid, Textes Arabes et Études Islamiques 18 (Cairo: Institut Français dʾArchéologie Orientale du Caire, 1981), p. 13. In Taqī al-Dīn Aḥmad Ibn ʿAlī al-Maqrīzī, *Ittiʿāẓ al-ḥunafāʾ bi-akhbār al-aʾimma al-fāṭimīyyīn al-khulafāʾ*, ed. Jamāl al-Dīn al-Shayyāl and Muḥammad Ḥilmī Muḥammad Aḥmad, 3 vols. (Cairo: Lajnat Iḥyāʾ al-Turāth al-Islāmī, 1967–73), vol. II, p. 227, the said help is 100,000 qafiz of wheat; Hinz calculates 90 litres or 70 kilograms of wheat for an irdabb. See Walther Hinz, *Islamische Masse und Gewichte: umgerechnet ins metrische System* (Leiden: E. J. Brill, 1970), p. 39; Wolfgang Felix, *Byzanz und die islamische Welt im frühen 11 Jarhundert: geschichte der politischen Beziehungen von 1001 bis 1055*, Byzantina Vindobonensia 14 (Vienna: Verlag der Österreichischen Akademie der Wissenschaften, 1981), pp. 119–23.

unfortunate case of repeated hungers, the rhythm of the crises and the increasing dimensions of the events were as important as what occurred during the famines themselves. The resilience of administrations is determined not only by the intensity of the hunger but also by the degree of preparedness and by the amount of food they could have hoarded during periods of plenitude.

## SPATIAL ANALYSIS OF A CLIMATIC DISASTER: DROUGHTS IN THE NILE VALLEY

It is hard to pinpoint when the ecological disaster of the tenth and eleventh centuries began. Severe cold spells were recorded in the northern regions of the eastern Mediterranean in AD 855, long before they began affecting the structure of local societies. Similarly, the 'unprecedented' cold waves that hit Mesopotamia, Iran and the Lower Volga basin in the 920s caused both the Tigris and the Euphrates to freeze to such an extent that pack animals could have crossed them.[17] The only region of the eastern Mediterranean in which both the beginning and the end of a food crisis are unequivocal is the Nile Valley. Likewise, no climate crisis in the eastern Mediterranean can attain its calamitous nature if Egypt, the age-old exporter of grain to all the region, is not hit by a famine.

The role of Egypt as the 'granary of the ancient Mediterranean' supplying ancient Greece, Rome and Byzantium with food cannot be underestimated. 'Every year', writes the fourth-century anonymous author of the *Expositio Totius Mundi et Gentium*, 'this productive land is of great benefit to the other provinces;

[17] Bulliet, *Cotton, climate, and camels*, p. 79; Aḥmad Ibn Faḍlān, *Ibn Faḍlān's journey to Russia: a tenth-century traveler from Baghdad to the Volga River*, trans. Richard N. Frye (Princeton, NJ: Markus Wiener Publishers, 2005), pp. 30–1.

Constantinople in Thrace is almost wholly supported by it, as are the eastern lands . . . because no other province could support this endeavour except Egypt'.[18] Egypt served as a shock absorber securing a minimal amount of grain supply even when the other regions of the eastern Mediterranean were hit by famines. It was totally independent of the regime of cyclones and anti-cyclones of the Mediterranean climate, and its yields were dependent solely on the monsoons of eastern Africa. The fact that the food supply of the Mediterranean depended on two, totally independent, sources facilitated the creation of empires such as Greece, Rome and Constantinople in this region. The fear of hunger, leading to disorders, pestilences and possible coup d'états, was reduced in comparison to any other region of the world. The simultaneous failure of both the Mediterranean and eastern Africa to supply the centres of the region with food was very unlikely, and a failure of both of them to provide food for an extended period of time was highly improbable.

Egypt continued to supply grain to its neighbours long after the export to Constantinople was halted in the seventh century. Egyptian surplus was exported to Arabia, Nubia, Palestine and North Africa, ensuring also the peaceful behaviour of the nomads, who were totally dependent on this surplus.[19] In any event, until the mid tenth century the supply of food from the Nile was highly reliable and no extended period of drought was recorded before the tenth century or after the second half of the eleventh century.

[18] *Expositio Totius Mundi et Gentium*, ed. Jean Rougé, Sources chrétiennes 124 (Paris: Éditions du Cerf, 1966), pp. 15–19.

[19] John L. Teall, 'The grain supply of the Byzantine Empire, 330–1025', *Dumbarton Oaks Papers* 13 (1959), 87–139; Michel De Boüard, 'Sur l'évolution monétaire de l'Égypte médiévale', *L'Égypte Contemporaine* 30 (1939), 427–59; Gaston Wiet, 'L'Égypte musulmane de la conquête arabe jusqu'à la conquête ottomane', in *Précis de l'histoire de l'Égypte*, 3 vols. (Cairo: Institut Français d'Archéologie Orientale, 1932), vol. III, p. 13.

Droughts in the Nile Valley are easy to follow because they are always the result of insufficient risings of the Nile, which has to attain a minimum height for the canals spreading the water to be opened and ensure a minimum amount of cultivated land.[20] The rise of the Nile was measured regularly,[21] and the 'plenitude' of the rise of the Nile was officially declared each year during the Coptic agricultural New Year[22] that also marked the beginning of a new tax year.[23]

The height of the Nile was measured in 'cubits' (approximately 0.541m) and 'fingers' and a plenitude of 16 cubits was considered, during the eleventh century, enough to ensure a stable supply of food in the coming year. A rise of 17 or 18 cubits ensured a year of opulence, while any plenitude of less than 14 or of more than 19 cubits was considered a catastrophe.[24] Therefore, it is easy to follow

[20] Hassanein Rabie, 'Some technical aspects of agriculture in medieval Egypt', in *The Islamic Middle East, 700–1900*, ed. Abraham L. Udovitch (Princeton, NJ: Darwin Press, 1981), pp. 59–90; Tsugitaka Sato, 'Irrigation in rural Egypt from the 12th to the 14th centuries – especially in the case of the irrigation in Fayyum Province', *Orient* 8 (1972), 81–92.

[21] William Popper, *The Cairo nilometer: studies in Ibn Taghri Birdi's Chronicles of Egypt* (Berkeley and Los Angeles: University of California Press, 1951), vol. I, pp. 57–63.

[22] On the Coptic celebrations of the New Year that coincided with the measurement of the plenitude of the Nile in the Mamluk period, see Taqī al-Dīn Aḥmad Ibn ʿAlī al-Maqrīzī, *Kitāb al-sulūk li-maʿrifat duwal al-mulūk*, ed. Muḥammad M. Ziyāda and Saʿīd ʿAbd al-Fattāḥ ʿĀshūr, 4 vols. in 12 parts (Cairo: National Library Press, 1934–73), vol. IV, part 2, pp. 618, 728, 881, 903, 927, 1164; see also Boaz Shoshan, 'The Festival of Nawruz: a world turned upside down', in *Popular culture in medieval Cairo* (Cambridge University Press, 1993), pp. 40–51.

[23] Al-Maqrīzī, *Kitāb al-sulūk*, vol. IV, part 2, p. 875.

[24] *Anonymi auctoris chronicon ad AC 1234 pertinens, II*, translated by Albert Abouna with an introduction and notes by Jean M. Fiey, Corpus Scriptorum Christianorum Orientalium, 354 (Scriptores Syri, 154) (Louvain: Secrétariat du Corpus SCO, 1974), p. 13:

> If the river attains only 14 cubits, only a small part of Egypt is irrigated, there are no crops of grain, and the tax is not collected in this year. If the river attains 15 or 16 cubits, the harvest is mediocre and the tax is collected accordingly. If the Nile reaches 17 or 18 cubits, then all of the land of Egypt is irrigated, and the tax is collected in full. If the Nile rises by more than 20 cubits it will flood the land and there will be no crops in that year . . .

See also *Chronique de Michel le Syrien*, ed. Jean-Baptiste Chabot, 5 vols. (Paris, 1899–1924; reprinted Brussels, 1963), vol. III, p. 82.

Fig. 2.1 A Nilometer in a fifth-century mosaic from the Nile House, Zippori. The mosaic depicts a young boy standing upon the shoulders of another boy, carving the figure '17' (cubits), the water level of the Nile in particularly abundant seasons.

events of droughts and food crises in the Nile Valley, and during such an event there is almost no difference between the situation in one part of the country and that in another.

Modern studies have relied on fifteenth-century testimonies to calculate the rises of the Nile since the beginning of the Islamic period. The figures provided by later chroniclers often contradict each other and should be calibrated with the rise of the riverbed of the Nile due to the continuous deposit of alluvium.[25] Pliny the Elder attests that during the first century AD a rise of only 14 cubits would signal a good year, while a drop below 12 cubits would lead to famine.[26] It is clear, therefore, that the level of the riverbed of the Nile was augmented by about two cubits or one metre between the first and the eleventh centuries AD, and it probably continued to be augmented thereafter. Therefore, in the present study each testimony of insufficient rise of the Nile is checked vis-à-vis other testimonies of contemporaneous sources. The books written by al-Maqrīzī (1364–1442), especially the one describing the 'famines that took place in Egypt', were found more reliable.[27] Al-Maqrīzī was the *muḥtasib* (the official in charge of the regular grain supply of the country), and therefore knew more about the interrelationship between droughts and the rise of the Nile than many of his contemporaries.[28]

The credibility of al-Maqrīzī's descriptions of incidents of famine and dearth is further corroborated by other medieval and even contemporary testimonies, such as those written by Sawīrus Ibn

[25] Popper, *Cairo nilometer;* Mamdouḥ Shāhīn, *Hydrology of the Nile basin*, Developments in Water Science, 21 (Amsterdam: Elsevier, 1985); William H. Quinn, 'A study of southern oscillation-related climatic activity for AD 622–1900 incorporating Nile River flood data', in *El Niño – historical and paleoclimatic aspects of the southern oscillation*, ed. Henry F. Diaz and Vera Markgraf (Cambridge University Press, 1992), pp. 119–50.

[26] Pliny the Elder, *Natural history with an English translation in ten volumes*, vol. II, *Libri III–VII*, trans. Harris Rackham, Loeb Classical Library (London: Heinemann and Cambridge, MA: Harvard University Press, 1961), 5.58: 263: 'in xii cubitis famem sentit, in xiii etiamnum esurit, xiv cubita hilaritatem adferunt, xv securitatem, xvi delicias. Maximum incrementum ad hoc aevi fuit cubitorum xviii Claudio principe, minimum v Pharsalico bello'.

[27] Taqī al-Dīn Aḥmad Ibn ʿAlī al-Maqrīzī, *Ighāthat al-umma bi-kashf al-ghumma* (Cairo, 1956); for a translation, see Gaston Wiet, 'Le Traité des famines de Maqrīzī', *Journal of the Economic and Social History of the Orient* 5.1 (1962), 1–90.

[28] Jere L. Bacharach, 'Circassian Mamluk historians and their quantitative economic data', *Journal of American Research Center in Egypt* 12 (1975), 77.

al-Muqaffaʿ, Yaḥyā Ibn Saʿīd al-Anṭākī, ʿIzz al-Mulk Muḥammad Musabbiḥī and the Genizah documents, or by Yaʿlā Ibn al-Qalānisī, Ibn al-Jawzī and Sibṭ Ibn al-Jawzī, Ibn al-Athīr and many later authors such as Qalqashandī and Ibn Taghrībirdī.

The exhaustive lists prepared by Dionysios Ch. Stathakopoulos and Ioannes G. Teleles enumerating droughts and pestilences that hit the eastern Mediterranean and the Byzantine Empire until AD 750 (Stathakopoulos) and AD 1500 (Teleles) clearly show that the droughts and insufficient rises of the Nile during the tenth and eleventh centuries were indeed exceptional.[29]

Out of all the events mentioned in these two lists only *nine* events of drought hit the Nile Valley between AD 300 and 900, six of which lasted for one year each and two for two-year periods. Altogether there were eleven years of drought in the Nile Valley, an average of one drought year every fifty-four years in the six hundred years that preceded the period to which I point in my own research.[30]

[29] Dionysius Ch. Stathakopoulos, *Famine and pestilence in the late Roman and early Byzantine Empire: a systematic survey of subsistence crises and epidemics*, Birmingham Byzantine and Ottoman Monographs, 9 (Aldershot: Ashgate, 2004); an average of two events in a decade. Many of the events, however, are different references to other events in the list. The statistics of Ioannes G. Teleles, *Meteorologika phainomena kai klima sto Byzantio* [Meteorological phenomena and climate in Byzantium] (Athens: Akademia Athenon, 2004), takes into account the number of references only.

[30] For the shortage and epidemic of 346, see Stathakopoulos, *Famine and pestilence*, pp. 184–7 (nos. 7 and 8); for the insufficient rise of the Nile in 383–5, see pp. 207–8 (no. 29). For the rise of the Nile in 392, see Teleles, *Meteorologika phainomena*, vol. I, pp. 127–9; for the shortage of 463, see pp. 171–2. See also *Chronicon Paschale*, 593; Gilbert Dagron (ed.), 'La Vie ancienne de Saint Marcel l'Acémète', *Analecta Bollandiana* 86 (1986), 308–9. For the shortage in 515–16, see John Malalas, *Excerpta de insidiis*, ed. Carl de Boor (Berlin, 1905), p. 41. For the crop failure in Alexandria in 619, see Stathakopoulos, *Famine and pestilence*, pp. 342–6 (no. 174). For the drought of 645 in Upper Egypt, see Sāwīrus Ibn al-Muqaffaʿ, *History of the patriarchs of the Coptic Church of Alexandria*, 1/4, edited, annotated and translated by Basil Evetts, *Patrologia Orientalis* 1.4 (Turnhout: Brepols, 1904), p. 501: 'a great dearth . . . the like of which had not been seen from the time of Claudius the unbeliever . . . For all the inhabitants of Upper Egypt came down to the Delta in search of provisions'. For the famine of 706, see Wiet, 'Traité', especially 12, n. 3. For the dearth of

On the other hand, no less than nine events, lasting together for twenty-six years, affected Egypt between 950 and 1072. In other words, during the period of 122 years between 950 and 1072 the average number of droughts in the Nile Valley rose tenfold in comparison to the previous 650 years – from one drought year every 54.5 years to one year of famine every 4.63 years, and during the period of 21 years between 1052 and 1072 there were no less than 11 years of drought. One year on average every two years. There were droughts in 338H/949 and between 341H/953–343/954–5; a cycle of a six-year-long drought between 352/963 and 358/969, and a one-year drought in 387/997. The eleventh century was even more destructive: an interrupted cycle of four years' drought (395/1004/5–399/1009); another cycle of three years (414–16/1023–6); and a third drought that lasted between 444/1052 and 447/1056. The final blow to the stability of a country – a famine of the biblical dimensions of seven years (457–64/1065–72) – led to an unprecedented economic crisis, described by the chroniclers of the time as the 'great calamity' (*al-shidda al-ʿuẓma*) or as the famine that led to the 'destruction of Fustat'.

The recurrence of the droughts and their length left very little time for the Egyptian governments to recover and refill state granaries and to be prepared for an extended catastrophic period that was very difficult to suppress.

715, see Sāwīrus Ibn al-Muqaffaʿ, *Patrologia Orientalis* 4.1, pp. 67–8. For the drought of 834, see *Chronique de Michel le Syrien*, vol. III, p. 83 and vol. IV, p. 527. For the cold-induced famine and plague of 745 that spread to Egypt, see Sāwīrus Ibn al-Muqaffaʿ, *Patrologia Orientalis*, 4.1, p. 97: 'In the first year the land was dried up ... And many men and cattle died ... In the second year, there came a pestilence upon Egypt, such as had not been before'. See also *Patrologia Orientalis*, 4.1, p. 115. For the shortage in Constantinople in 581–2 that led to increased importing of grain from Egypt, resulting in famine there, see *Chronique de Michel le Syrien*, vol. II, pp. 351–2; John of Ephesos, *Historia Ecclesiastica, II*, ed. Ernest W. Brooks, Corpus Scriptorum Christianorum Orientalium, 3 (Scriptores Syri,3) (Louvain: Brepols, 1936), pp. 133–4; Stathakopoulos, *Famine and pestilence*, p. 318 (no. 148).

Fig. 2.2 David Roberts (1796–1864), *The Nilometer on the Isle of Rhoda*, Cairo, 1838

The long period of 122 years, during which Egypt was not only deprived of its traditional ability to export food and of being a regional buffer, preventing widespread hunger, also made it unable to feed its own citizens. The absence of Egypt from the grain market, combined with extended periods of droughts in Syria, Palestine and Mesopotamia, ensured dearth. No other source, no

Table 2.1 *Droughts in the Nile Valley*

| Between AD 283 and 850 | Tenth and eleventh centuries |
|---|---|
| 383–5 A two-year-long drought | 949 A one-year-long drought |
| 346 A one-year-long drought | 954–5 A two-year-long drought |
| 463 A one-year-long drought | 963–9 A six-year-long drought |
| 515–16 A two-year-long drought | 997–8 A one-year-long drought |
| | 1004–5 A one-year-long drought |
| 645 A one-year-long drought | 1007–8 A two-year low Nile |
| 706 A one-year-long drought | 1009 A one-year-long drought |
| 715(?) A one-year-long drought | 1023–6 A three-year-long drought |
| 745 A one-year-long drought | 1052–6 A four-year-long drought |
| 834 A one-year-long drought | 1065–72 The 'great calamity' or 'destruction of Fustat' |

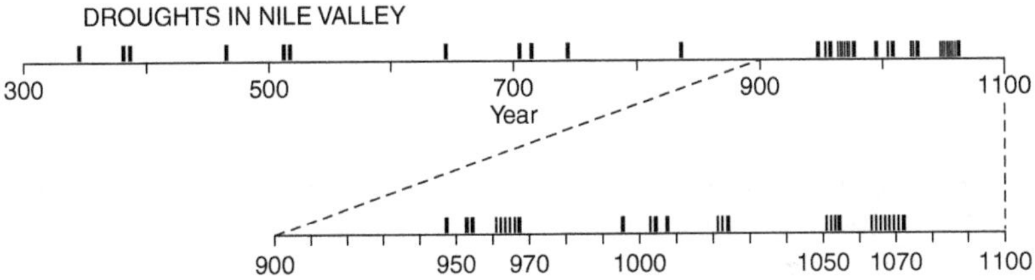


Fig. 2.3 Years of droughts in the Nile Valley, between 200 and 1072 (*above*) and between 900 and 1072 (*below*).

other country was able to replace Egypt as an exporter or distributor of such a great amount of food.

Therefore, despite the earlier periods of freeze-induced hunger that affected the Trans-Oxonian steppes, Iran, Khurasan and Mesopotamia in the first half of the ninth century, the crisis of the eastern Mediterranean became regional, affecting the whole region only when the first of the recurring droughts in the Nile Valley was recorded (in 338/949 and again in 341–3/953–5) and it started having disastrous effects when an extended hunger of biblical dimensions hit Egypt between 352/963 and 358/969.

## EARLIER COLD SPELLS IN IRAN AND MESOPOTAMIA

Severe cold waves were recorded in the eastern Mediterranean in the eighth and ninth centuries, but their number, length and intensity increased considerably during the tenth and eleventh centuries.

Five events of lingering, extensive and severe cold that hit Mesopotamia, the Jazira and Armenia were recorded during the seventh century.[31] Four additional events were listed in the eighth century, including the cold wave and famine of 743 and 745 that was coupled by an insufficient rise of the Nile,[32] and the freezing weather of 749–51 that led the inhabitants of Armenia to flee 'en masse to Syria (Bilad al-Sham) to escape starvation but their sheer

31 Michael G. Morony, 'Michael the Syrian as a source for economic history', *Hugoye* 3.2 (2000), n.p. This is a special issue devoted to Michael the Syrian. For the freezing of the Euphrates in 607, see *Chronique de Michel le Syrien*, vol. II, p. 378; Bar Hebraeus (Abū al-Faraj), *The Chronography*, translated from the Syriac by Ernest A. Wallis Budge, 2 vols. (Oxford University Press, 1932), vol. I, p. 86; Teleles, *Meteorologika phainomena*, pp. 283–8. For the cold spell that induced famine in Armenia and Marash in the 650s, see Robert W. Thomson, *The Armenian history attributed to Sebeos*, 2 vols. (Liverpool University Press, 1999), vol. I, p. 146; *Chronique de Michel le Syrien*, vol. IV, pp. 431, 433. For the very severe winter of 684 when the Euphrates froze over for six days and people and domestic animals died of the cold, see *Chronique de Michel le Syrien*, vol. IV, p. 444, and for the cold wave of 669, see p. 436. Famines that were not related to cold occurred also in 611, 687 and 694; see *Chronique de Michel le Syrien*, vol. IV, pp. 403 and 447.

32 For the famine of 720–1, see *Chronique de Michel le Syrien*, vol. IV, p. 456. For the famine in Edessa in 786, see Bar Hebraeus, *Chronography*, vol. I, p. 118. For a series of cold spells that induced famine between 742 and 745, see *Le Chronique de Denys de Tell-Mahré, Quatrième Partie*, 112, ed. and trans. Jean-Baptiste Chabot (Paris: Ǧ. Bouillon, 1895), pp. 29–30, 34–5; *The chronicle of Zuqnin, Parts III and IV, AD 488–775*, trans. Amir Harrak (Toronto: Pontifical Institute of Mediaeval Studies, 1999), pp. 165–6, 167; *Chronique de Michel le Syrien*, vol. II, pp. 506–8, vol. IV, pp. 464–6; Sāwīrus, *History of the patriarchs*, vol. III, p. 115; see also Michael W. Dols, 'Plague in early Islamic history', *Journal of the American Oriental Society* 94 (1974), 380; Lawrence I. Conrad, 'Ṭaʿūn and Wabāʾ: conceptions of plague and pestilence in early Islam', *Journal of the Economic and Social History of the Orient (JESHO)* 25 (1981), 268–307, especially 294–6; Lawrence I. Conrad, 'Arabic plague chronologies and treatises: social and historical factors in the formation of a literary genre', *Studia Islamica* 54 (1981), 51–93, especially 56, 85.

number aggravated the famine . . . that existed in Syria as well'.[33] The frequency of droughts and cold spells increased considerably during the ninth and early tenth centuries, reaching an average of one drought every ten years.[34] The severe cold in 855, for example, spread from the 'lands of the Turks' to Khurasan and onwards to Iran and Mesopotamia, killing many people.[35]

The freezing weather that hit Baghdad in 307–8/919–21 induced shortage, led to riots and famine,[36] and was also felt north of the Black Sea, where it was described as 'unprecedented'.[37] The famine

[33] *Chronique de Denys de Tell-Mahré*, pp. 50–1; *Chronicle of Zuqnin*, pp. 184–6; Morony prefers to date this event to 750–4. The Arabic sources, however, date the beginning of the plague to 748. See Conrad, 'Ṭaʿūn and Wabāʾ', 304; Conrad, 'Arabic plague'; Dols, 'Plague', 380. The extreme cold that affected central and northern Europe between 762 (or even 761) and 764 (or even 765), however, is not even mentioned by eastern chroniclers; see Michael McCormick, Paul E. Dutton and Paul A. Mayewski, 'Volcanoes and the climate forcing of Carolingian Europe, AD 750–950', *Speculum* 82 (2007), 865–95. The last drought of the eighth century hit Mosul, the entire Jazira and Syria during 772–3: see *Chronique de Denys de Tell-Mahré*, pp. 136, 145–6; *Chronicle of Zuqnin*, pp. 266, 274–6; 287, 289, 296.

[34] For the cold wave of 808 or 810 that influenced Mosul and the northern Jazira, see *Chronique de Michel le Syrien*, vol. IV, p. 490; Bar Hebraeus, *Chronography*, vol. I, p. 122. In 819 or 821 there was no rain and no harvest in the East as well as in the West; see *Anonymi auctoris chronicon ad AC 1234 pertinens*, vol. II, p. 10 (ch. 203); for a drought and famine in Salakh in 819, see *The book of the governors: the Historia monastica of Thomas, bishop of Marga, AD 840*, ed. Ernest A. Wallis Budge, 2 vols. (London: Kegan Paul, Trench, Trübner & Co., 1893), vol. I, p. 168 and vol. II, pp. 337–8. For the 'great famine' of Khurasan, see *Chronique de Michel le Syrien*, vol. IV, pp. 524–45; for the drought in Egypt in 834 see *Chronique de Michel le Syrien*, vol. III, p. 83 and vol. IV, p. 527. The severe winter of 842 was also accompanied by famine and pestilence: see *Chronique de Michel le Syrien*, vol. IV, pp. 541–2. Bar Hebraeus, *Chronography*, vol. I, p. 140, describes how the Persian army was frostbitten while fighting the Kurds: 'The severe famine and pestilence [caused] . . . tribulation [in] . . . Dara, Nisibis and Amedia and plunder'.

[35] Ḥamza Ibn al-Ḥasan al-Iṣfahānī, *Kitāb Taʾrīkh sanī mulūk al-arḍ wal-anbiyāʾ* (Berlin: Maṭbaʿat Kāwiyāni [1340] [1921 or 1922]), p. 122, as quoted by Bulliet, *Cotton, climate, and camels*, p. 77, n. 16.

[36] Rioting broke out in Baghdad in 307/919–20 and ended only when the Caliph opened the granaries of the princedom and sold wheat and barley at subsidized prices; see Marius Canard, 'Baghdad au IVe siècle de l'Hégire (Xe siècle de l'ère chrétienne)', *Arabica* 9 (1962), 267–87, especially 282. Bulliet noted that even the summer of 308/920 was very cold following a cold winter, and that the 'dates and trees, and a lot of snow fell'; Bulliet, *Cotton, climate, and camels*, p. 71.

[37] Bulliet, *Cotton, climate, and camels*, p. 79; Ibn Faḍlān, *Ibn Faḍlān's journey*, pp. 30–1.

of 312/925 in Baghdad was also accompanied by agitation, followed in January 313/926 by such freezing weather and heavy snow that the Tigris and the Euphrates froze over completely so that pack animals could have crossed them.[38]

The cold spells and famines that hit Mesopotamia and Iran from the mid tenth century onwards led to widespread brigandage, clashes between military and civilians, and the desertion of the stronger populations.[39] The Jews and Zoroastrians began deserting Baghdad after the cold spell of 332–4/943–6,[40] when its citizens were reduced to eating dogs and even to devouring human flesh, and looting was widespread.[41]

The severe cold that affected Mesopotamia in 331/942–3 was also recorded in Isfahan. An Isfahani chronicler attested that the amount of snow in the city that year was 'so great that people were not able to move around' and that 'we [Isfahanis] never had such a snow . . . in the springtime'.[42]

Gruesome details of the famine that followed the cold spell of 334/944–5 are provided by Yaḥyā Ibn Saʿīd[43] and by Bar Hebraeus, who writes that

[38] Canard, 'Baghdad', 282; Ibn al-Jawzī, Abū al-Faraj ʿAbd al-Raḥmān Ibn ʿĀlī, *al-Muntaẓam fī ta'rīkh al-mulūk wal-umam*, 11 vols. in 6 vols. (Ḥyderabad: al-ʿUthmānīyya, 1357–59/1938–40), vol. VI, pp. 201–2; Bulliet, *Cotton, climate, and camels*, p. 80.

[39] Muḥammad Ibn Yaḥyā al-Ṣūlī, *Akhbār al-Rāḍī bi-llāh wa'l-Muttaqī bi-llāh: histoire de la dynastie abbaside de 322 à 333/934 à 944*, trans. Marius Canard, 2 vols. (Algiers, 1946–50).

[40] Eliyahu Ashtor, 'Un Mouvement migratoire au haut Moyen Age: migrations de l'Irak vers les pays Méditerranéens', *Annales: Histoire, Sciences Sociales* 27 (1972), 185–214; al-Ṣūlī, *Akhbār*, p. 251. This event was a part of an extended period of drought that lasted between 330/941–2 and 334/945–6.

[41] Canard, 'Baghdad', 282–3.

[42] Bulliet, *Cotton, climate, and camels*, p. 79, pointed to the connection between the cold spell and the drought in Baghdad; see Ḥamza al-Iṣfahānī, *Ta'rīkh* (n. 36 above), p. 124.

[43] Yaḥyā Ibn Saʿīd al-Anṭākī, *Histoire de Yahya-Ibn Saʿīd d'Antioche*, ed. and trans. Ignace Kratchkovsky and Alexander Vasiliev, *Patrologia Orientalis* 18.5 (Turnhout: Brepols, 1924), pp. 744–5.

there was a great famine in Baghdad . . . houses, vineyards, and gardens were sold for joints of meat and cakes of bread. And men used to pick out the grains of barley from the dung of horses and asses and eat them . . . [and finally they were reduced to cannibalism]. And very many died during that famine, and [their bodies] were devoured by the dogs because there was no one to bury them.[44]

According to Matthew of Edessa, there was an additional lengthy and disastrous famine that hit the Jazira during the 340s/950s lasting for seven years. 'The dearth', he writes, 'stayed in that country for seven years . . . Many went mad and attacking one another mercilessly and savagely, devouring each other . . . Many villages and regions became uninhabited, and nothing else has been built [in them] to the present day'.[45]

Sectarian fights in Baghdad (Hanbalis against Shafiʿis and Sunnis against Shiʿis) usually followed periods of dearth and gave rise to bloodshed and destruction. The conflicts between the Shiʿis and the Sunnis became usual occurrences from the famine of 338/949, when the district of Karkh was pillaged,[46] and they were repeated in 348/959 and again in 362/971 when 17,000 people perished and 300 shops, many houses, and 33 mosques were burnt down.[47]

The famine of the 950s is also mentioned in Jewish documents. A letter sent by an unknown writer in 953 from Mesopotamia to Spain recounts the history of the Jewish academies of Sura and Pumbedita in those years. The writer refers to a contribution that arrived two

[44] Bar Hebraeus, *Chronography*, vol. I, p. 164; for the same events in Baghdad as recorded by Muslim chroniclers, see Canard, 'Baghdad', 282–3.

[45] Matthew of Edessa, *Armenia and the Crusades, tenth to twelfth centuries: the chronicle of Matthew of Edessa*, trans. Ara E. Dostourian (Lanham, MD: University Press of America, 1993), 1.1, p. 19.

[46] Ibn al-Jawzī, *Muntaẓam*, vol. VI, p. 363–364.

[47] Ibid., vol. VI, p. 390 and vol. VII, p. 60; ʿIzz al-Dīn Abū al-Ḥasan ʿAlī Ibn al-Athīr, *al-Kāmil fī'l-Taʾrīkh*, ed. Carl J. Tornberg, 13 vols. (Leiden: E. J. Brill, 1862–71; reprinted Beirut: Dār Ṣādr and Dār Bayrūt, 1965–7), vol. VIII, p. 619.

years earlier from Spain to the academies, 'but we were robbed and received only a small amount ... we have been oppressed and bowed to the ground ... our lands were destroyed during those evil years which we experienced; our money and lands have disappeared. We have been spilled like sacred stones in all the streets and have given our precious things in exchange for food to restore our souls'.[48]

The consequences of the long cold-induced famines of the 940s included inability of governments to provide food, decline of public order, emigration of elites and depopulation of the countryside. These consequences were magnified by the later climatic disasters of the tenth and early eleventh centuries.

## DOMINO EFFECTS

The chaotic mechanisms of domino effects are not easily theorized, although they do have repeated patterns and logics and their spread is not infinite. These mechanisms – the regional price rise of foodstuffs, pestilences and invading nomads that know no borders – can easily lead to the collapse of economies and bureaucracies and to radically changed cultures in regions not directly affected by the climatic calamities themselves.

Traditional, direct mechanisms, however, are only part of the game. Periods of dearth are usually followed by intensification of existing and dormant dissensions and by the deepening of division lines that were kept in low profile for years – even for generations – and deteriorated into open violence that can tear fragile societies apart.

[48] Sherira ben Hanina, Gaon, *Igeret Rav Sherira Ga'on* [The Epistle of Rav Sherira Gaon], ed. Binyamin M. Lewin (Haifa: Hevra le-Safrut Ha-Yahadut, 1921), app. XXIII–XXIV (Hebrew).

Therefore, although the direct mechanisms were the most important agents spreading the damages of the dearth and weakening societal institutions, they were not the only – and certainly not the last – domino stones participating in the game. In many of the cases secondary processes were as important, initiating and intensifying inactive political, economic and cultural conflicts and inflicting damage that in certain cases was so substantial as to lead to the collapse of crumbling administrations or feeble societies.

On the other hand, domino effects are very often also ephemeral occurrences that do not last longer than the dearth that created them and are usually brought to abrupt conclusions. Regular rains and ascertained supply of food lead to the decrease of food prices, to the end of social agitations, and to the pacification of the nomads. The dissensions that existed before the beginning of the crisis are abated and are once again manageable.

The geographical significance of the climatic crises that affected the eastern Mediterranean during the eleventh century can be divided into three circles. The first circle includes regions that were affected directly by the crisis (the inner circle), including the cold-stricken Trans-Oxonian provinces, Khurasan, Iran, the Lower Volga and the Balkans, on the one hand, and the Nile Valley, on the other.

The second circle is composed of the regions that border on the first and were affected by the dislocations, nomadizations and other forms of 'domino effects' and shock waves. It includes Mesopotamia, the Jazira, Armenia, Asia Minor and occasionally also northern Syria in the north, and Sinai and North Africa in the south. The borders of the second zone or circle were not stable and occasionally they overlapped the inner or the outer zones.

The third circle or zone includes the regions of the Mediterranean coast (Palestine, Syria, Lebanon and Cilicia) that

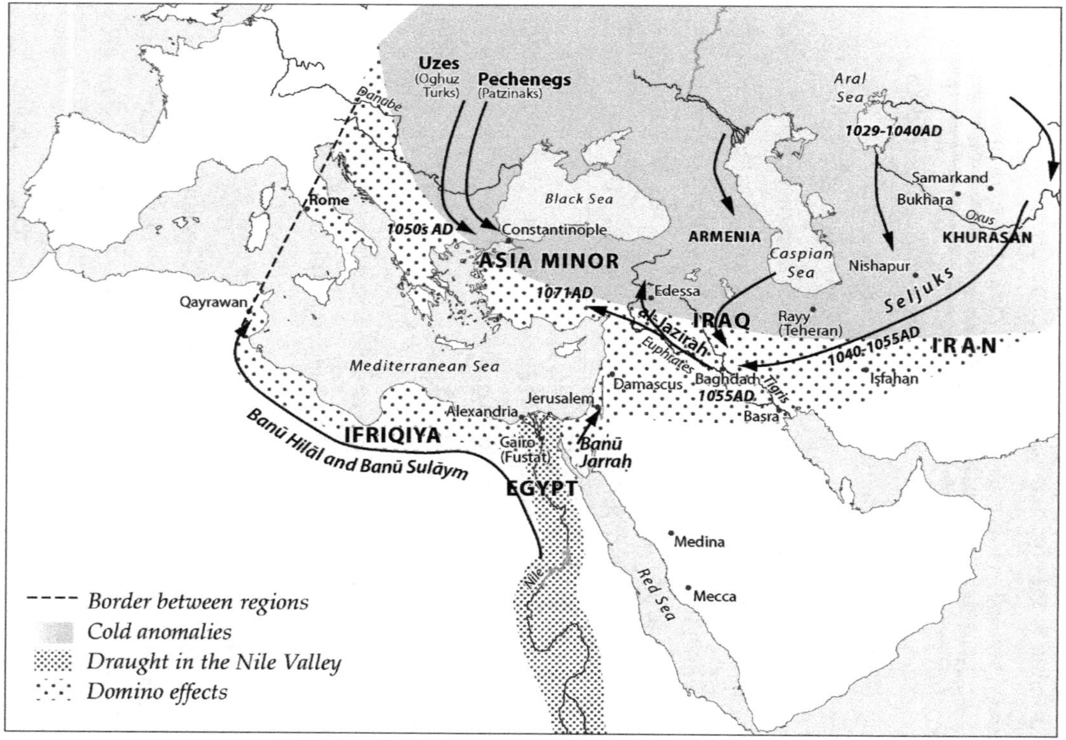


Map 2.1 Zones of effective influence of climatic disasters.

were affected indirectly by the droughts in the Nile Valley, on the one hand, or by cold spells in the north, on the other.

The inner diversity in these countries is an important factor ruling out any generalization about the regional dimensions of climatic disasters. The southern provinces of the 'third circle', including the south of Palestine and Jordan, or some of the eastern provinces of Syria, are more vulnerable to droughts and famines. For centuries these regions were the transitional zone that serves as a border between the sedentary and well-watered lands of the coast and the semi-desert, populated mainly by pastoral nomads. The zone separating nomads from peasants was never stable, and its location depended mainly on the amount of rainfall but also on the existence of a central government and law and the technological and organizational abilities of the population to efficiently accumulate rain-water and use it for agriculture. It can be safely claimed, however, that any serious drop below the average annual rainfall would extend the 'desert-line' and bring regions which were formerly cultivated within the desert-line, thus forcing many of those who formerly depended on a mixed economy to prefer the greater flexibility provided by pastoral nomadism or by raiding.[49]

Any drop in the annual rainfall beneath the average will usually lead to a drought along the desert-line and its proximity and to the temporary migration of at least some of the nomads from beyond it to the sedentary land. In the well-watered provinces, such as the northern provinces of Palestine or those of western Syria that lie along the coastline, even a decline of 30 per cent in the annual rainfall will not lead to a drought or stop the cultivation of grain, although springs and underground reservoirs will be severely

[49] Norman N. Lewis *Nomads and settlers in Syria and Jordan, 1800–1980* (Cambridge University Press, 1987).

depleted. Droughts that hit Syria or Palestine do not have a similar effect as those that hit Egypt or the cold spells of the north, and only parts of these countries will be affected by an extended decline in rainfall. A sharp decrease in the annual amount of rainfall will lead to a change in the desert-line and to the migration of pastoralists who will try to benefit from the comparative abundance of grain that the inhabitants of the central coastal plain (in the case of Palestine) or the west of the country (in the case of Syria and Lebanon) continue to raise. In short, it is mainly those who live south (or east, when referring to Syria and Lebanon) who will be affected by lingering droughts. On the other hand, the impoverishment of springs and water reservoirs is expected to influence urban centres, whose high standard of living is highly dependent on the availability of running water, and villages in the mountainous areas, whose agriculture is dependent on irrigation and on perched springs that cease to function during the summers that follow periods of drought.

The facts and arguments presented above lead us to the following summation. Despite the regional nature of the climatic disaster, its effects resulted no less from its repetitive nature and from the escalating magnitude of the events than from their concurrence and from the hunger that prevailed throughout the region. During any of the most difficult moments in each of the subregions there was a neighbouring subregion to which the refugees from the currently most hard hit could have escaped. The temporary refuges did not enjoy any abundance and the incoming emigrations brought each of them to the brink of hunger and famine, leading to violence between the 'newcomers' and the sedentary populations that dwelled there beforehand. The overall picture, however, was of hunger, dislocation, violence and dearth.

## CHAPTER THREE

# 950–1027: an impending disaster

### EGYPT: SEVEN BAD YEARS (963–9)

The regional calamity began when Egypt was hit for the first time in centuries by a series of insufficient rises of the Nile. The first event, which was preceded by a cold spell that hit Mesopotamia in the late 940s, was in 338/949. The second began four years later, in 341–3/953–5. These two short periods of famine were enough to create a shortage of bread in Cairo and to induce the population to rise against the ruling Ikhshidid dynasty.[1] The longer, devastating famine of the 960s (352/963 to 358/969), however, resulted in the collapse of the Ikhshidid dynasty, the first administration to be toppled during the crisis, and the rise of the Fatimids. The famine started with an insufficient rise of the Nile (15 cubits and 4 fingers) continued by an additional deficiency a year later (353/964), when 'the famine was all over the country ... causing restlessness and plunder of corn in many places'. The Nile was even lower in 354/965, descending further in 355/966 and reaching a catastrophic level

[1] Gaston Wiet, 'Le Traité des famines de Maqrīzī', *Journal of the Economic and Social History of the Orient* 5.1 (1962), 13. For an earlier description of the country as being very prosperous, see al-Masʿūdī, *Murūj al-dhahab*, *Les prairies d'or*, ed. and trans. Berbier de Meynard and Pavet de Courteille, 9 vols. (Paris, 1861–76), vol. II, pp. 356–441; for the description by Ibn Hauqal, written before this drought and updated after the Fatimid conquest, see Ibn Hauqal, *Configuration de la terre (Kitāb Ṣūrat al-arḍ)*, vol. I, ed. and trans. by Johannes H. Kramers and Gaston Wiet (Beirut and Paris: Commission Internationale pour la Traduction des Chefs-d'Œuvres, G. P. Maisonneuve & Larose, 1964), pp. 131–62.

of 12 cubits and some fingers in 356/967, a level unprecedented since 'the rise of Islam'. It was said that 600,000 inhabitants died in Fustat or deserted the city.[2] Markets were plundered and institutions set ablaze. Terror reigned, and the Egyptian possessions in Syria became vulnerable. Anyone who tried to restrain the rebels was killed.[3]

The death of the black eunuch Kāfūr, who efficiently ruled Egypt at the time, attempting to manage the crisis, brought the disorder to its highest level. The army was split in two, one part supporting the minor who was the legitimate successor to the throne while the other plotted with Fatimid caliph al-Muʿizz of North Africa. The latter benefited from the power vacuum and the absence of the commander of the first party and would-be regent, who departed for Palestine (*jund Filasṭīn*), which was also hit by the famine, sending his armies to Egypt and conquering Fustat, which surrendered in July 969.

The extended famine in Egypt, like any other previous or future extended Egyptian famine, weakened the Syrian provinces as well, enabling Byzantium to reconquer regions that were not under its direct rule for centuries. The emperor Nicephorus II Phocas (963–9) succeeded in conquering Cilicia, Tarsus and Cyprus and in

[2] Stanley Lane-Poole, *A history of Egypt in the Middle Ages*, 2nd edn (London: Methuen, 1914), pp. 89, 100ff.; Yaḥyā Ibn Saʿīd al-Anṭākī, *Eutychii Patriarchae Alexadtrini Annales, II*, Corpus Scriptorum Christianorum Orientalium, 51 (Scriptores Arabici, 7), ed. Louis Cheikho et al. (Louvain: Secrétariat du Corpus SCO, 1960), pp. 129–30; Aḥmad Ibn ʿAlī al-Maqrīzī, *al-Mawāʿiẓ wal-iʿtibār*, ed. Muḥammad al-ʿAdawī, 2 vols. (Cairo: Būlāq, 1853–54), vol. I, pp. 329–30 and vol. II, p. 27; Abū al-Maḥāsin Yūsuf Ibn Taghrībirdī, *al-Nujūm al-Zāhira fī mulūk miṣr wal-qāhira*, 16 vols. (Cairo: Dār al-Kutub al-Miṣriyya, 1929–72), vol. III, p. 326 and vol. IV, p. 18; Aḥmad Ibn ʿAlī al-Qalqashandī, *Maʾāthir al-ināfa fī maʿālim al-khilāfa*, ed. ʿAbd al-Sattār Aḥmad Farrāj, 3 vols. (Kuwait, 1964), vol. I, p. 305 relates that the price of wheat in 358/969 rose to 2 dinars for a *wayba* (approximately 12 kg) and the cost of a *raṭl* of bread (approximately 450 gms) was 2 dirhams, while that of an egg was 1.33 dirhams.

[3] Maqrīzī, *Mawāʿiẓ*, vol. II, p. 27.

969, the same year the Ikhshidids were replaced by the Fatimids in Egypt, the Byzantine Empire succeeded in subjugating Antioch and the region of Aleppo.

The lengthy drought was also associated with the decline of some of the Christian communities in Egypt and with inter-religious strife in the provinces. Sāwīrūs Ibn al-Muqaffaʿ reports:

> The famine did not cease until the end of seven successive years, and it was great in all of Egypt, so that the land was depopulated ... and the hunger ... prevailed ... A number of the Episcopal sees were abandoned ... joining the populated sees which were neighboring to them.[4]

Severe anti-Christian riots erupted in Jerusalem in May 966, one of the worst years of the famine. The rioters set the Church of the Holy Sepulchre on fire, causing its dome to collapse, and looted it. They also robbed and burnt down the Church of Holy Zion. The patriarch of Jerusalem was killed and his body tied to a pillar and set on fire. The Jerusalem riots testify to other facets of the domino effect of a continuing famine: the rise of fanaticism, the increasing power of the mob, and the incompetence of the central authorities to enforce internal security and order.[5] The connection between periods of hunger, desertion of Episcopal sees and the destruction of Christian institutions was to be repeated during the following outbreaks of hunger.

The ascendance to power of the Jewish renegade YaṬqūb Ibn Killis sheds light on a strange but recurring archaeological

[4] Sāwīrūs Ibn al-Muqaffaʿ, *History of the patriarchs of the Egyptian Church: known as the history of the Holy Church*, vol. II, part 2, *Khae'l III – Shenouti II (AD 880–1066)*, translated and annotated by Aziz Suryal Atiya, Yassa ʿAbd al-Masīḥ and Oswald H. E. Burmester, Publications de la Société d'Archéologie Copte, 3–5, 11–15, Textes et Documents (Cairo: Société d'Archéologie Copte, 1948–59), pp. 134–45.

[5] Yaḥyā Ibn Saʿīd al-Anṭākī, *Histoire de Yahya Ibn Saʿīd d'Antioche*, ed. and trans. Ignace Kratchkovsky and Alexander Vasiliev, *Patrologia Orientalis*, 18.5 (Turnhout: Brepols, 1924), pp. 101–4.

discovery that was made at sites which were abandoned during the crisis. Yaīqūb Ibn Killis was born in Baghdad and his family left for Ramla during the great desertion that followed the above-mentioned hunger of 943–6 (see p. 34). When he grew up he moved to Egypt, serving under the Ikhshidid vizier Kāfūr and assuming important roles in the government of the country, including the responsibility for tax collection. According to Ibn al-Ṣayrafī, Yaʿqūb began his rise to power by reporting to Kāfūr about a hoard of 30,000 dīnārs that was hidden in the house of a certain Ibn al-Baladī, who died in Ramla without leaving heirs. Later he reported to the same Kāfūr about yet another hoard, hidden in the house of a Jew who lived and died in al-Faramā.[6]

The two hoards were hidden in cities that suffered from the extended period of drought and were most probably the property of people who died without heirs. Hoards are a recurring phenomenon in the archaeological sites of the eleventh century. Archaeologists tend to ascribe them to the fear of conquests, or to earthquakes, but, as we can see from the examples given here, they can also characterize periods of famine, when no money can buy food and when heads of families, in their quest for bread, leave their families behind or abandon their urban dwellings, leaving behind valuables that can only endanger them along the unsafe roads. People who go and look for food tend to believe that they are going to return soon, but famines and pestilences such as those that prevailed in Egypt and Palestine during the 960s took heavy tolls on human life, often resulting in the death of both those who went to look for food and their families that were left behind. Yaʿqūb Ibn Killis, who knew about some of these hidden treasures,

[6] ʿAlī Ibn al-Ṣayrafī, *al-Ishāra ilā man nāla ʾl-wizāra* (Cairo: al-Maʿhad al-ʿIlmī al-Faransī lil-āthār al-Sharqīyya, 1924) (*Bulletin de l'Institut Français d'Archéologie Orientale du Caire* 25 [1925], 92–4), pp. 19–21.

used them to acquire power, while other hoards were stolen by greedy neighbours or remained hidden and untouched in the walls for future archaeologists to reveal. No less than thirty hoards, a record number in any period, were found in the excavations of Fatimid strata in Israel.

The Fatimid regime, which ascended to power following a long famine, took measures to prevent similar occurrences in the future. They certainly and justifiably believed that adequate administrative acts could meet the needs of the population even in times of famine, frequently evoking the biblical story of Joseph to prove their assumption. One of the first acts of the new regime was, therefore, to send ships loaded with grain from their native country in North Africa to relieve the immediate hunger.[7] Later, they appointed a *muḥtasib* whose duties were to supervise the grain market,[8] prevent private and illegal hoarding and excessive prices, designate spaces for grain markets and inflict punishment on offending millers and grain dealers.[9] Following the age-long Egyptian tradition, the Fatimids, too, accumulated grain in state granaries[10] and took measures to ensure an adequate supply

[7] De Lacy O'Leary, *A short history of the Fatimid khalifate* (London: Trübner, 1923), p. 106.

[8] For the appointment of the *muḥtasib* in 358/969, see Taqī al-Dīn Aḥmad Ibn ʿAlī al-Maqrīzī, *Ittiʿāẓ al-ḥunafāʾ bi-akhbār al-aʾimma al-fāṭimiyyīn al-khulafāʾ*, ed. Jamāl al-Dīn al-Shayyāl and Muḥammad Ḥilmī Muḥammad Aḥmad, 3 vols. (Cairo: Lajnat Iḥyāʾ al-Turāth al-Islāmī, 1967–73) , vol. I, pp. 117, 122; al-Maqrīzī, *Ighāthat al-umma bi-kashf al-ghumma* (Cairo, 1957), p. 13; Boaz Shoshan, 'Fatimid grain policy and the post of the *muḥtasib*', *International Journal of Middle East Studies* 13 (1981), 181–9; Yaacov Lev, 'The suppression of crime, the supervision of markets, and urban society in the Egyptian capital during the tenth and eleventh centuries', *Mediterranean Historical Review* 3.2 (1988), 71–95; Emile Tyan, *Histoire de l'organisation judiciaire en pays d'Islam*, 2nd edn (Leiden: E. J. Brill, 1960), pp. 616–48; for the biblical story of Joseph, see Genesis 41; Quran, Sura 12.

[9] See al-Maqrīzī, *Ittiʿāẓ*, vol. I, pp. 120, 122; al-Maqrīzī, *Ighātha*, pp. 15–16.

[10] For state granaries in Fatimid Egypt, see al-Maqrīzī, *Ittiʿāẓ*, vol. II, pp. 224, 226; vol. III, pp. 72, 86, 165–6, 341. According to al-Maqrīzī, the Fatimid granaries had stored as much as one million irdabbs or 70,000 tons during the vizierate of al-Afḍal (487/1094–515/1121); al-Maqrīzī, *Ittiʿāẓ*, vol. III, p. 72.

of grain and appropriate seasonal shipping from Upper Egypt to Fustat.[11]

The first drought that hit Fatimid Egypt, and therefore the first drought after that of the 960s, was short-lived, lasting for only one year. It occurred in 387/997 due to an insufficient rise of the Nile, and the Fatimid administration succeeded in diminishing its negative results.[12]

## CONSECUTIVE FAILURES OF THE NILE, 1004–9

The drought and famine of 395–9/1004–9 was certainly a bigger challenge to the efficiency of the Fatimid administration, being the second long-term devastating drought within less than four decades.

The crisis began as early as 395/1004 with an insufficient rise of the Nile; the situation was better for two years, but the Nile continued to be too low in 397/1007 and 398/1008, and the famine continued in 399/1009 as well, although the canal was opened in that year.[13]

The Fatimids met the crisis by tightening the state monopoly on grain and conferring upon the *muḥtasib* compelling powers. Dealers and brokers were forced to sell their merchandise directly to the

[11] Market inspectors were therefore appointed on the docks of the Nile near Cairo, where ships loaded with grain used to arrive from Upper Egypt; al-Maqrīzī, *Itti῾āẓ*, vol. II, p. 31 s. a 390/1000; Shoshan, 'Fatimid grain policy', 185–6.

[12] Al-Maqrīzī, *Ighātha*, p. 13 dates this event to the period of administration of Muḥammad Ḥasan Ibn ῾Ammār, which supports the reliability of his claim. Ibn ῾Ammār was entrusted with the administration of Egypt in 997; see Ibn Taghrībirdī, *Nujūm*, vol. IV, p. 122; al-Maqrīzī, *Itti῾āẓ*, vol. I, pp. 132–3, 146, 229, 277; Ḥamza Abū Ya῾lā Ibn al-Qalānisī, *Dhayl ta'rīkh Dimashq*, ed. Henry F. Amedroz (Beirut and Leiden: E. J. Brill, 1908), pp. 44–5; Yaacov Lev, 'Army, regime, and society in Fatimid Egypt, 358–487/968–1094', *International Journal of Middle East Studies* 19 (1987), 337–65, especially 346. For the famine, see Yaḥyā Ibn Sa῾īd, *Eutychii Patriarchae Alexadtrini Annales*, ed. Cheikho et al., p. 164. For the creation of a state monopoly during this crisis, see al-Maqrīzī, *Itti῾āẓ*, vol. I, p. 291.

[13] Al-Maqrīzī, *Itti῾āẓ*, vol. II, p. 74.

government, hoarders were severely punished, and the devaluation of the dinar was decelerated by coins provided directly from the state coffers. Rising prices, however, and stagnation in the market continued to loom.[14]

In addition, this drought was accompanied by anti-Christian riots and an outburst of religious afflictions and oppression of the Christian subjects originating with the Caliph himself. The religious frenzy culminated in an order issued by Caliph al-Ḥākim on 28 September 1009 to destroy the Church of the Holy Sepulchre in Jerusalem. The order was issued only weeks into the new agricultural and tax year and the third successive year of very low 'plenitudes'.[15] Ibn al-Athīr describes the event very briefly, without mentioning the year: al-Ḥākim ordered that after the destruction of the Church of the Resurrection in Jerusalem, *all* the churches in the realm be destroyed – and this was done – and that the Jews and the Christians were then to accept Islam or emigrate to Byzantine lands – and many did convert. Many of the converted Christians and Jews returned to their original faith when the decrees were abolished, following the end of the persecutions, although many of the Jews 'generally managed to evade the decree to convert to Islam and only a few of them did convert and although many other Jews converted to Islam'.[16]

[14] Al-Maqrīzī, *Ighātha*, pp. 15–17. See also Thierry Bianquis, 'Une Crise frumentaire dans l'Egypte Fatimide', *Journal of the Economic and Social History of the Orient* 23 (1980), 67–101, especially 91.

[15] For the destruction, see Yaḥyā Ibn Saʿīd, *Eutychii Patriarchae Alexadtrini Annales*, ed. Cheikho et al., pp. 283ff; ʿIzz al-Dīn Abū al-Ḥasan ʿAlī Ibn al-Athīr, *al-Kāmil fī ʾl-taʾrīkh*, ed. Carl J. Tornberg (Leiden: E. J. Brill, 1862–71; reprinted Beirut: Dār Ṣāder and Dār Beyrouth,1965–7), vol. IX, pp. 208–9; al-Maqrīzī, *al-Mawāʿiẓ*, vol. II, p. 287; Moshe Gil, *A history of Palestine, 634–1099* (Cambridge University Press, 1992), pp. 374–5.

[16] According to Ibn al-Athīr, *Kāmil*, vol. IX, p. 209. Al-Maqrīzī, *Mawāʿiẓ* , vol. II, p. 495, and Bar Hebraeus (Abū al-Faraj), *The chronography*, translated from the Syriac by Ernest A. Wallis Budge, 2 vols. (Oxford University Press, 1932), vol. I, p. 184 speak about thousands of churches that were destroyed in the Fatimid kingdom at the time. See also Yaḥyā Ibn Saʿīd al-Anṭākī, *Histoire*, 511; Gil, *History of Palestine*, pp. 376–7.

A letter sent from Elḥanan b. Shemaria to the community of Jerusalem, probably not earlier than 1011, describes the edicts that had been imposed on the Jews of Egypt in the previous years, claiming that 'Many have left behind their creed and dropped their religion'. The decrees were revoked during the lifetime of al-Ḥākim himself, who allowed the restoration of the destroyed churches and synagogues, except those which had been sold in order to raise money for the regime's empty treasury.[17]

The drought of 1004–9 was accompanied by the penetration of nomadic tribes into Palestine and Syria. 'From then onwards', writes Yaḥyā Ibn Saʿīd, 'they became the rulers of the country ... They even attempted to capture coastal strongholds but did not succeed'. In 1011, he reports, they started minting coins of their own, and were suppressed by the Fatimid army only in July 1013.[18] The nomads (Bedouins, and in a way the Qarmatians too)[19] who established a loose coalition with the local Christians and obtained the support of the Byzantines, tried to chase the Jews, who supported the Fatimids, out of Jerusalem.[20] According to Salmon

17 Gil, *History of Palestine*, pp. 377–8. For the letter see Moshe Gil, *Palestine during the first Muslim period*, 3 vols. (Tel Aviv University Press, 1983), vol. II, pp. 41–3 (no. 26) (Hebrew). According to the *Le Synaxaire arabe jacobite (rédaction copte)*, texte Arabe publié, traduit et annoté par René Basset, *Patrologia Orientalis* 1.3 (Turnhout: Brepols, 1904), p. 560, the persecution lasted for seven years, and according to another version eight years and a month.

18 Al-Anṭākī, *Histoire de Yaḥyā Ibn Saʿīd d'Antioche*, facsimile 2, *Patrologia Orientalis*, 23.3, pp. 295–8; for the entry of tribes into Palestine, see Yehoshua Frenkel, 'The Seljuks in Palestine, 1071–1098', *Cathedra* 21 (1981), 63–72 (Hebrew).

19 For Muslim sources describing the Qarmatians as completely rejecting Islam and representing Persian political aspirations, see Abū Jaʿfar Muḥammad b. Jarīr al-Ṭabarī, *Tāʾrīkh al-rusul wal-mulūk*, ed. Michael J. De Goeje (Leiden: E. J. Brill, 1964 [1879–1901]), 3rd series, p. 2128; al-Muʾayyad ʿImād al-Dīn Ismāʿīl Abū ʾl-Fidāʾ, *Al-Mukhtaṣar fī akhbār al-bashar* (Cairo: al-Ḥusayniyya [AH 1325]), vol. II, p. 55; ʿAbd al-Raḥmān Ibn Khaldūn al-Maghribī, *al-ʿIbar wa-dīwān al-mubtadaʾ wal-khabar* (Beirut: Dār al-Kitāb al-Lubnānī, 1957), vol. III, p. 705.

20 Gil, *History of Palestine*, pp. 347–8; Georges Vajda, *Deux commentaires Karaïtes sur l'Ecclésiate* (Leiden: E. J. Brill, 1971), p. 42, n. 4; see also Yefet b. ʿAlī in his commentary on Psalms 11:1: 'for the Byzantines do not demand that we leave all of Palestine, only Jerusalem', MS Paris 286, fol. 70 as quoted by Gil, *History of Palestine*, p. 348. For the Jewish community supporting the Fatimids, see Gil, *Palestine*, vol. II, pp. 116–19.

b. Yeruḥam, in his commentary on Psalms written in Jerusalem during this period, 'the uncircumcised beat us in order to oust us from Jerusalem by force and separate us from the city'.[21]

## COLD SPELLS IN BAGHDAD, 398/1007, AND IN SOUTHERN ITALY, 398/1007–402/1012 AND 1017

The Egyptian drought of the first decade of the eleventh century was also accompanied by severely cold weather that hit Baghdad and Mesopotamia in 398/1007, causing severe drought and famine there too. Snow accumulated, not melting for weeks, and riots erupted in the ranks of the army as well as among civilians. Sibṭ Ibn al-Jawzī says that snow was not recorded in Baghdad since 296, one hundred years earlier, and that it was as far south as Basra.[22] Sectarian fights (Hanbalis against Shafiʿis and Sunnis against Shiʿis) gave rise to bloodshed and destruction. The shortage led the Bedouins to plunder the Hajj caravans of July–August 397/1007 and July August 398/1008, leaving the pilgrims naked, hungry and thirsty, and unable to reach their destination.[23] The drought of 400/1009–10 resulted in an unprecedented low level of the Tigris, so low that boats had to be towed.[24] The cold spell that continued to hit Khurasan in 401/1011 was felt in eastern Iran, where the Sultan tried to meet the hunger with administrative measures:

[21] In the commentary on Ecclesiastes 9:6, he writes: 'they want to evict us from Jerusalem and place a heavy iron yoke around our necks'. See Gil, *History of Palestine*, pp. 346–7; Jacob Mann, *Texts and studies in Jewish history and literature*, 2 vols. (Cincinnati: Hebrew College Press, 1931–35), vol. II, p. 18.

[22] Sibṭ Ibn al-Jawzī (Yūsuf Ibn Qazughlī), *Mirʾat al-ẓamān fī taʾrīkh al-aʿyān: al-ḥiqba 345–447 H*, ed. Janān Jalīl Muḥammad al-Hamawundī, (Baghdād: al-Dār al-Waṭaniyya, 1990), pp. 273–4; Ibn al-Athīr, *Kāmil*, vol. IX, p. 208.

[23] Sibṭ Ibn al-Jawzī, *Mirʾat al-ẓamān*, pp. 271, 273; for similar events in 403/1012 and 404/1013, see pp. 287, 289; for cancellation of the Hajj in 406/1016 (because of the thirst) and between 408–12/1018–22, see pp. 299, 304.

[24] Ibid., p. 280.

A wide-spread famine, and a frightful and calamitous scarcity occurred ... in the district of Nishapur, nearly 100,000 men perished, and there was nobody to bury them ... and the Sultan ... commanded ... that the revenue officers ... should empty the granaries of corn, and distribute amongst the poor and wretched ... until the produce of the year 402/1012 arrived ... and that extremity was remedied.[25]

The return to order in Baghdad included prohibition of the Sunnis and Shiʿis from publicly observing their religious ceremonies, and an order to match the capture of a Sunni bandit with that of a Shiʿi one and to drown them together in the Tigris in broad daylight.[26]

A very harsh winter was recorded in southern Italy in the year 1009, which led to the outbreak of a revolt in the coastal cities of Apulia. For several months and possibly longer, the cities of Bari and Trani were in the hands of the rebels and special reinforcements despatched from Constantinople were needed to suppress the uprising. Simultaneously, Muslims from Sicily attacked northern Calabria, sacking Cosenza.[27]

[25] Muḥammad Ibn ʿAbd al-Jabbār ʿUtbī, *The Kitab-i-Yamini: historical memoirs of the Amir Sabaktagin, and the Sultán Mahmúd of Ghazna, early conquerors of Hindustan, and founders of the Ghaznavide dynasty*, trans. James Reynolds, Oriental Translation Fund, Publication 72 (London: Oriental Translation Fund, 1858), ch. 33.

[26] Hilāl al-Ṣabī, in Henry F. Amedroz and David S. Margoliouth (eds. and trans.), *The eclipse of the Abbasid caliphate: original chronicles of the fourth Islamic century*, 7 vols. (Oxford: Basil Blackwell, 1920–1), vol. III, pp. 439–42, 458; Ibn al-Jawzī, Abū al-Faraj ʿAbd al-Raḥmān Ibn ʿĀlī, *al-Muntaẓam fī ta'rīkh al-mulūk wal-umam*, 11 vols. in 6 vols. (Hyderabad: al-ʿUthmānīyya, 1357–9/1938–40), vol. VII, p. 222; al-Dawādārī, Abū Bakr Ibn ʿAbd Allāh, *Kanz al-durar wa-jāmiʿ al-ghurar*, ed. Ṣalāḥ al-Dīn al-Munajjid (Cairo: Deutches Archäologisches Institut, in Komission bei Harrassowitz Wiesbaden, 1961), vol. VI, p. 319.

[27] Graham A. Loud, 'Southern Italy in the eleventh century', in *The new Cambridge medieval history*, vol. IV, *c. 1024–c. 1198*, ed. David Luscombe and Jonathan Riley-Smith (Cambridge University Press, 2004), part 2, pp. 94–119, especially p. 95; *Annales Barenses*, ed. Georg H. Pertz, Monumenta Germaniae Historica, Scriptores 5 (Hanover, 1844), p. 53.

The first rebellion of the Normans in Apulia against the Byzantine lords of the region in 1017 was also preceded by an unexpected and unprecedented severe cold spell. William of Apulia refers in his book, written during the 1090s, to the deterioration of agricultural products that eventually hastened the advance of the Normans that followed it: 'At this time the Italians were astounded by the fall of an extraordinary and up to then unprecedented quantity of snow, which killed the bulk of the wild animals and cut down trees, never to grow again'.[28] The small number of Norman rebels participating in the uprising (between 300 and 2,500) emphasizes the fragility of the Byzantine government in periods of dearth.[29]

## EGYPT IN THE MID 1020S

The period between 1013 and 1023 was comparatively calm and no dearth is mentioned, but the period between 414 and 416/1023–6 is often described as one of the most difficult in the history of Fatimid Egypt, exemplifying, once again, the immediate domino effect of droughts.[30] The crisis began in September 1023/414 when the canal (the Khalīj) was opened (on 2 September) but, according to al-Maqrīzī, the water level in it went down two weeks later. The ensuing famine was soon followed by pestilence, with many people, especially the poor, dying of hunger or disease. The events during this year were typical for years of famine – citizens who could not obtain bread rioted, and unpaid soldiers rebelled, complaining that

28 Guillaume de Pouille, *La Geste de Robert Guiscard*, ed. Marguerite Mathieu (Palermo: Istituto Siciliano di Studi Bizantini e Neoellenici, 1961), c. 1, pp. 100–2, 47–51.

29 Loud, 'Southern Italy'; Amatus de' Monte Cassino, *Storia de' Normanni*, ed. Vicenzo de Bartholomaeis, *Fonti per la Storia d'Italia* (Rome: Tipografia del Senato in Roma, 1935), vol. LXXVI, pp. 30–1.

30 Bianquis, 'Crise frumentaire'; Lev, 'Army', 337–65.

they were reduced to eating dogs.[31] The soldiers marched on Fustat, setting houses on fire, plundering the city's grain port, stores and a supply of meat intended for the Caliph.[32]

The riots soon spread across the country: soldiers demanding a raise in their wages looted the cities of Tinnis[33] and Ashmunayn, cooperating with the Bedouins, who appeared on the scene as the crisis progressed.[34] Rebellions were reported from Upper Egypt[35] and even among the soldiers of the palace guard, who clashed with the Turkish regiment and unsuccessfully attacked the Hajj caravan.[36]

The Fatimids' belief that an efficient administration could prevent hunger regardless of the rise of the Nile is exemplified in a dialogue conducted between the Caliph and his *muḥtasib* in 415/1025. The *muḥtasib* was reminded that upon receiving the office he had committed himself to seeing that grain and bread were available to all, and that since he had failed to keep his promise, the Caliph accused him of 'starving the people to death and destroying the country'.[37]

In 1024/5 the Caliph therefore ordered the seizure of all ships transporting grain from Upper Egypt and the transfer of the grain to the palace. When the agitation continued, he opened 150 granaries and their content was sold to millers and bakers at a fixed price, instructing them to do the same with the public.[38]

31 ʿIzz al-Mulk Muḥammad Musabbiḥī, *al-Juzʾ al-arbaʿūn min akhbār miṣr*, ed. Ayman F. Sayyid and Thierry Bianquis, 2 vols. (Cairo: Institut Français d'Archéologie Orientale du Caire, 1978–84), vol. I, pp. 87–8. (The surviving part of the chronicle of al-Musabbiḥī [366–420/977–1030] covers a period from 1 Jumādā II 414 to the end of 415 [August 1023–March 1025].) Al-Maqrīzī, *Ittiʿāẓ*, vol. II, pp. 134–5.

32 Musabbiḥī, *Akhbār miṣr*, vol. I, pp. 68, 81–2, 87–8; al-Maqrīzī, *Ittiʿāẓ*, vol. II, pp. 164–5.

33 Musabbiḥī, *Akhbār miṣr*, vol. I, p. 57. 34 Ibid., vol. I, p. 82. 35 Ibid., vol. I, p. 21.

36 Musabbiḥī, *Akhbār miṣr*, vol. I, pp. 69, 74; Lev, 'Army', 344, 361.

37 Al-Maqrīzī, *Ittiʿāẓ*, vol. II, p. 165; Bianquis, 'Crise frumentaire', 84; Shoshan, 'Fatimid grain policy', 185–6.

38 Al-Maqrīzī, *Ittiʿāẓ*, vol. II, pp. 144–5.

The drought and pestilence soon spread to neighbouring countries as well. It is interesting, perhaps, to note that a severe drought was felt for the first time in Ifriqiya (North Africa) in 413/1022, a year before it was experienced in Egypt. The concurrence of a drought in North Africa and Egypt was a rare occasion; Ifriqiya, like the rest of the coastal plain of North Africa, is usually affected by the southern Mediterranean climate and by rains coming from the west, unlike the rise of the Nile, which is affected only by the monsoon rains in East Africa. Ifriqiya, like Egypt's other neighbours, depended upon the Egyptian supply only as a buffer, in years of dearth. Ibn al-Athīr mentions an extreme drought in Ifriqiya in 413 (which began on 6 April 1022), but says that nobody died of hunger.[39] The drought in Ifriqiya is also mentioned in the letters of the Geniza. A letter that was sent from Qayrawan when the drought was over (1024?) and written by two merchants, Joseph and Nissim, sons of Berekhiah, states clearly that the 'kingdom' (of Ifriqiya) is in a state of anarchy; the place had suffered heavily during the previous year. Although in the present year there was rain again, they say that in the far Maghrib, such as Sijilmasa and other places, people died 'by the famine and by the sword'.[40] Another letter sent from Qayrawan says that wheat was sold for a price that was 20–24 times higher than the price that was paid for it in years of abundance.[41]

In Palestine, as elsewhere, the first domino effect of the dearth was a price rise and the violence of the nomads. In 415/1024 the Bedouins of Palestine joined forces with local Christians, attacking

[39] Ibn al-Athīr, *Kāmil*, vol. IX, p. 329; Moshe Gil, 'Institutions and events of the eleventh century mirrored in Geniza letters (part I)', *Bulletin of the School of Oriental and African Studies* 67.2 (2004), 151–67, especially 161–3.

[40] Sijilmasa, a trade entrepôt at the western edge of the Maghreb, now in Morocco; Gil, *History of Palestine*, p. 149a, lines 31–8.

[41] Ibid., p. 139b, line 12; for the lower price, see p. 660b, lines 9–10 (5–6 qafizs for a quarter of a dinar).

regions bordering the desert, and during the summer, when the famine increased, the situation in Palestine became very tense. The Bedouins overran Ramla twice or thrice, occupied it for two months, killed many of the inhabitants, sacked property and maltreated women. Earlier they attacked and pillaged al-Aylah, abandoning the city in return for money and agricultural products, continuing with a similar maltreatment in al-ʿArish. Tiberias was also sacked and the inhabitants were slaughtered mercilessly.[42] The soldiers sent to suppress them had to be supplied with extra money and horses and personal rations of bread because it was impossible to purchase bread on the site.[43] The revolt continued, however, and in January 415/1025 hundreds of horsemen belonging to the al-Jarrāḥ tribe raided cities in Sinai, demanding control of Jerusalem and Nāblus in return for peace.[44]

The weakened and bankrupted Fatimid government of Palestine imposed special taxes, attempting to meet the needs of the army who were suppressing the riots and the hungry population. Both the taxes and the pressure of the government are described in letters written by the heads of the Jerusalem Academy to Fustat, referring to the desertion of the cities of Ramla and Jerusalem by their Jewish population following the hunger, attacks by the Bedouins and the special taxes, and detailing the atrocities and their cruel mistreatment.[45] The representative of the head of the Academy warns the governor of Jerusalem that if the demand of a special tax of 2,500 dinars is materialized, 'half the population will flee and the city will

[42] Ibid., p. 387; Musabbiḥī, *Akhbār miṣr*, vol. I, pp. 34–5, 43–4, 47–54, 57f., 65, 76, 83–4, 89, 98; al-Maqrīzī, *Ittiʿāẓ*, vol. II, pp. 151–7.

[43] Musabbiḥī, *Akhbār miṣr*, vol. I, pp. 35, 68. [44] Ibid., vol. I, pp. 36, 52–3, 58, 76.

[45] Mann, *Jews in Egypt*, vol. vI, pp. 179–80 and the discussion in vol. I, p. 160; Gil, *Palestine*, vol. II, pp. 83–4 (no. 49). See also Mann, *Jews in Egypt*, vol. I, pp. 160–1 and vol. II, pp. 180–2; Gil, *Palestine*, vol. II, pp. 85–7 (no. 50).

be destroyed in front of your eyes'.[46] At about the same time we are informed about another special tax of 15,000 dinars that is imposed on the entire city of Jerusalem and an additional tax of 6,000 dinars imposed on the Jews only. The Jews were not able to collect the entire sum and as a result some were imprisoned and others forced to sell or mortgage their property, 'until we went out of everything we had. [We were] empty, naked, sad, poor and nothing remained to a man in his house even a dress for himself or house ware'.[47] Solomon ha-Kohen further notes that many of the Jews in Jerusalem died 'in the plague that happened in the city'.[48]

Between 1026 and 1030 the famine abated, the pressure of the Bedouins was gradually reduced, and peace and calm slowly returned to the Levant. The year 1030, however, was still one of dearth. In another letter written by ha-Kohen to his son on 1 May 1030 he still mourns the extended poverty of the Jews in Ramla and their lingering dearth. The winter, he says, was particularly hard and he himself had to spend all his money and sell his household goods. 'When this year arrived, I had to sell everything that remained in the house ... and would not have thought that the year will pass and we are still alive'. Most of the fields, he says, lie fallow and the remnants of the community in Ramla are miserably poor. He talks of the terrible starvation, for 'there is nothing in the whole land of the Philistines (*Jund Filasṭīn*)'.[49]

[46] Gil, *Palestine*, vol. II, pp. 59–60 (no. 36). [47] Ibid., vol. II, pp. 83–4 (no. 49).

[48] A plague seems more plausible to me in the context of Mann's reading of dying people than Gill's reading of the same word as 'thing'. See Jacob Mann, *The Jews in Egypt and in Palestine under the Faṭimid caliphs*, 2 vols. (New York: Ktav, 1970 (reprinted Oxford University Press, 1920–2), vol. I, p. 106; Gil, *Palestine*, vol. II, pp. 97–8 (no. 57).

[49] Gil, *Palestine*, vol. II, pp. 151–5 (no. 83b), mentions the reduction of his livelihood; in no. 88, p. 163, he writes: 'we, the people of the Holy City, the congregation that dwindled and bowed down, of which we remained but a few'. For the cold winter of 1030, see Gil, *Palestine*, vol. II, p. 167 (no. 90l, line 17); see also Shelomo Dov Goitein, *Palestinian Jewry in early Islamic and Crusader times in the light of the Geniẓah documents* (Jerusalem: Yad Izhak Ben-Zvi, 1980), pp. 98–9 (Hebrew).

The early 1030s were years of restoration and renovation, both in Jerusalem, where the walls were renewed and where the reconstruction of the Dome of the Rock was completed in 424 H/1032, and in Ramla, where reconstruction immediately followed the defeat of the Bedouins.

The alignment of the reconstructed walls of Jerusalem was considerably shorter than the previous one, and a considerable portion of the southern part of the city was left outside the line of the walls and was therefore undefended. The works were probably completed during the mid 1050s, but the alignment of the walls points to the weakening of the city, especially of its Christian community, and to the desertion of a considerable part of its former population that had lived in the unfortified parts.

The severe crises that hit Ifriqiya in 1022–3 and Egypt in 1023–5 were followed by an even more disastrous crisis that plagued the countries of the north (Iran and Mesopotamia) and lingered on for many more years. Such climatic crises, however, did not hit Egypt and the Levant for almost three consecutive decades. The dislocated nomads that had made life difficult to bear in the mid 1020s now settled down, and Egypt enjoyed sufficient rises of the Nile to enable it to supply its neighbours with sufficient amounts of grain. Egypt was so prosperous, in fact, that the sufferings of 1004–9 and of the mid 1020s, including the attacks of the nomads, the desertions of cities and agricultural provinces and the persecutions of the Jewish and Christian communities, were forgotten. The Fatimid administration of these three decades is thus considered to be an exemplary bureaucracy, and historians often tend to ignore the short periods of disorder that coincide with periods of dearth. The situation was diametrically different in the northern regions of the eastern Mediterranean (or of southwestern Asia), which suffered, at the same time that Egypt enjoyed wealth and order, from extended periods of freeze. This led to the arrival of waves of dislocated nomads, which gradually transformed Iran, Mesopotamia and the Byzantine Empire, enforcing on them the same miserable situation that characterized Egypt in the periods of extended hunger.

PART TWO

# *Regional domino effects in the eastern Mediterranean: 1027–60 AD*

CHAPTER FOUR

# The collapse of Iran

## THE CLIMATIC CRISIS OF 1024–71

The disorder, anarchy, plunder, looting and anti-Christian riots that followed the droughts and the pestilences of the 960s and of 1004–11 were resumed during the climatic disaster that started in the late 1020s and reached its most negative manifestations in the mid 1050s. The climatic disturbances of the 1020s to the 1050s were associated with a wave of dislocation and nomadization that transformed the formerly pastoralist societies of the steppes and other nomadic tribes into agents of destruction.

Pastoralist economies are dependent on seasonal migration. Each summer the herds are driven out of their winter grounds to pastures and sources of water. But the extended cold waves and the hunger prevented the nomads from maintaining their regular habits. The flocks froze to death during the winters, and the pastures dried out during the summers. The nomads were compelled to look for pastures further west and south, in the valleys of Iran, Khurasan and later even in Mesopotamia, Armenia and Anatolia.[1]

[1] My interest in pastoralist economies was raised while following the graduate seminar of Professor Anatholy M. Khazanov at the Hebrew University of Jerusalem in 1986. See Anatholy M. Khazanov, 'Pastoral nomads and anthropology', *Nomadic Peoples* 4 (2000), 5–22. For the nomadization of agriculturalists, see Owen Lattimore, 'The geographical factor in Mongol history', *Geographical Journal* 91 (1938), 1–20.

The regions of the south, however, were also drought-stricken and could not sustain the numbers of newly arrived nomads, who turned to violence and aggression, looting and plundering the regions that were supposed to sustain them. The damage the nomads spread in the neighbouring countries was worse than that which they inflicted on their countries of origin.

The migration of the dislocated pastoralists was not organized or conducted from above. The nomads who penetrated Iran, Khurasan, Azerbaijan or the Balkans were divided into groups that operated simultaneously but independently in various parts of the region. Even the Oghuz tribes that penetrated Iran from 1027 onwards and were known later as the 'Seljuks', were divided into (at least) three groups, whose advance can be followed in detail. Each group of tribes roamed a different region, spreading destruction and havoc wherever it went. Stronger tribes or coalitions of tribes often penetrated the roaming 'territories' of the weaker ones, causing a further movement and extending the 'domino effect' to the neighbouring regions. Eventually, the weaker groups among the tribes that penetrated Iran and Khurasan accepted the leadership of the strongest clan, that of the Seljuks, and of their leader Tughril Beg, and those who refused to do so deteriorated and vanished.

Three phenomena were repeated during the climatic disasters of the late 1020s to the end of the 1050s in the north:

1. There is a strong connection between events of severe cold that led to famine and the arrival of the dislocated pastoralists. Invasions of nomads were recorded only during the most severely cold years.
2. There is a strong connection between cold and famine, on the one hand, and the violence of the nomads, on the other. Even when the Seljuks acquired legitimacy and became acknowledged

rulers, they returned to pillage and plunder during severe cold spells and hunger. The opposite is also true: their attacks were considerably reduced in years of comparative opulence.

3. Both the penetration of the nomads from the north, and the violence of the nomads who immigrated to the south, ended when the cold spells abated and when climate and winter rain returned to normal.

Edmund Bosworth, one of the most important scholars dealing with the early history of the Turkic tribes, does not mention climate change in general or cold spells in particular as a possible reason for the migration of the Ghuzz. These incursions from Inner Asia, he says 'had effects on the older Islamic lands – in the case of the Mongol invasions, cataclysmic ones – but in the longer term, the perdurable absorptive powers of Islamic religion and culture exercised their effects on the incomers'.[2] Bertold Spuler, in his article about the disintegration of the Caliphate in the first edition of the *Cambridge History of Islam*, also ignored the role of climate in the advance of the Oghuz Turks.[3]

Richard Bulliet was the first (and so far probably the only) scholar to interpret some of the social, economical and cultural transformations that occurred in Iran and in the steppes during the tenth and eleventh centuries as the results of what he labels the 'Big Chill' – a long period of cold spells that hit these regions during the same time. In his *Cotton, climate, and camels* he argues

[2] Edmund Bosworth, 'The steppe peoples in the Islamic world', in Michael Cook (general ed.), *The new Cambridge history of Islam*, vol. III, *The eastern Islamic world, eleventh to eighteenth centuries*, ed. David O. Morgan and Anthony Reid (Cambridge University Press, 2010), pp. 21–77.

[3] Bertold Spuler, 'The disintegration of the caliphate in the east', in *The Cambridge history of Islam*, ed. Peter. M. Holt, Ann K. S. Lambton and Bernard Lewis, vol. I, *The central Islamic lands from pre-Islamic times to the First World War* ( Cambridge University Press, 1970), pp. 143–74.

that the decline of the cotton industry in Iran and the stability it provided to the local elites resulted from the 'chill'.[4] The migration of the Oghuz Turks to the south emanated, according to Bulliet, from the physiological needs of the one-humped camel that the Turkic people have bred since the arrival of the Arabs to their regions. The new breed was larger and stronger than both of its one- and two-humped precedents, but it was less adapted than the two-humped breed to the cold, and the Oghuz were forced to migrate to the warmer countries to rescue their new breed of camels.

This is not the first time that Bulliet bases an important argumentation on the abilities and availabilities of camels. But whereas his previous *Camel and the Wheel* volume was a convincing study in technological history,[5] his present 'camel oriented', deterministic theory for the migration of the Oghuz Turks to the south is not supported by any historical or archaeological documentation. In the following pages I will try to claim that the Turkic incursions of the eleventh century were the direct result of climatic disturbances.

## THE COLLAPSE OF IRAN

In the year 417/1027, writes Ibn al-Jawzī, 'continuously from November to January, came a cold that no one had ever known before. *Water froze solid throughout this period, including the shores of the Tigris and the wide canals*'.[6] Bar Hebraeus also refers to the intense cold that prevailed in Baghdad in that same year: '[that] the

[4] Richard W. Bulliet *Cotton, climate, and camels in early Islamic Iran: a moment in world history* (New York: Columbia University Press, 2009).

[5] Richard W. Bulliet, *The camel and the wheel* (Cambridge, MA: Harvard University Press, 1975).

[6] Ibn al-Jawzī, Abū al-Faraj ʿAbd al-Raḥmān Ibn ʿAlī, *al-Muntaẓam fī taʾrīkh al-mulūk wa-al-umam*, 11 vols. in 6 vols. (Hyderabad: al-ʿUthmānīyya, 1357–9/1938–40), vol. VIII, p. 25; emphasis the present author.

farmers were unable to sow seed'.[7] The intense cold of 417/1027 was only the first of years of severe cold that hit the eastern and northeastern countries between 417–30/1027 and the late 1050s.[8] In 419/1028–9 there was a strong cold 'black wind' and the water froze, ice accumulated and palm dates 'were burned'. The following year (420/1029–30) there was a hailstorm in Baghdad and every piece of hail was as big as 'a standing ox'.[9] The cold made life in the Trans-Oxonian steppes insupportable and spurred the nomads to move on to Khurasan, Iran and later to Baghdad.

Ibn al-Athīr dates the first appearance of the Seljuks to 420/1029 (i.e., two years after the beginning of the freeze) and relates the severe measures that Maḥmūd of Ghazna, the leader of the Ghaznavid dynasty (who died in April 1030), took against the 'followers of Arslan Ibn Saljūq the Turk, who had been in the desert around Bukhara'. Maḥmūd, who himself penetrated the territory of the Buyids, appreciated the 'offensive capacity and great numbers' of his Seljuk adversaries but declined the advice 'to cut off their thumbs or to drown them in the Oxus'. He decided, instead, to arrest their leader Arslān and scatter his men far and wide in the regions of Khurasan. Later he arrested Arslān's son, Tughril Beg, plundering his tents and massacring many of his followers, and driving the rest away from Khurasan.[10] The severe measures were not enough, and Maḥmūd had to repeat his struggle against the Oghuz Turks, who 'caused

[7] Bar Hebraeus (Abū al-Faraj), *The chronography*, translated from the Syriac by Ernest A. Wallis Budge, 2 vols. ( Oxford University Press, 1932), vol. I, p. 191.

[8] Ibn al-Jawzī, *Muntaẓam*, vol. VIII, pp. 28–9, 36; Sibṭ Ibn al-Jawzī (Yūsuf Ibn Qazughlī), *Mir'at al-ẓamān fī ta'rīkh al-a'yān: al-ḥiqba 345–447 H*, ed. Janān Jalīl Muḥammad al-Ḥamawundī (Baghdad: al-Dār al-Wataniyya, 1990), pp. 342, 344.

[9] Sibṭ Ibn al-Jawzi, *Mir'at al-ẓamān*, pp. 342, 344.

[10] ʿIzz al-Dīn Abū al-Ḥasan ʿAlī Ibn al-Athīr, *al-Kāmil fī al-ta'rīkh*, ed. Carl J. Tornberg, 13 vols. (Leiden: E. J. Brill, 1862–71; reprinted Beirut: Dār Ṣāder, Dār Beyrouth, 1965–7), vol. IX, pp. 377–8; vol. I, p. 13; see also Dickran K. Kouymjian, 'Problems of medieval Armenian and Muslim historiography: the Mxitʿar of Ani fragment', *International Journal of Middle East Studies* 4 (1973), 465–75, especially 467–9.

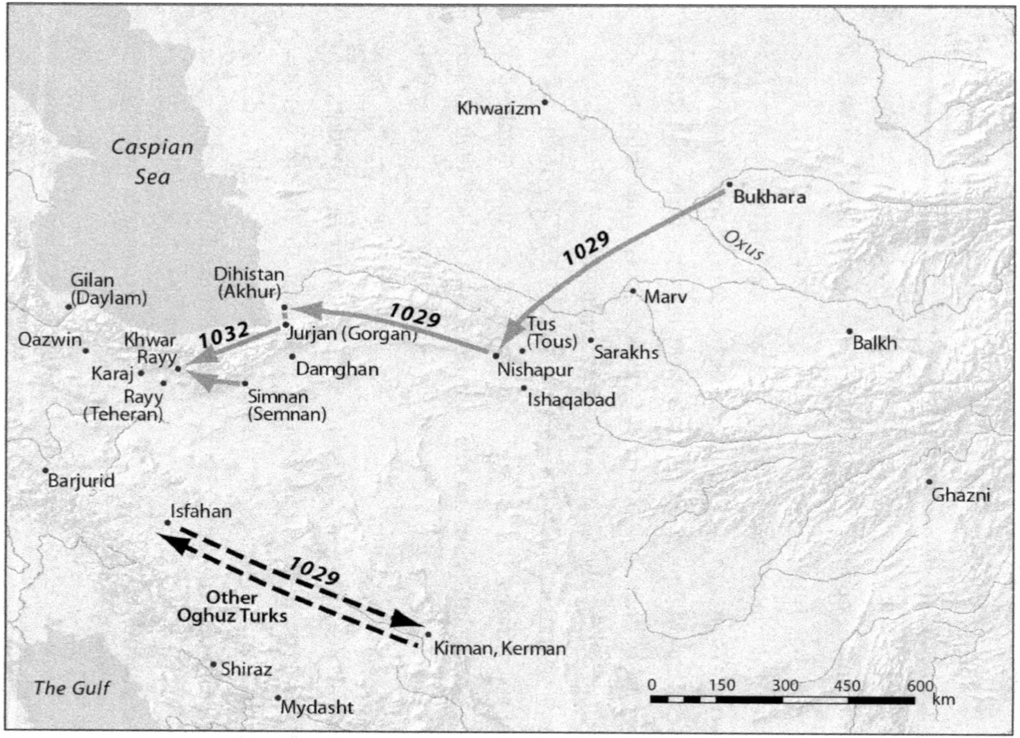


Map 4.1 The advance of the Seljuks between Bukhara, Nishapur and Rayy (ancient Teheran) and of 'two thousands tents' of the Oghuz Turks in central Iran between Kirman and Isfahan before they left for Azerbaijan.

disturbances and indulged in pillage'. Initially he dealt with two thousand tents only, a number of nomads small enough to be suppressed. But it soon became clear that 'More [Oghuz Turks] . . . came down from the mountain into the [neighbouring] regions, where they plundered and wreaked havoc and murder.' The attempt to limit these cold- and famine-driven nomads was doomed to failure. More nomads appeared every day, and the promises they made to be 'loyal and behave well' were not fulfilled.[11]

It is usually not so easy to keep track of all the comings and goings of the Turkmen and their migrations into northern Iran after AD 1027.[12] However, the coherent, detailed and reliable descriptions of the advance of the Oghuz into Iran and Khurasan provide us with an unprecedented anatomy of a quasi-epic historical collapse and with clear evidence of the concurrence between outbursts of cold, famine and pestilence and the violence and plunder that followed them. Therefore, I will detail these migrations, including exact names and locations, to strengthen the connection between causes (cold winters) and effects (outbursts of violence among the pastoralists).

The existence of different and independent nomadic groups in Iran and Khurasan is manifested in 1029 when the Ghaznavid leader, Maḥmūd of Ghazna, pursued the Seljuks westwards, 'from Nishapur to Dihistan [and] to Jurjan', while another group of 'two thousand tents', to whom Ibn al-Athīr later refers as the 'Iraqi Oghuz', was roaming in the south, but also similarly proceeded westward from Kirman to Isfahan on their way to Azerbaijan. When the members of the second group were expelled from Isfahan, they 'plundered every village they passed, until they

[11] Ibn al-Athīr, *Kāmil*, vol. IX, p. 379; English translation, vol. I, p. 14.

[12] For a helpful if slightly outdated guide, see Clifford E. Bosworth, *The Ghaznavids: their empire in Afghanistan and Eastern Iran, 994–1040*, 2nd edn (Beirut: Librairie du Liban, 1973).

eventually came to ... Azerbaijan ... [but] more remained in Khurasan than had gone to Isfahan'.[13]

The lingering cold spell and hunger of the 1030s accelerated the arrival of additional groups of nomads, spreading havoc and destruction along their advancing trails. Bar Hebraeus clearly points to the lingering nature of the hunger and the connection between the freeze, the famine and the arrival of the nomads:

In 423/1031 *the water froze in Baghdad* ... and the trees were destroyed and produced no fruit at all. *And there was so great a famine in the wilderness that the nomads who lived there ate their camels and their horses, and even their children* ... And they were in tribulation not only because of the famine (or want of food), but also through thirst which was due to the scarcity of water, and they came and camped by the canals which were in the neighborhood of the towns and villages.[14]

In December 423/1031 the inhabitants of Baghdad were still praying for rain.[15]

Matthew of Edessa refers to the lingering nature of the famine in his description of the following year, 424/1032–3: 'there was a severe famine throughout the entire land. Many people died ... selling their women and children for want of bread ... the land was consumed by famine'.[16] A pestilence, which is almost the natural consequence of a famine, spread in Khurasan, Iran and Mesopotamia causing 'forty thousand' funerals in Isfahan in 423/1032–33[17] and 'seventy thousand'

[13] Ibn al-Athīr, *Kāmil*, vol. IX, p. 378; English translation, vol. I, p. 14.

[14] Bar Hebraeus, *Chronograpy*, vol. I, pp. 193–4; for the famine in Baghdād, see Sibṭ Ibn al-Jawzī, *Mir'at al-zamān*, p. 358; emphasis the present author.

[15] Sibṭ Ibn al-Jawzī, *Mir'at al-zamān*, p. 358.

[16] Matthew of Edessa, *Armenia and the Crusades, tenth to twelfth centuries: the chronicle of Matthew of Edessa*, trans. Ara E. Dostourian (Lanham, MD: University Press of America, 1993), 1.60, p. 55.

[17] Sibṭ Ibn al-Jawzī, *Mir'at al-zamān*, p. 361; Matthew of Edessa, *Armenia and the Crusades*, 1.60, p. 55: 'And there was a pestilence in India and in all Persia; forty thousand biers with dead men were taken out from Isfahan in one week. And in Baghdad also there was not a single house left in which there was not wailing.'

dead in 425/1033–4.[18] The famine was also felt in Ghazna and in 'the land of the Indians'.[19]

In 1033–4 the Seljuks crossed the Oxus back into Khwarizm, where they tried to find refuge. The ruler, however, expelled them, leaving their children in captivity. The Seljuks crossed the desert to Marv, where they 'did not cause anyone any trouble',[20] but many of them continued to roam in Iran and Khurasan and were still persecuted.

Although the two groups, the Seljuks who plundered the north-east and the Iraqi Oghuz who were active in Khurasan, belonged to the same ethnic 'Oghuz' stock, they often operated against each other. The Seljuks were even ready to collaborate with Masʿūd, the son of Maḥmūd of Ghazna, against the other group, promising him to 'drive them out and fight them', if he – Masʿūd – guaranteed the security of the Seljuks. Masʿūd refused, met the Seljuks in battle, routed them temporarily, and was later defeated. The Seljuks reverted once again to their traditional habit of attacking cities in the east, and Balkh, Nishapur, Tus (Tous) and Jurjan were among their victims.[21]

The extreme cold and the violent behaviour of the nomads encouraged millenarian tendencies and apocalyptic interpretations of the events among the Christians.[22] Matthew of Edessa refers to a (apparently anachronistic) prophecy that was ostensibly made three or four years later, in 1036–7, relating the severe cold and harsh famine to the invasion by the Seljuks:

[18] Abū al-Faḍl Bayhaqī, *The history of Bayhaqi*, trans. and with commentary by Clifford E. Bosworth, rev. Mohsen Ashtiany, Persian Heritage series, 3 vols. (New York: Mahtab, 2009), vol. II, p. 209.

[19] Sibṭ Ibn al-Jawzī, *Mirʾat al-zamān*, p. 361.

[20] Ibn al-Athīr, *Kāmil*, vol. IX, p. 476; English translation, vol. I, p. 35

[21] Ibn al-Athīr, *Kāmil*, vol. IX, pp. 477–8; English translation, vol. I, p. 35; al-Ḥusaynī, ʿAlī Ibn Nāṣir, *Akhbār al-dawla al-saljūqiyya*, ed. Muḥammad Iqbāl (Lahore: University Press of the Panjab, 1933), p. 32: 'The Sultan's army fled to Nishapur'.

[22] Bar Hebraus, *Chronography*, vol. I, p. 194.

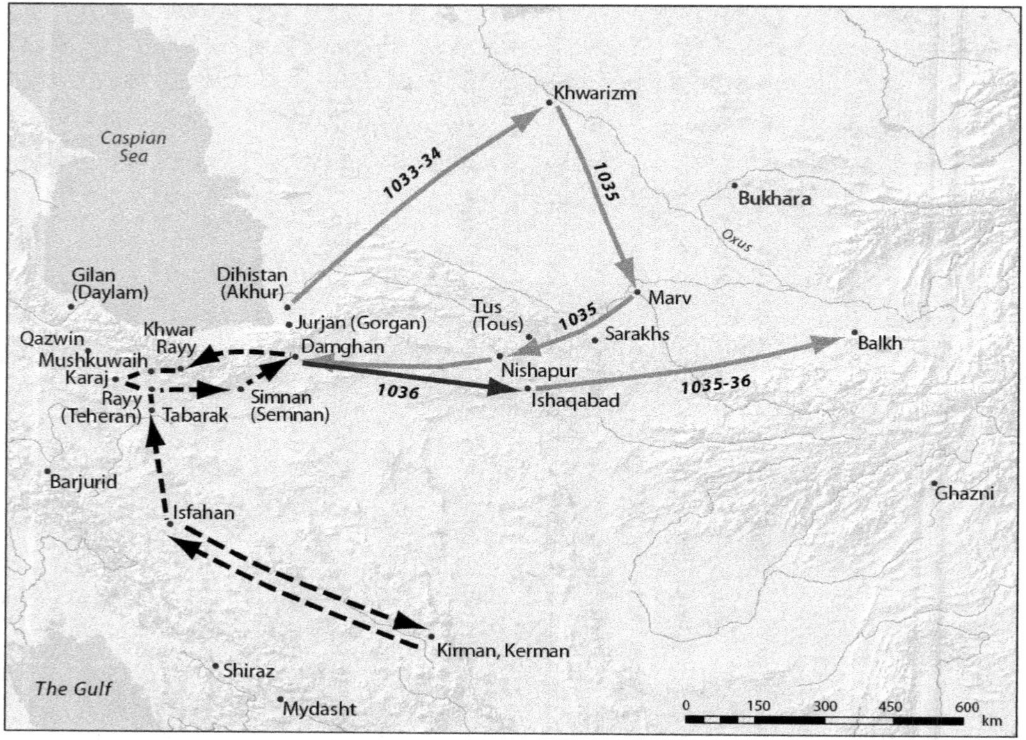


Map 4.2 The circular migration of the Seljuks in 1033–6, according to Ibn al-Athīr, from Rayy to Khwarizm, back to Nishapur, and again to Rayy and Balkh. Cities and villages were plundered on the way.

> There will take place invasions by ... the abominable forces of the Turks ... against the Christian nations; and the whole land will be consumed by the sword. All the nations ... will suffer through famine ... Many regions will become uninhabited ... and many churches will be destroyed to their foundations ...[23]

People believed, says Michael the Syrian 'that ... the end of the world' was coming.[24]

Meanwhile, while the Seljuks were roaming to and fro, between Khwarizm and Marv, attacking time and again the cities of eastern Iran, the 'Iraqi Oghuz' advanced in 1035 and 1036 from Isfahan towards Azerbaijan, plundering cities and overcoming military attempts to hinder them. They arrived in Rayy (present-day Teheran), plundering neighbouring cities on their way.[25]

The nomads, writes Ibn al-Athīr, continued 'their repeating attacks and plundering of villages which were on their way'. The recurrence of the raids and the number of marauders, he says 'was increasing'.[26] In 426/1034, while the Iraqi Oghuz were attacking the city of Rayy, they numbered 5,000 men, whereas when they took it a year later, in 427/May 1035, it became clear 'that every time there was trouble with them they grew stronger and [their adversaries] weaker'. When the governor of Rayy abandoned his city in 1035, 'they entered it, sacking and enslaving women ... so that

[23] Matthew of Edessa, *Armenia and the Crusades*, 1.64, pp. 56–9; Bar Hebraeus, *Chronography*, vol. I, pp. 193–4, describes an event that occurred in Baghdad in 1033–4, 'when a woman gave birth [to a being] which was like an ill-formed serpent ... when he fell upon the ground he spoke and said, "Four years from now a famine shall make an end of the children of men, unless men, and women, and children, and the beasts go forth and weep before the Lord"'.

[24] *Chronique de Michel le Syrien*, edited by Jean-Baptiste Chabot, 5 vols. (Paris, 1899–1924; reprinted Brussels, 1963), vol. III, p. 136 and vol. IV, pp. 559–60.

[25] Damghan, Simnan, Khwar Rayy, Ishaqabad, Mushkuwaih and Tabarak.

[26] Ibn al-Athīr, *Kāmil*, vol. IX, p. 379; English translation, vol. I, p. 15.

the womenfolk took refuge in the main mosque . . . It was even said that some Fridays there were only fifty souls in the main mosque'.[27]

Rayy was the first major city of Iran that was taken and sacked by the nomads, but the victory of the '"Iraqi Oghuz" did not stop their trail of murder and pillage'.

During this time cold spells continued hitting the region, extending from north Afghanistan to the Jazira. They were mostly felt in 1036, 1037 and 1038, when the violent activities of the nomads attained its peak.[28] The correlation between periods of extreme cold and famine and periods of increasing violence of the nomads is always apparent.

In 428/1037, says Ibn al-Athīr, when the Seljuks were chased by Masʿūd of Ghazna, who tried to expel them from the country, 'the land [of Khurasan] was devastated and . . . supplies and provisions became short . . . The Seljuks did not care too much about that because they were content with little'.[29] In May 1037 the Seljuks succeeded in defeating the Ghazanavid army near Sarakhs 'because of the cold, the thirst, and the exhaustion of his own soldiers'.[30]

27 Ibid., vol. IX, pp. 380–4; English translation, vol. I, pp. 15–17.

28 429/1037: 'During the whole time I was in the service of this great dynasty, I never witnessed a winter at Ghazna as hard as this year'; Bayhaqī, *History*, vol. II, p. 209, quoted Bulliet, *Cotton, climate, and camels*, p. 81. According to Ibn Funduq, a local historian of the Bayhaq district just west of Nishapur, the famine had begun in 428/1036 when food was imported to Nishapur from the Caspian coast. For 430/1038: 'It was bitterly cold, colder than anyone could remember in their lifetime . . . the cold there was of another degree of intensity, and snow fell continuously. The army suffered more on this expedition than on any other'; Bulliet, *Cotton, climate, and camels*, p. 81 quoting Bayhaqī, *History*, vol. II, pp. 247–8. In October of the same year Bayhaqī describes a defeated Turkish army fleeing across the frozen Oxus River. Wilhelm Barthold commented on this: 'This story evokes some doubt: it is strange that as early as October a whole army could cross the Amu-Darya on ice.' Wilhelm Barthold, *Turkestan down to the Mongol invasion*, 2nd edn (London: Luzac & Co., 1928), p. 298, n. 4.

29 Ibn al-Athīr, *Kāmil*, vol. IX, p. 480; English translation, vol. I, p. 37.

30 See also Bundārī, al-Fatḥ Ibn ʿAlī, *Kitāb zubdat al-nuṣra wa-nukhbat al-ʿuṣra. Histoire des Seldjoucides de l'Irâq d'après Imâd al-Dīn al-Isfahānī*, ed. M. Th. Houtsma (Leiden: E. J. Brill, 1889), p. 6; Ibn al-Athīr, *Kāmil*, vol. IX, pp. 480–1; English translation, vol. I, pp. 37–8.

The intense freeze of 430/1038 was severely felt in Mesopotamia, where heavy snow fell in Baghdad twice and remained for days in the bazaars, and Bar Hebraeus reports that 'in the month of [December] there came intense cold and the waters [in Baghdad] froze for six days'.[31]

When arriving back in frozen and famine-stricken Khurasan in 1037–8, the Seljuks 'caused trouble [and] plundered and ruined the land'. The impoverishment of the country is also apparent from the descriptions of the expedition mounted by Masʿūd of Ghazna himself against the Seljuks in Ramadan 429/June 1038. Masʿūd was determined to stop 'what the Oghuz had done to the land and the people, the destruction, murder, enslavement and conquest', but the upkeep of his army 'bore heavily on the lands . . . [and] ruined what had escaped ruin by the Oghuz'.[32] The Seljuks, however, were victorious and their leader, Tughril Beg, even succeeded in temporarily conquering the city of Nishapur to become the master of the second major city that was held by a group of Oghuz Turks.[33]

During the cold spell of the year 429/1038 the Oghuz entered the city of Maragha, burning its main mosque and slaughtering many of its inhabitants. They tried to besiege the city of Hamadhan, but failed. They sacked and 'perpetrated abominable deeds' in Karaj, and in the winter months of 430/1039 they finally succeeded in taking Hamadhan 'in an atrocious fashion that was not used in other cities'. Two other parties of Oghuz horsemen that were active in the same geographical region and who probably belonged to the confederation of the 'Iraqi Oghuz' attacked neighbouring regions,

[31] Bar Hebraeus, *Chronography*, vol. I, p. 199: 'And in this year the Sultan Masud left and went to the country of India, in the winter season . . . because of the intensity of the cold of the country of Khawarazm'.

[32] Ibn al-Athīr, *Kāmil*, vol. IX, p. 458; English translation, vol. I, p. 26; compare with the other, slightly different, version, vol. IX, pp. 463–4; English translation, vol. I, pp. 28–30.

[33] Ibn al-Athīr, *Kāmil*, vol. IX, p. 481; English translation, vol. I, p. 39.

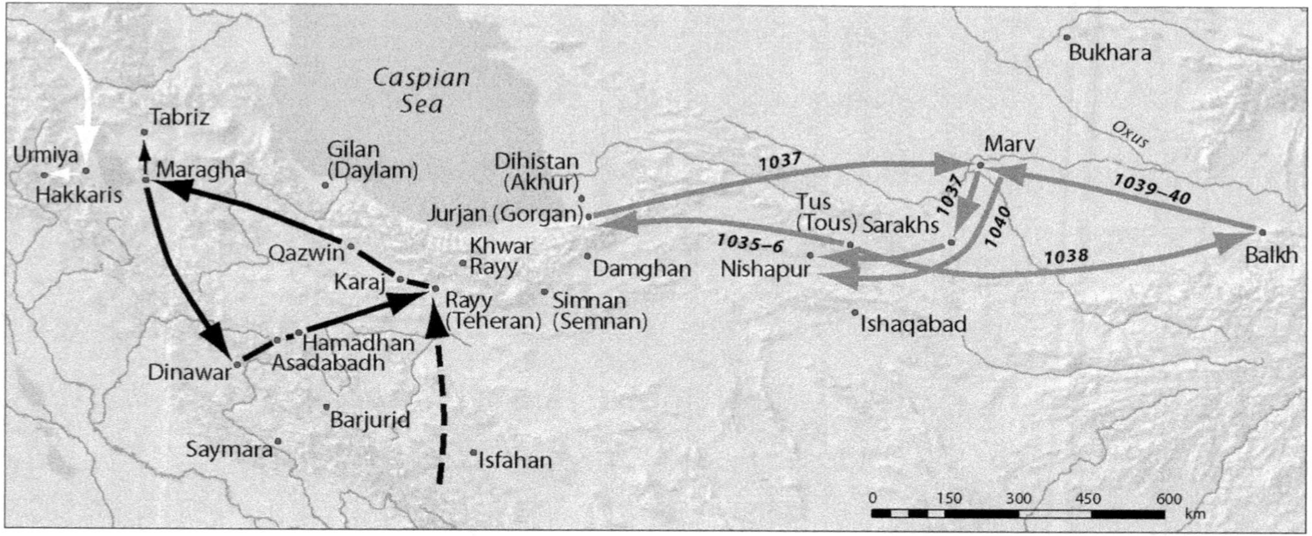


Map 4.3 Cities plundered by the Seljuks in 1037–40. The migration and havoc continued as before.

which 'were given to pillage and rapine'. The city of Qazwin was forced to pay them a ransom of 7,000 dinars.[34] A different group, which operated elsewhere and is mentioned here for the first time, arrived probably from Azerbaijan, invading the districts of Urmiya, on the border of Armenia, slaying a large number of local Kurds and plundering their lands.

The struggle between the unequal forces of the Ghaznavid Empire, on the one hand, and the Seljuks, on the other, continued until 431/1040. Masʿūd reassembled his armies in order to pursue the nomads, forcing the Seljuks to withdraw and abandon any city which Masʿūd approached, attempting to avoid a direct encounter. But Masʿūd was very slow and hesitant in his manoeuvres, allegedly because of the cold and the lack of provisions. Finally, in the spring of 431/1040, the Seljuks successfully dragged the reluctant Ghazanvid army into a desert trap without sufficient water and food, and routed it in the Battle of Dandanqan in 431/1040.[35]

When the victorious Tughril entered Nishapur in 341/1040 he found a partially deserted city ravaged by repeated struggles and agitations. Ibn al-Athīr describes the situation in Nishapur in 431/1040:

> The urban gangs ... had been causing great trouble and had grown very powerful. The inhabitants ... suffered increasing hardship through them and because of their seizing of property, killing of persons, and shameful treatment of women.[36]

Later the same year, Bayhaqī described Nishapur from a more personal viewpoint, but drew a similar image of the city:

> Nishapur was not the city I knew from the past: it now lay in ruins with only vestiges of habitation and urban life ... Property owners had torn off the

[34] Ibn al-Athīr, *Kāmil*, vol. IX, pp. 383–4; English translation, vol. I, pp. 17–19.
[35] Omeljan Pritsak, 'Die Karahaniden', *Der Islam* 31 (1953/4), 17–68.
[36] Ibn al-Athīr, *Kāmil*, vol. IX, p. 483; English translation, vol. I, p. 40.

roofs of their houses and sold them. A great number of people, together with their families and children, had died from hunger. The price of landed property had plummeted ... the weather was bitterly cold and life was becoming hard to bear. Such a famine in Nishapur could not be recalled, and large numbers of people died, soldiers and civilians alike ... It goes without saying that the Turkmens did not harass or hover around us, since they too were taken up with their own welfare, since this dearth and famine had spread everywhere.

Sarakhs (in Khurasan) suffered from the same fate:

[The city] ... looked parched and in ruins, and there was not a single shoot of corn anywhere. The inhabitants had all fled, and the plains and mountains looked scorched, with not a speck of vegetation in sight. ...The beasts ... died from hunger.[37]

## NOMADS ACQUIRE POLITICAL POWER

The decisive victory over the Ghazanvids in Dandanqan transformed the status of Tughril Beg from a mere chieftain of a persecuted tribe to a respectable territorial sovereign who fostered political ambitions of replacing the Buyids of Baghdad. It is usually not easy to determine the exact moment when hunger-stricken marauders who have been chased and persecuted by all the political powers are transformed into a legitimate political power themselves. It is clear, however, that being Muslim was a major precondition for their being accepted in one of the existing political alliances. The decision whether to follow a Shiʿi or a Sunni tradition, however, seems to be part of their introduction into the political game and not a precondition of any of the existing powers.

[37] Bulliet, *Cotton, climate, and camels*, pp. 81–3, quoting Bayhaqī, vol. II, pp. 299, 304; Peter Christensen, *The decline of Iranshahr: irrigation and environments in the history of the Middle East, 500 BC. to AD 1500* (Copenhagen: Museum Tusculanum Press, 1993).

Masʿūd, who was aware of Tughril's potential to become a powerful player in the political game, threatened him with menacing letters. Tughril's response, written by his 'prayer leader', was polite but not grovelling, reminding Masʿūd of the temporariness of power and intentionally using a citation from the Quran: 'Only God, he wrote, gives power over everything'.[38] Consequently he started, in 434/1042–3, to create the machinery of his future administration, imitating the Perso-Islamic monarchical tradition: he started minting coins and nominated a vizier and a *raʾīs al-ruʾsāʾ*.[39]

Consequently, Tughril Beg started acquiring territorial strength in central Iran. For the first time since their arrival in Iran, the Seljuks began emerging from the confines of the eastern provinces and started moving westwards and southwards towards Hamadhan. The other group of Iraqi Oghuz, who previously occupied the regions, were forced to move towards the northwest for fear of the Seljuks, at the expense of cities that had not yet experienced their violence.[40] Tughril himself attempted to increase the number of cities that paid him tribute and to compel the members of his own family to abandon territories and hand them over to him. He did not abandon his eastern and northern estates, however, and returned in 433/1041–2 to Jurjan and Tabaristan, and a year later to Khwarizm, invading the north, while his nephew Ibrāhīm Yināl was conquering, plundering and perpetrating atrocities in Rayy (which Tughril had just left), Barujird and Sabur Khwast.[41]

38 Quran 3:26; Ibn al-Athīr, *Kāmil*, vol. IX, p. 478; English translation, vol. I, p. 35.

39 George C. Miles, *The numismatic history of Rayy* (New York: American Numismatic Society, 1938), pp. 196–7.

40 Ibn al-Jawzī, *Muntaẓam*, vol. VIII, p. 116: 'Tughril Beg arrived in the Uplands, and a letter of his from Rayy came to Abū Ṭāhir Jalāl al-Dawla who was the Buyid amir of Iraq (1027–44)'. See also Ibn al-Athīr, *Kāmil*, vol. IX, p. 507; English translation, vol. I, p. 49.

41 Ibrāhīm Yināl may have been a cousin and half-brother on Tughril's mother's side, but his precise position within the family was never fully cleared: see Vladimir Minorsky, 'Äinallu/Inallu', *Roczṇik Orientalistyczṇy*, 17 (1951/2), 5–6.

It is clear from this chaotic outcome of Tughril's advance that despite the change in his status, he still acted in the same way as when he was mere chieftain of a dislocated and persecuted tribe. In periods of dearth he plundered cities that had been plundered in the past and sometimes even plundered cities that paid him tribute. His people, however, proceeded westwards, taking Qazwin, the region of Gilan (Daylam) and the town of Tarn, exacting heavy taxes from them. Later they proceeded to Hadadhan and Dihistan, reaching Kirman and plundering and sacking its suburbs.[42]

At the same time, the Iraqi Oghuz, who were forced to flee Rayy as early as 433/1041–2 for fear of Ibrāhīm Yināl, moved on to Diyar Bakr, plundering the vicinity of Mosul and of Jazirat Ibn Umar (modern Cizre) in their quest for food. Another probably independent group of nomads who resided in the region of Urmiya moved to Hakkaris (Mosul area), defeating the local Kurds and 'seizing their encampments, flocks, women, and children'.[43]

The attacks against cities intensified during the cold spells of 435/1043–4 and 437–9/1045–8 that also brought in their wake new waves of incoming nomads. These were the years when the behaviour of the nomads was most violent.[44] The contemporaneous sources provide us with detailed descriptions of the newly arrived dislocated pastoralists, who were soon converted to Islam. Ibn al-Athīr writes:

In Safar [435/September–October 1043], ten thousand tents of the Turks, who used to attack Islamic lands in the regions of Balasaghun and Kashgar[45]

[42] Ibn al-Athīr, *Kāmil*, vol. IX, pp. 509–10; English translation, vol. I, p. 51.
[43] Ibn al-Athīr, *Kāmil*, vol. IX, p. 385; English translation, vol. I, p. 19.
[44] For the famine of 438/1047–8, see Bar Hebraeus, *Chronography*, vol. I, p. 205; *Chronique de Michel le Syrien*, vol. III, pp. 277 and 282–3, vol. IV, pp. 638, 640–1: 'A general drought and the springs dried up, and many places without rivers and fountains were deserted'.
[45] Oasis city in today's Xinjiang, Uyghur autonomous region.

raiding and causing havoc, converted to Islam. On the fest of the Sacrifice they slaughtered 20,000 head of sheep. Thus God saved the Muslims from their wicked ways.

They used to pass the summer around Bulghar and winter in the region of Balasaghun. After their conversion they scattered throughout the lands. Each district had 1,000 tents, more or less, because they now felt secure.[46]

Bar Hebraeus provides us with an insightful description of nomads joining Tughril Beg, the victorious leader of the Seljuks, during the cold spell of 1043, shedding new light on the meaning of 'a new wave of nomads' and on the mechanism that enabled the Seljuks to multiply within less than a decade from a tribe of no more than two thousand tents to a confederation that was able to defeat empires. The new arrivals, he says, sat in groups of two thousand men, at a certain distance from the Sultan, not daring to approach or speak to him. They only kissed the land upon which he stood, waiting quietly for a hint that would tell them that their request to join the Seljuks was granted.

In every place where his troops meet together they plunder, and destroy and kill, *and no district (or quarter) is able to support them for more than one week because of their vast number. And from sheer necessity they are compelled to depart to another quarter in order to find food for themselves and their beasts.*[47]

It is clear from this description that the newly dislocated pastoralists were forced to abandon their traditional way of life and that they were looking for the protection of the charismatic leader, who could have ensured their lives and the lives of their beasts.

The freeze of 1043–4 affected the Bedouins as much as it did the Turks, and intensified activities and conflicts with the Oghuz. Ibn al-Athīr refers to the seasonal migration of the Bedouins ('the

[46] Ibn al-Athīr, *Kāmil*, vol. IX, p. 520; English translation, vol. I, p. 56.
[47] Bar Hebraeus, *Chronography*, vol. I, p. 202; emphasis the present author.

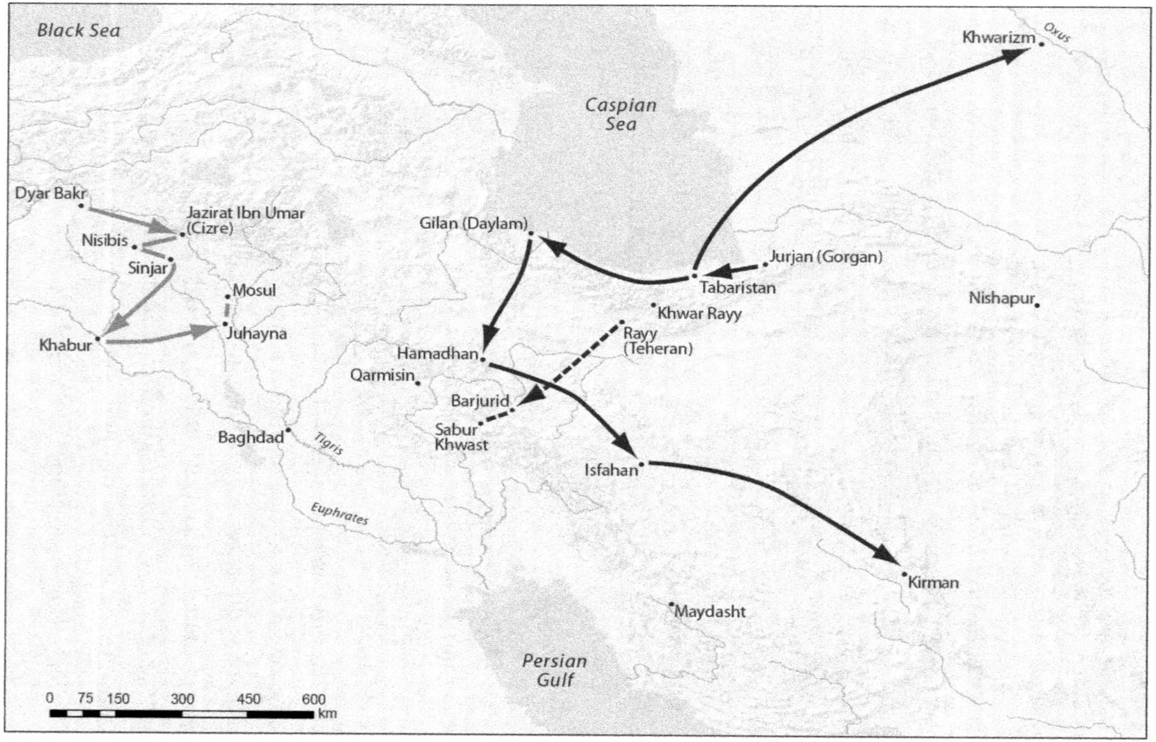


Map 4.4 Oghuz raids in Iran and the Jazira in 1040–4, showing the raid of Tughril and his Seljuks against Hamadhan, Isfahan and Kirman and in a different raid against Khwarizm; Ibrāhīm Yināl abandoning Rayy to Tughril and pillaging the borders of Mesopotamia; and the ʿIraqi Oghuz' plundering the Jazira.

Arabs') while describing the violent activity of the Iraqi Oghuz: 'The Arabs set out for al-ʿIrāq to winter there, while the Oghuz devastated Diyar Bakr, plundering and murdering.' The violence intensified as the cold spell lingered, and in 1043,the Oghuz 'plundered Nisibis, Sinjar and Khabur and Juhayna [south of Mosul on the Tigris] and the valley district'. In 1044 they finally entered Mosul itself, plundering one of the major cities of Mesopotamia. 'The Oghuz entered the city, plundering and robbing the possessions of the ruler: money, jewels, finery, clothes and furniture. They acted abominably towards the population, murdering, raping women and plundering property'.

The local population rose up and drove them out of the city, but on 25 Rajab 435/27 February 1044 they returned, taking prisoners, plundering property and killing for twelve days. They also carried out raids on the lands of the Armenians, plundering and taking captives.

Tughril Beg did not miss the opportunity to strengthen his image within the regional politics and to present himself as leader of all the Oghuz. From his place of residence (far from Mosul) he attempted to intervene in the events, writing a letter to the Buyid prince Jalāl al-Dawla in which he claimed:

> these Turkomans [the Iraqi Oghuz] were slaves and servants of ours ... who obeyed our command and served our princely state. When we undertook to manage the problems of the house of Maḥmūd [of Ghazna] and we were commissioned to deal with Khwarizm, they withdrew to Rayy and made mischief and created disturbances there. We marched with our troops from Khurasan against them ... Inevitably we shall again make them subservient to our banners and in our might make them taste the reward of rebels, be they near or distant, in the valleys or on the heights.

The Buyid prince was not convinced by this letter of flattery presenting Tughril's interpretation of the recent events, and did not offer him the role of peace-keeper. In the battle that ensued on 22 April 1044 between the Iraqi Oghuz and a combined force that included the Buyids, the Bedouins of Banū ʿUqayl and the Kurds, Turghil defeated the Iraqi Oghuz, executing their leaders, while the Bedouins took their property and tents. 'The [Iraqi Oghuz] were dispersed all over West Mesopotamia and the Jazira. Some of them plundered Diyar Bakr, others turned against Armenia and plundered Byzantine territories, the rest moved into Azerbaijan.' But, says Ibn al-Athīr, 'this is the history of the 'Iraqi' Oghuz ... their power did not endure long enough for its events to be related in the fashion of annals'.[48]

The mild break of 436/1044–5 was followed by a new severe cold spell and famine in 437–9/1045–7[49] that led to the arrival of yet another wave of nomads, who invaded the Trans-Oxonian regions, pillaging Bakhara, Samarkand and Khwarizm. Later, after reaching Iran, the invaders looted Rayy and Isfahan and moved on to Azerbaijan, Armenia and the Byzantine Empire.[50]

The area engulfed by the cold spell of 1045–7 was so vast that nomads came from as far away as Tibet:

> From the land of Tibet ... came a great horde of Turks beyond number. They made contact with Arslān Khān, the ruler of Balasaghun, thanking him for the good way he ruled his subjects. They caused no trouble or harm to his lands but took up residence there. He sent to them and called them to convert to Islam. They did not accept but remained friendly.[51]

The severe cold spell of 1045–7 caused the Seljuks to revert once again from their temporary status as rulers to their old habits of

[48] Ibn al-Athīr, *Kāmil*, vol. IX, pp. 388–91; English translation, vol. I, pp. 20–3; Bar Hebraeus, *Chronography*, vol. I, p. 202.

[49] 'In Mosul people ate the dead, and only 400 Muslims were able to pray in the mosque, all the other citizens died'; Sibṭ Ibn al-Jawzī, *Mirʾat al-zamān*, p. 395; Ibn al-Jawzī, *Muntaẓam*, vol. VIII, p. 132; Bar Hebraeus, *Chronography*, vol. I, p. 202.

[50] Sibṭ Ibn al-Jawzī, *Mirʾat al-zamān*, pp. 392–3, 395.

[51] Ibn al-Athīr, *Kāmil*, vol. IX, p. 535; English translation, vol. I, p. 62.

marauding, attacking innocent cities and leaving behind a trail of destruction. Ibrāhīm Yināl attacked Hamadhan in the winter of 1045, marching later on Dinawar and Qarmisin (present-day Kermanshah), where he arrived in January 1046. The defenders of Qarmisin were 'too weak to hold out against him', so he sacked the city, killing and expelling many of the defenders. In February he sacked Saymara (Simareh); in early March he arrived in Sirawan, sacking, destroying and razing it to the ground. Other groups of Oghuz plundered the inhabitants of Hulwan, reaching Maydasht, which they sacked and raided.

It was during a repeated attack on Nishapur in that year that Tughril Beg was told by his kinsman, Ibrāhīm Yināl, that 'this land is ruined and cannot sustain us. Ask for the land of the Byzantines that can better sustain us'. Therefore, writes Sibṭ Ibn al-Jawzī, they turned to the Byzantine territory, 'killing, arresting, pillaging and returning to Armenia. Some said they reached the Bosporus. Muḥammad the son of Ibrāhīm b. Yināl was with them, and his cattle alone were more than one hundred thousand.'[52]

The freeze and famine of the late 1040s were also felt in the delta of the Nile, spreading from there throughout the region.[53] The drought of 1047 was followed by a plague that began in 440/1048,

[52] Sibṭ Ibn al-Jawzī, *Mir'at al-zamān*, p. 395; Ibn al-Jawzī, *Muntaẓam*, vol. VIII, pp. 127, 130; Ibn al-Athīr, *Kāmil*, vol. IX, pp. 528–9. Ibn al-Athīr related the same story to Ibrāhīm b. Yināl himself in 1048–9: 'During his raid against the Byzantines this year, Ibrāhīm Yināl won a victory over them and took booty. This came about because a large number of the Oghuz in Transoxania came to join him and he said to them 'My lands are too small to accommodate you and to provide what you require. The best plan is for you to go and raid the Byzantines to strive on the path of God and to gain booty. I shall follow in your tracks and aid you in your enterprise". This they did.' Ibn al-Athīr, *Kāmil*, vol. IX, p. 546; English translation, vol. I, p. 67.

[53] Gil, *History of Palestine*, pp. 602a, lines 5–7 and 603a, lines 15–16; see also Moshe Gil 'Institutions and events of the eleventh century mirrored in Geniza letters (part I)', *Bulletin of the School of Oriental and African Studies* 67.2 (2004), 161–2.

'in all countries: in Mecca, Iraq, Mosul, the Jazira (Mesopotamia), al-Shām (Syria, Palestine), Egypt'.[54]

The cold and hunger that continued to loom during 1047–8 led Ibrāhīm Yināl and his tribesmen to look for plunder in the north of Mesopotamia, starting with Hamadhan and continuing with Bandanijin, where 'dreadful deeds were perpetrated: plunder, murder, rapine and torture to extract money'. A request sent to Baghdad for reinforcements was not met because of 'a complete lack of authority in Baghdad and [because the] affairs [there] were in chaos'.[55] In January 1048 the Oghuz continued plundering the regions northeast of Baghdad in the region of Jalula, slaying a vast multitude of Kurds and seizing their flocks. Cities bordering Iran and Iraq were plundered. At this stage rumour reached Baghdad that Ibrāhīm Yināl was intending to attack the city, creating panic amongst the populace. The emirs and the army commanders came together in order to march out to forestall Ibrāhīm Yināl. But only a small handful of emirs left the city, the rest making no move at all.

The freeze and cold affected the armies of Baghdad as much as it did the nomads, and when the Buyid king, Abū Kālījār, received information about the approach of the nomads, he found it hard to make a stand against them:

> The information reached . . . Abū Kālījār . . . who gave orders for his troops to prepare for a campaign against them, but they were unable to mobilize because of the great number of their horses that had died. . . . He set out towards Fars with the army carrying their baggage on donkeys.[56]

Ibn al-Athīr provides us with a possible explanation:

[54] Ibn al-Athīr, *Kāmil*, vol. IX, p. 552 [no translation].
[55] Ibn al-Athīr, *Kāmil*, vol. IX, p. 537–8; English translation, vol. I, p. 64.
[56] Ibn al-Athīr, *Kāmil*, vol. IX, pp. 537–8, 529; English translation, vol. I , pp. 58–9.

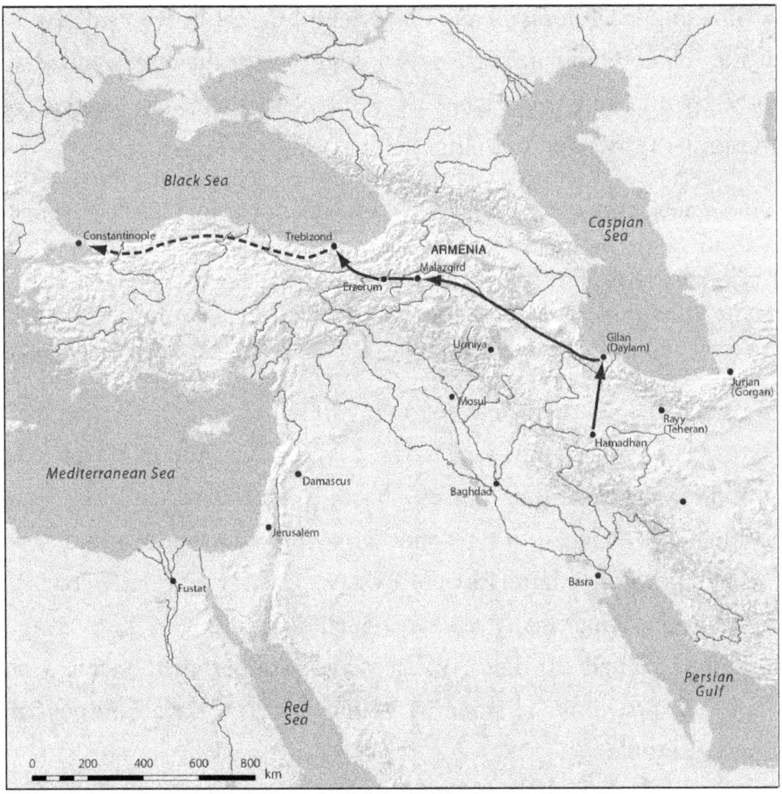


Map 4.5 Ibrāhīm Yināl invading Armenia and Asia Minor for the first time in 1046–7.

This year in Baghdad and Mosul and in the rest of Iraq and Mesopotamia there was a serious famine, in which people were reduced to eating carrion. This was followed by a raging epidemic as a result of which many people died. The markets were deserted, and the prices of necessities for the sick rose steeply.

The results were obvious: 'Masses of people perished in the devastated areas, some put to the sword, some drowned and others killed by the sword'.[57]

[57] Ibn al-Athīr, *Kāmil*, vol. IX, pp. 539, 541–2; English translation, vol. I, pp. 65–6.

The lingering hunger caused many Oghuz Turks who still dwelt in the Trans-Oxonian regions to immigrate to the south and join forces with Ibrāhīm Yināl, who directed them to attack the Byzantine territories as well:

> A large number of the Oghuz in Transoxania came to join him and he said to them 'My lands are too small to accommodate you and to provide what you require. The best plan is for you to go and raid the Byzantines to strive on the path of God and to gain booty. I shall follow in your tracks and aid you in your enterprise.' This they did.[58]

The year 1048 marks the beginning of Seljuk raids on Armenian, Georgian and Byzantine territories. The attack begun in Malazgird, continued in Erzerum, passed through Qali-qala (in the same region) and ended in Trebizond. The newly arrived Oghuz succeeded in beating a large force of Byzantines and Georgians, slaying many and taking many captives including the Georgian king. Ibrāhīm b. Yināl continued raiding and plundering the shores of the Black Sea until he came to within a fifteen days' journey of Constantinople.

The death of the Buyid king on 15 October 1048, coinciding with a year of pause in the hunger, was the signal for the Oghuz to start intervening in the politics of Baghdad and to try and inherit the Buyid dynasty.

'The Seljuk invasion', says Khazanov, 'was neither premeditated, nor thought out and planned in advance. It was a chain reaction of events and the unexpected weakness of the Middle Eastern states that led to the creation of the Seljuk Empire'.[59] Evidence shows with certainty that not only was the Seljuk invasion not 'premeditated,

[58] Ibn al-Athīr, *Kāmil*, vol. IX, p. 546; English translation, vol. I, p. 67.
[59] Anatoly M. Khazanov, *Nomads and the outside world*, trans.Julia Crookenden, foreword Ernest Gellner, 2nd edn (Madison: University of Wisconsin Press, 1994), p. 264.

thought out or planned in advance', but that it was a 'chain of reaction of events' that was rekindled whenever there was a severe cold spell followed by famine and pesitilence in the north. When such misfortunes occurred, they led more pastoralists to abandon their habitual seasonal migrations, to cross the Oxus, and to try find pastures, fodder and food for their households and for themselves in the south. The central sedentarized powers of the region tried to force them to pull out, but their efforts were in vain.

The most important confederation of Oghuz to invade Iran and Khurasan was that of the Seljuks, who early on exceeded beyond their pasturing/pillaging premises of eastern Iran and northeastern Khurasan, roaming – at least until 1040 – mainly in the parallelogram comprising Balkh–Marv–Nishapur and Jurjan.

Ibrāhīm Yināl, who formally belonged to the clan of Tughril, conducted a separate policy, roaming, pillaging and pasturing his herds away from Tughril until he finally broke off completely from his kinsman. When Tughril extended his territory to the mountainous area between Rayy and Hamadhan, and from there to Isfahan and Kirman, he moved away to the borders of Iraq, thereby pillaging a region that had not been plundered in the past.

A totally independent group of dislocated Oghuz, the 'Iraqi Oghuz', were pushed further away by the more dominant Seljuks and the Oghuz of Ibrāhīm Yināl, and were finally known to have pillaged cities and agricultural regions in the north of Iraq and in the Jazira.

The collapse of Iran can be depicted as a wave, or as a domino effect, of several groups of nomads (at least three, but probably more) that were forced to push each other until the final collapse of the central government in this country in the late 1040s.

CHAPTER FIVE

# The fall of Baghdad

The disastrous climatic events continued to loom over the eastern Mediterranean during the 1050s. Simultaneous famines, resulting from waves of severe cold in the north and extended periods of drought in Egypt, Palestine and Syria, led to one of the worst periods of regional distress. It seems, however, that the centre of the cold shifted westwards during the 1050s, affecting the northern shores of the Black Sea and the Balkans rather than Khurasan and eastern Iran. In any event, more instances of dislocated pastoralists who crossed the Danube to the south and attacked Byzantium are recorded than cases of their kinsmen crossing the Oxus, although Mesopotamia was still affected by the hunger.[1]

If a date is needed to signify the year in which the climatic disasters of the eleventh century attained their maximal societal effects, transforming political, economic and cultural structures of some of the most complex civilizations of the time, then 1055 is a symbolic watershed. In the following four chapters I will summarize four examples of 'domino effects' that attained their most disastrous impact between 1054 and 1056, leading to complete or partial collapses of economies, societies and civilizations.

[1] Bulliet noticed that the 'Big Chill' is not mentioned any more in Iran during the 1050s. See Richard W. Bulliet, *Cotton, climate, and camels in early Islamic Iran: a moment in world history* (New York: Columbia University Press, 2009), pp. 84–6.

The present chapter deals with the events that led to the takeover of Baghdad by the Seljuks in 1055, the civil war that followed it, and the establishment of a nomadic statehood in Mesopotamia. Chapter 6 will deal with the situation in the Byzantine Empire during the first half of that same decade. The Byzantine Empire, which suffered from a continuing dearth from the late 1020s until the mid 1070s, faced, like its counterparts in Iran and Iraq, recurrent invasions of Oghuz nomads, who repeatedly defeated it. The incessant wars and cold waves led to a reduction in the empire's income, to an enormous rise in military expenditure, and to an inevitable economic crisis manifested in an unprecedented devaluation of the Byzantine currency. The devaluation was accelerated between 1054 and 1056, reaching the lowest rate – 27 per cent below the rate in 1040 – by the end of the 1050s. The monetary and economic collapse rekindled a traditional struggle between the military and the administration over the division of the budget, and led to the dismissal of the last descendant of the Macedonian dynasty that successfully ruled the empire since 867. Neither of the generals who ascended the throne after the coup d'état of 1055 was able to reverse the inferiority of the empire vis-à-vis the nomads or to divert enough resources to save the crumbling empire from decimation and additional defeats. The situation was reversed only at the beginning of the 1080s, when mild weather returned to Asia Minor and the Balkans – but the area, the might and the glory of the empire in 1025 were never restored.

Chapter 7 is based on the results of the extensive archaeological excavations conducted in Israel, Jordan and elsewhere since 1995. It shows that some of the thriving urban centres of the region, which flourished economically and demographically during the late 1020s, declined abruptly between the mid 1050s and the early 1060s. Cities as big and prosperous as Ramla, then the capital of Palestine and four times the size of contemporary Jerusalem, virtually ceased to exist, and the same is true of Tiberias, Caesarea and Jerusalem. In Chapter 9 I suggest an explanation for the neglect of the aqueducts of the eastern Mediterranean during the eleventh century, following the depletion of springs and underground reservoirs.

Chapter 8 will deal with the hunger that prevailed in Egypt during the 1050s, compelling its rulers, for the first time in their country's recorded history, to plead for grain and to react violently when their request was refused. The Egyptian famine of the mid 1050s also led to the dislocation of the Bedouin tribes of the Banū Hilāl and the Banū Sulaym, who plundered the formerly prosperous agricultural province of North Africa together with its capital Qayrawan, leading to the permanent desertification of Ifriqiya.

### POLITICAL EVENTS AND CLIMATIC DISASTERS

The political collapse of the Buyid dynasty in Baghdad began when it was no longer able to rule the multi-level and diversified Iranian and Mesopotamian societies that it had ruled, quite efficiently, since 934. For more than a century the Shiʿi Buyids cooperated with the Sunni caliphs to foster a policy of religious equilibrium and to conduct the affairs of this enormous state together.

During the development of the climatic crisis the Buyids gradually lost their efficiency, and from the late 1040s onwards were no longer able to impose law and order. On the other hand, the Abbasid caliphs, dazzled by the opportunity of ridding themselves of their Shiʿi protectors and by the possibility of acquiring more independence, plotted together with the Seljuks in order to create an all Sunni administration. The coup d'état, led by the Caliph, was only one of the attempts of various political and ethnic groups to acquire influence and power. Agitations, riots and internal conflicts were very common in Mesopotamia between the late 1020s and late 1050s, coinciding with the years of extreme dearth and reaching their most influential effects in the mid 1050s. The reasons for the agitations were diverse: there were riots over religious issues (between the Sunnis and the Shiʿis and between the Muslims and the Christians); over rising prices; even over Muslim theological issues, mainly among the Sunnis themselves. Hanbali leaders attempted to prevent rationalism and to enforce rigid orthodoxy by persecuting 'sinners' who dared to drink wine, sing songs, play musical instruments or even innocently attend lessons taught by teachers of other intellectual traditions.[2] The ability of the Buyids to prevent such agitations, to hinder persecutions against Christians and to delimit the territorial expansionism of ambitious '*ʿayyārūn*' was steadily diminishing.

The concurrence of these social and religious agitations with outbursts of cold spells is quite evident. A previous wave of agitations was recorded during the cold waves of 1007–10, but both the dearth and the agitations were abated for two decades. Riots reappeared in Baghdad in 1024 and did not cease until the late 1050s when the dearth was also abated. Testimonies of bandits raiding and burning houses and plundering property of rich people or torturing them in order to reveal their hidden treasures appear in 1026, immediately after the beginning of the crisis.[3] During the reign of the Buyid amir of Iraq, Jalāl al-Dawla, between 1027 and 1044, there were no less than five rebellions of unpaid Turkish mercenaries that actually forced the impoverished amir to flee his capital and attempt to pay

[2] George Maqdisi, 'Nouveaux détails sur l'affaire d'Ibn ʿAqīl', in *Mélanges Louis Massignon* (Damascus: Institut Français de Damas, 1957), vol. III, pp. 91–126; George Maqdisi, *Ibn ʿAqīl et la resurgence de l'Islam traditionaliste au XIe siècle* (Damascus: Institut Français de Damas, 1963); Daphna Ephrat, *A learned society in a period of transition: the Sunni ʿulamaʾ of eleventh-century Baghdad* (Albany: State University of New York Press, 2000).

[3] ʿIzz al-Dīn Abū al-Ḥasan ʿAlī Ibn al-Athīr, *al-Kāmil fī al-taʾrīkh*, ed. Carl J. Tornberg, 13 vols. (Leiden: E. J. Brill, 1862–71; reprinted Beirut: Dār Ṣāder, Dār Beyrouth, 1965–7), vol. IX, p. 353; Mafizullah Kabir, *The Buwayhid dynasty of Baghdad (334/946–447/1055)* (Calcutta: Iran Society, 1964), p. 100.

their salaries. These events coincided with the peak years of the hunger (in 423–4/1032–3, 427–8/1035–6, 431/1039–40). The unpaid soldiers plundered gold and silver ingots kept for minting coins as well as for the poll tax, robbed commodities imported from Mosul and removed horses from the amir's stables.[4] 'It would be no exaggeration to say,' writes Mafizulla Kabir, 'that during the whole reign of Jalāl al-Dawla in Baghdad there was hardly any effective government in the city.'[5]

The terror of the *ʿayyārūn* is another good example of the concurrence of periods of dearth and social violence. The ʿayyārūn were a divisive social element that prospered in periods of dearth and calmed down in periods of abundance. They appear in Baghdad as early as the beginning of the ninth century, but between 1027 and 1060 they were more active than ever before. Moreover, they were organized for the first time in bands, trained in a military fashion, bore arms and perpetrated organized banditry in open defiance of authority.[6] They kept the people of Baghdad in constant terror between the 1030s and the late 1050s, levying tolls on markets and roads, robbing wayfarers, spreading havoc and burning quarters and markets.[7] The situation became all the more complicated when the ʿayyārūn joined forces with the revolting leaders of the army or when the Shiʿi–Sunni riots provided them with further opportunities for justifiable plundering. Their activities continued throughout

[4] Ibn al-Jawzī, Abū al-Faraj ʿAbd al-Raḥmān Ibn ʿAlī, *al-Muntaẓam fī ta'rīkh al-mulūk wal-umam*, 11 vols. in 6 vols. (Hyderabad: al-ʿUthmāniyya , 1357–9/1938–40), vol. VIII, pp. 35, 72–3, 78; Ibn al-Athīr, *Kāmil*, vol. IX, pp. 366, 423–4, 431–2; Kabir, *Buwayhid dynasty*, pp. 102–4.

[5] Kabir, *Buwayhid dynasty*, p. 102.

[6] Franz Taeschner, 'ʿAyyār', *Encyclopaedia of Islam*, 2nd edn, ed. Peri J. Bearman, Thierry Bianquis, Clifford E. Bosworth, Emeri van Donzel and Wolfhart P. Heinrichs (Leiden: E. J. Brill, 2010); Ibn al-Jawzī, *Muntaẓam*, vol. VII, p. 174; Ibn al-Athīr, *Kāmil*, vol. IX, p. 106.

[7] Ibn al-Jawzī, *Muntaẓam*, vol. VII, pp. 153 and 220, and vol. VIII, pp. 21–2, 44–5, 46–7, 50–1, 54–7, 59–60, 72–6, 78–9, 88–9, 142, 160–1.

the whole period of dearth, stopping only when the hunger was over in the early 1060s.[8]

Outbursts of clashes between the Shiʿis and the Sunnis also coincided with the years of dearth. The serious clashes between them were renewed in the winter of 1029 after more than two decades of relative peace. Another outburst was recorded in 422/1031 when nearly the whole of Baghdad was involved in fierce fighting, while all communication between the two banks was severed by the destruction of the bridges.[9] The ʿayyārūn came on the scene in 425/1033, intensifying the struggle, but the situation became hard to bear for both sides, especially for the Shiʿis, between 441/1049 and 447/1055. The Shiʿis were forced to build a protective wall around their quarter in order to defend themselves from the daily harassment of Hanbali extremists. The latter did not hesitate to put the tombs of the Buyid princes, and even the tomb of Shiʿi imams, to the torch.[10]

The concurrence of political agitations, the activities of the ʿayyārūn and the outbursts of religious extremism with periods of dearth and hunger is no coincidence. Division lines that threatened the coherence of law and society were established long before the beginning of the climatic crisis, but hunger led to renewed outbursts of violence and to the deepening of the existing division lines. The periods of extreme dearth led Iraqi society into an incessant struggle and to the verge of a societal collapse. The concurrence of the political collapse of the Buyids with the appearance of the ʿayyārūn or renewed fierce struggles between the Shiʿis and the Sunnis were different manifestations of the same crisis. The climatic crisis led to

[8] Ibid., vol. VIII, pp. 91, 72.
[9] Ibn al-Jawzī, *Muntaẓam*, vol. VIII, pp. 41–5, 55; Ibn al-Athīr, *Kāmil*, vol. IX, pp. 418–20.
[10] Ibn al-Jawzī, *Muntaẓam*, vol. VIII, pp. 19, 21–5, 149–51; Ibn al-Athīr, *Kāmil*, vol. IX, pp. 561, 595–7.

the deterioration of the economy, to the weakening of the agencies of law and order and to the inability of the central government to sustain its army and bureaucracy. From this point onwards, the way to imminent political collapse was very short.

The famine of 1053–4 emptied the coffers of the Buyid state, led to riots and accentuated the behaviour of extremist groups. The authorities failed to establish law and order in the provincial centres of Basra and Ahwaz, were unable to stop the advance of a Kurdish prince who 'murdered, raped virgins and seized money and goods', or to prevent new eruptions of religious riots in Baghdad. In short, the inability of the Buyid administration to govern Iraq, eventually leading to its imminent collapse, was clearly manifested during the famine of 1053–4, two years before the Buyid's deposition.[11]

The situation worsened during the winter of 1054/5 when 'reports came to Baghdad that bands of Kurds and of Arabs had caused disturbances' and the Buyid ruler was not able to stop them or even 'to follow the marauders because of the flood'. The Buyid ruler of Baghdad failed to pay the salaries of his Turkish mercenaries, leading to an open revolt of the unpaid soldiers, who 'rode to the Christian quarter [Dār al-Rūm] and sacked it, burning churches and monasteries'. Ibn al-Athīr describes the year's events in Baghdad in the following words:

> Order broke down, and the [Turkish soldiers] robbed everyone arriving at Baghdād. Prices soared and there was a shortage of food stuffs . . .
>
> [Even after] the vizier . . . settled the [soldiers'] outstanding pay from his own money . . . they continued with their disorderly and violent behavior. The Kurds and the Arabs . . . resumed their raids, their plundering and killing, so that the land became ruined and the inhabitants scattered.

[11] Ibn al-Athīr, *Kāmil*, vol. IX, pp. 588–90, 593; for an English translation see *The Annals of the Saljuq Turks: Selections from al-Kāmil fī'l-ta'rīkh of 'Izz al-Dīn Ibn al-Athīr*, translated and annotated by Donald S. Richards (London: Routledge Curzon, 2002), pp. 86–9.

[Kurds] . . . came down from Mosul in hope of booty. They raided the settlements . . . and plundered them . . . The news reached Baghdād, and the people became even more fearful of the mob and the Turks. The decline in the authority of the Caliphate had become really serious. This is the dire result of dissension.[12]

The Seljuks were also affected by the dearth of 1054–5 and Tughril was therefore still hesitant about entering Iraq, preferring to stay in Azerbaijan from where he raided Asia Minor as far as Erzerum, retreating only because of the coming winter and promising to return when the cold was over.[13]

It was during this period, and probably earlier, that the Abbasid caliph started to negotiate with Tughril, attempting to draw him over to his own camp, thereby harnessing his growing military power to the caliph's interests. He therefore suggested bestowing upon him the title of Sultan in return for loyalty. The title itself, originally meaning 'power and authority', was transformed during the late tenth and the eleventh centuries to denote personal and official status. Both the heads of the Buyid and the Ghaznavid dynasties bore the title, and Tughril was probably tempted to acquire a similar status, which would pave his way to becoming a legitimate ruler of Iraq and of Iran.[14] The Caliph of Baghdad, who was the only authority that could bestow such a regal title, corresponded with Tughril, attempting to set the rules and to get the best reward for the 'honorific titles which may be legally applied to kingship'.

Tughril was expected to adhere to the Caliph's authority; to cease harming Muslim territories; to commit to a legal oath; to

[12] Ibn al-Athīr, *Kāmil*, vol. IX, pp. 596–8; English translation, vol. I, pp. 91–3.

[13] Ibn al-Athīr, *Kāmil*, vol. IX, pp. 598–9; English translation, vol. I, p. 93.

[14] August Müller, *Der Islam in Morgen-und Abendland* (Berlin: G. Grote, 1858), vol. I, p. 568. According to Ibn al-Athīr, *Kāmil*, vol. IX, p. 130, Maḥmūd of Ghazna obtained the title of Sultan from the Caliph.

accept the supremacy of the Caliph in religious matters; to dismiss unbelievers from his retinue; and not to act as a tyrant.[15] He refused to accept these preconditions but nevertheless received the title later, probably on the eve of his entry into Baghdad in December 1055, and from then onwards he was referred to as the 'lawful king'. Gradually he stopped attacking Muslim cities and, from the late 1050s onwards, he and his kinsmen directed most of their violence against Christian property.

According to Bar Hebraeus, however, Tughril started employing honorific titles and a calligraphic signature (*ṭughra*) well before his entry into Baghdad in 1055.[16] Nevertheless, in acknowledging him as a legitimate sultan and in promising to promote him to a status equal to that of the Buyids and the Ghazanvids, the Caliph paved the way for the political rise of the Seljuks and the potential creation of the all-Sunni government that he cherished, instead of the two-headed Shiʿi–Sunni government to which he was presently subject.

## THE CIVIL WAR (1055–60)

The general dearth and communal strife were in the background of the civil war that tore Iraqi society apart between 1055 and 1060. Two coalitions participated in that war. One was led by a certain al-Basāsīrī, a former Turkish slave who became a chief military leader in the Buyid administration and was supported by Iraqi and Bedouin forces, by the remnants of the overthrown Buyid

[15] Bar Hebraeus (Abū al-Faraj), *The chronography*, translated from the Syriac by Ernest A. Wallis Budge, 2 vols. (Oxford University Press, 1932), vol. I, pp. 227–8. Bar Hebraeus, however, dates the correspondence to 1044.

[16] Bar Hebraeus, *Chronography*, vol. I, p. 206. For the use of the *tughra* during the later eleventh century, see Claude Cahen, 'La ṭuġrā seljuḳide', *Journal Asiatique* 234 (1943–5), 167–72; Osman Turan, 'Les Souverains seldjoukides et leurs sujets non-musulmans', *Studia Islamica* 1 (1953), 65–100, especially 69.

dynasty and by the Fatimids of Egypt.[17] The other coalition was initiated by the Abbasid caliph and by his chief vizier (the Raʾīs al-Ruʾasāʾ), who openly collaborated in the usurpation against the Buyid amir, but after the deposition of the Buyid it was headed by Tughril.

A detailed analysis of the struggle between the two coalitions shows that many of the manoeuvres were determined by the need to feed the armies and by the chaotic waves of hunger, pestilence and mass death. The relative strengths of both parties, and of the one which temporarily took the upper hand, were determined by the ever-changing balance of power. No party was significantly stronger or better equipped than its rival.

The political rivalry between the two coalitions was apparent before the arrival of the Seljuks. Al-Basāsīrī, who was well aware of the Caliph's negotiations with Tughril, accused the Raʾīs al-Ruʾasāʾ of summoning the Oghuz. The Raʾīs retorted by instigating Sunni extremists against him, by seizing one of his ships carrying wine, and by publicly breaking the wine jars that belonged to Christian merchants, although the wine and the merchants were protected by Islamic law. The Caliph and his vizier further denigrated al-Basāsīrī by accusing him of communicating with the Fatimid caliph al-Mustanṣir.

Tughril was aware of the struggle and of the chaos. Feeling that the time was ripe for intervention, he declared his intention of passing through Baghdad on his way to perform a pilgrimage to Mecca. He also promised to proceed to Syria and Egypt in order to dethrone the Fatimid caliph. His declared wish for a 'very short stop-over' in Baghdad resulted in a real usurpation. His name was proclaimed in the Friday prayers of 15 December 447/1055, three days before his solemn entry into the capital. The entry was

[17] Maurice Canard, 'Al-Basāsīrī , Abu ʾl-Ḥārith Arslān al-Muẓaffar', *Encyclopaedia of Islam*.

revolutionary indeed: a nomadic tribe seizing the capital of Islam without striking a blow. Several days later Tughril imprisoned the last descendant of the Buyid dynasty and became, for all practical purposes, the sole ruler of Baghdad.

Clashes between the population of Baghdad and their new rulers commenced almost immediately. Among other things, this was because the people of Baghdad did not comprehend the language of their new rulers, and so misunderstandings soon led to confrontations.

Tughril Beg began creating his own nomadic statehood by granting estates to his men, reconstructing mosques and repairing the royal palace (into which he himself moved in January 1056), on the one hand, and letting his kinsmen spread out in the fertile agricultural hinterland (the Sawād) around Baghdad, plundering as much as they could, on the other. 'Their pillaging was quite terrible. The price of an ox in Baghdad reached from five to ten qirāṭs, and of a donkey from two to five. The Sawād was ruined and the population fled from it,' reported al-Athīr. During the next year the 'prices were exceedingly high. Dates and bread were sold at a dinar for five rotls'.[18] Bar Hebraeus says that 'the master of Baghdad, appointed governors and tax-gatherers from among his own people'. But, he adds, the Seljuks 'laid [the country] waste. Agriculture came to an end'.[19]

An extended wave of famine and epidemic that hit the region from 448/1056 to 450/1058 led to a further deterioration of the economy of Mesopotamia and ultimately to temporary expulsion of the Seljuks from Baghdad. The famine of 1056 started with a cold wave:

18 Ibn al-Athīr, *Kāmil*, vol. IX, pp. 613, 624; English translation, pp. 102, 105.
19 Bar Hebraeus, *Chronography*, p. 208.

> The snow fell ... without interruption ... for sixty days ... thickly covering the face of the countryside [and] many quadruped animals, beasts and birds perished. Because of the severity of the heavenly wrath, they [the nomads] were unable to find food for themselves and being altogether prevented from roaming in fecund areas, were forced to take refuge with their enemies.[20]

The difficulty in feeding his men and governing the country led Tughril to leave Baghdad in January 1057 after staying there for thirteen months, 'during which, he had not met the Caliph'. It seems that the enthusiasm of the Caliph, who traded the weak Buyid amirs for the strong, coarse and potentially restrictive nomads, had lessened,[21] and his marriage politics with Tughril illustrates the situation. In 448/1056 the Caliph was still ready to marry a Seljuk princess, but four years later, in 452/1060, when Tughril himself aspired to marry a daughter of the Caliph, the latter objected to the union of an Abbasid gentle princess with the rough Turkmen. He yielded just two years later, after Tughril had threatened to confiscate his properties in Iran, but even then Tughril was only able to see his bride in 455/1063, and the marriage was never consummated.[22]

Meanwhile the coalition of al-Basāsīrī, including the Bedouins and the non-Seljuk Turks of Baghdad, that was supported politically and financially by the Fatimids of Egypt, succeeded in inflicting a defeat on the allies of the Seljuks near Mosul. In February

[20] Ibn al-Jawzī, *Muntaẓam*, vol. VIII, p. 170, 179; Bar Hebraeus, *Chronography*, p. 209; Ibn al-Athīr, *Kāmil*, vol. IX, pp. 631, 636. For the cold spell that led to this famine, see Matthew of Edessa, *Armenia and the Crusades, tenth to twelfth centuries: the chronicle of Matthew of Edessa*, trans. Ara E. Dostourian (Lanham, MD: University Press of America, 1993), 2.10, pp. 93–4.

[21] For the conflict of interests between the Caliph and Tughril, see Makdisi, *Ibn ʿAqīl*, p. 78.

[22] George Makdisi, 'The marriage of Tughril Beg', *International Journal of Middle East Studies* 1.3 (1970), 259–75.

1057, a month after Tughril left Baghdad, he and his Seljuks reverted to their previous violent behaviour, attacking and plundering towns such as Awānā and Takrīt. It was a time, says Ibn al-Athīr, 'of a general famine throughout the land, and the people of Takrīt told [Tughril] that their land is Basāsīrī's'. The Oghuz sacked the city, took women as captives, and killed many people. The famine of this year augmented the insecurity and there was 'fear in the roads'.[23]

The need for food and supplies is demonstrated when Tughril attempts to bestow the city of Balad to one of his protégées. His soldiers protested, demanding the looting of the city for provisions. Tughril gave in, ordering the population out of the city and letting his men into it; 'within an hour the city was a desert', says Ibn al-Athīr. The fighting between the two coalitions spread throughout the country; 'the land of al-ʿIrāq [was] ruined, property [was] lost and wherever the fighting [broke] out there [was] devastation'.[24]

The famine and the civil war exhausted the country and affected the nomads who supported al-Basāsīrī as much as they affected Tughril and his Seljuks. Finally the supporters of al-Basāsīrī gave up and were forced to tell Tughril, 'Our lands are ruined, our men killed and our women made captive because of you. War is a lottery. We don't know what will be.'[25] The dearth, the shortage, the epidemic and the fact that the lands were ruined are described by Ibn al-Athīr:

> This year [448/1057] all routes out of al-ʿIrāq were interrupted because of the fear of being plundered. Prices rose and there was a serious shortage.

[23] Sibṭ Ibn al-Jawzī, *Mir'at al-zamān*, the years 1056–86, ed. Ali Sevim (Ankara: Türk Tarih Kurumu Basimevi, 1968), p. 14; Ibn al-Athīr, *Kāmil*, vol. IX, p. 627; English translation (also of parallel quotes from Sibṭ Ibn al-Jawzī), p. 108.

[24] Ibn al-Athīr, *Kāmil*, vol. IX, pp. 628; English translation, pp. 109–10; Sibṭ Ibn al-Jawzī, *Mir'at al-zamān*, the years 1056–86, p. 17.

[25] Sibṭ Ibn al-Jawzī, *Mir'at al-zamān*, the years 1056–86, p. 18.

Provisions and all sorts of other things were not to be found. The people ate carrion and a terrible sickness ensued. There were so many deaths that the corpses were buried without being washed and wrapped in shrouds. A ruṭl of meat cost a qirāṭ . . . Other prices were comparable.

In Egypt also there was a severe epidemic. 1,000 people were dying daily. Later this spread everywhere, to Syria, Mesopotamia, Mosul, the Ḥijāz, Yemen and elsewhere.[26]

While besieging the city of Jazirat Ibn ʿUmar, Tughril's troops sacked the Nestorian monastery of Akhmūl, killing 120 of the 400 monks and ransoming the lives of the others for a huge amount of money.[27] Meanwhile, benefiting from the chaos, Tughril returned to Baghdad, entered it and received again the support of the Caliph in January 1058. But he was soon compelled to leave because 449/1058–9 was yet another year of famine and pestilence.

There was increasing famine in Baghdad and al-ʿIrāq . . . People ate . . . dogs and . . . sickness was so rife that people were incapable of burying the dead. They were put in communal pits . . . When Dubays [who ruled lands in the Jazira near Mosul] returned to his lands, [he] found them in ruin because of the large number of those who had died of the raging plague. There was nobody there.[28]

[26] Ibn al-Athīr, *Kāmil*, vol. IX, p. 631; English translation, p. 113. See also Ḥamza Abū Yaʿlā Ibn al-Qalānisī, *Dhayl taʾrīkh dimashq*, ed. Henry F. Amedroz (Beirut and Leiden: E. J. Brill, 1908), p. 86. Abū Bakr Ibn ʿAbd Allāh Ibn al-Dawādārī, *Kanz al-durar wa-jāmiʿ al-ghurar*, ed. Ṣalāḥ al-Dīn al-Munajjid (Cairo: Deutches Archäologisches Institut Kairo, in Kimmission Bei Harrassowitz Wiesbaden, 1961), vol. VI, pp. 369 and 371 says that in the famine of 448, 50,000 died every day in Baghdad, while in 450, 10,000 people died every day who left property, as well as many poor people who could not be counted.

[27] Ibn al-Athīr, *Kāmil*, vol. IX, p. 630; English translation, p. 111; Bar Hebraeus, *Chronography*, p. 210: 'When the Sulṭan was besieging al-Jazīra [Jazīrat Ibn ʿUmar], some of his troops went to the Monastery of Akmūl, where there were 400 monks. They slaughtered 120 of them. The remainder purchased their lives with six makkuks of gold and silver'. Compare Jean-Maurice Fiey, *Nisibe, metropole syriaque orientale et ses suffagants des origines à nos jours* (Louvain: Secrétariat du Corpus SCO, 1977), for the history of the Akhmūl monastery, see *passim*.

[28] Ibn al-Athīr, *Kāmil*, vol. IX, pp. 636, 637.

During the 'sickness and a great famine' of the same year 'one-third of the population perished'. In Bukhara there were 'eighteen thousand funerals in one day. And . . . in three months there were a million and six hundred and fifty thousand people [dying]. And in Samarqand, within two months, two hundred and thirty-six thousand people died.'[29] During this period 'many died in the land of Egypt', and the plague spread 'all over the world', 'killing ten thousand people every day'.[30]

The turmoil and civil war continued and more supporters joined the camp of al-Basāsīrī, including the nephew of Tughril, Ibrāhīm Yināl, who openly revolted against his kinsman. The skirmishes between the two coalitions were held in places as far apart as Baghdad, Mosul and the Jazira, with al-Basāsīrī arriving even in Syria.

Local Christian chroniclers detail the attacks committed by the new waves of Turkish nomads arriving from the north. For them, the cold spell of 1056–8 meant a 'horrible disaster and fatal calamity'. They detail, for example, the raid of the Seljuk tribesmen on Melitene (Malatya), a prosperous Christian commercial centre, in 1058, resulting in mass killing, the enslavement of citizens and the loss of property.[31]

[29] Bar Hebraeus, *Chronography*, p. 209; Ibn al-Athīr, *Kāmil*, vol. IX, p. 637; English translation, p. 116.

[30] Tāj al-Dīn Muḥammad Ibn ʿAlī Ibn Muyassar, *Al-Muntaqā min akhbār miṣr (Choix de passages de la Chronique d'Egypte d'Ibn Muyassar)*, ed. Ayman Fuʾād Sayyid, Textes Arabes et Études Islamiques 18 (Cairo: Institut Français d'Archéologie Orientale du Caire, 1981), p. 15, for 447/1055–6; for 448/1056, see Abū al-Maḥāsin Yūsuf Ibn Taghrībirdī, *al-Nujūm al-ẓāhira fī mulūk miṣr wal-qāhira*, 16 vols. (Cairo: Dār al-Kutub, 1963–72), vol. V, p. 59.

[31] Matthew of Edessa, *Armenia and the Crusades*, 2.11, p. 94; Bar Hebraeus, *Chronography*, p. 212; *Anonymi auctoris chronicon ad AC 1234 pertinens, II*, translated by Albert Abouna with an introduction and notes by Jean M. Fiey, Corpus Scriptorum Christianorum Orientalium, 354 (Scriptores Syri, 154) (Louvain: Secrétariat du Corpus SCO, 1974), 2:33 (p. 234). Bar Hebraeus relates other descriptions of these events: 'Joseph the monk . . . wrote three discourses on the event, and Mar John the son of Shoshan composed four discourses on the destruction of Melitene' , (*Chronography*, p. 213).

Monasteries were sacked and many monks were massacred during these raids. It seems that although the Seljuks did not refrain from attacking Muslim cities and property, and from murdering their residents, they preferred attacking Christian neighbourhoods. During the sacking of Melitene they destroyed the Monastery of Bar Gagai, which 'was never inhabited again'.[32] However, later, in 1058, they plundered the Muslim city of Sinjar, killing 4,000 people and destroying the mosque, although they looked for an excuse, accusing the citizens of insulting them in the past.[33]

In 1059 Tughril attempted to subdue Ibrāhīm Yināl, whom he feared more than al-Basāsīrī. He ordered the armies to join him, but the Caliph was prepared to replace Tughril and enthrone the son of Khātūn, Tughril's wife, in his place.[34] The plot was concocted by no less than Tughril's vizier Kundurī, by Khātūn and by the Caliph. It was exposed at the most inappropriate moment, when the Sultan was preparing himself for the final battle against Ibrāhīm Yināl. At his departure, noticing that he was followed by only 2,000 men, he reproached his vizier Kundurī, saying: 'Why did you not inform me so that I could wait until all the men were assembled?' Later at Hamadhan, when faced by the superior forces of Ibrāhīm Yināl, he asked his wife and his vizier to come to his aid, but they were sure that the victory would be Yināl's and so continued distributing money among the troops against Tughril. The plan, however, met with opposition from two of Tughril's generals, who refused to join at the last moment, and by Khātūn herself, who changed her mind

32 Bar Hebraeus, *Chronography*, p. 213.

33 Ibid., p. 210; Sibṭ Ibn al-Jawzī, *Mir'at al-zamān*, the years 1056–86, pp. 22–3; Ibn al-Athīr, *Kāmil*, vol. IX, pp. 630–1; English translation, p. 112, do not refer to the destruction of the mosque.

34 Sibṭ Ibn al-Jawzī, *Mir'at al-zamān*, the years 1056–86, pp. 31–3.

and remained loyal to her husband. Nobody was sure about the results of the battle.[35]

In December 1058 al-Basāsirī entered Baghdad, accompanied by four hundred Mamluks 'in a state of extreme hardship and poverty' and two hundred horsemen. He seized power, minted coins, appointed judges, arrested the Abbasid caliph, looted the latter's palace and proclaimed Fatimid al-Mustanṣir the Caliph of Egypt in the Friday prayers.[36] But this was the end of the support arriving from Egypt. The famine and the disastrous pestilence that hit the eastern Mediterranean during the winter of 1058/9 left little hope of further Egyptian support from al-Basāsīrī,[37] who was virtually abandoned by Cairo.[38] Without Egyptian help al-Basāsīrī was not able to retain his achievements and was compelled to leave Baghdad in December 1059. Meanwhile Tughril, after defeating and killing Ibrāhīm Yināl, was ready to reclaim power in Baghdad. He invaded Iraq approaching Baghdad and igniting riots that led to the further destruction of that city. Al-Basāsīrī was defeated a month later and was beheaded by Tughril's cavalry. Tughril entered Baghdad and assumed the position of Sultan.

The arrival of Tughril, says Ibn al-Athīr, signified the end of the drought.

> The year had been one of drought, in which no rain had been seen, but that night it came and the poets congratulated the Caliph and the Sultān on that circumstance. After the Caliph's return the rain lasted for thirty odd days. An untold number of people had perished through hunger and oppression.[39]

[35] Ibn Khallikān, *Wafayāt al-aʿyān*, trans. William MacGuckin de Slane (Paris: Oriental Translation Fund of Great Britain and Ireland, 1842–71), vol. III, pp. 290–5.

[36] Ibn al-Athīr, *Kāmil*, vol. IX, pp. 641–3; English translation, pp. 121–3; Sibṭ Ibn al- Jawzī, *Mirʾat al-zamān*, the years 1056–86, pp. 37–9.

[37] Ibn al-Athīr, *al-Kāmil*, vol. IX, pp. 631, 636. According to Ibn al-Athīr, a thousand people died every day in Fustat in 448/1056–7. Ibn al-Qalānisī, *Dhayl*, p. 86.

[38] The death of al-Yazūrī in February 1058 signifies the end of any possible Egyptian aid to Baghdad. See Ibn al-Athīr, *Kāmil*, vol. IX, pp. 635–6.

[39] Ibid., vol. IX, p. 648.

The rain of January and February 1060 was not only the end of that specific year's drought. It was, in fact, the end of more than thirty years of unremitting dearth and hunger; an end that in its abruptness emphasized the random and haphazard nature of the crisis. Many of the most important events during these thirty years were the result of unpredictable climatic catastrophes, including the initial crossing of the Oxus by the Oghuz, their outbursts of violence, and the chaotic nature of the collapse of Iran. All these events followed climatic disasters and years of freeze, and none of them could have been planned in advance. The takeover of Baghdad by the Seljuks in 1055 was probably schemed in advance, but its materialization was totally lacking any rational order and was the result of incidental opportunities. The political crisis ended when the drought and hunger were over and when sufficient and timely rain saturated the fields, putting an end to one of the longest periods of unremitting dearth and poverty in the region.

Tughril's own men were uncertain, until the very last minute, of his prospects of winning the battle against al-Basāsīrī; it was probably because al-Basāsīrī was abandoned by his impoverished Egyptian sponsors and was forced to quit Baghdad and seek his fortune elsewhere that Tughril won the day. Tughril's entry into the capital in December 1059 put him, therefore, in a better position to benefit from the return of the rain in January 1060. The picture could have been reversed if the drought crisis had come to an end a month earlier, and if al-Basāsīrī and not Tughril was ruling the capital at such a crucial moment.

The seesaw of power that started with Tughril's entry into Baghdad in 1055 and ended very dramatically during the winter of 1060 was therefore not decided because of Tughril's superiority in manpower or his strategic and tactical abilities; it was influenced by the end of the hunger that prevailed in Iraq until then.

## NOMADIC STATEHOOD

The takeover of Baghdad by the Seljuks in 1060 also marks the end of the first period of the 'nomadic statehood' that was established in Baghdad after the nomads gained control of the city. It also marks the transformation of the tribal aristocracy that ruled the city into an incipient ruling class of an established empire, and the transformation of the nomadic statehood itself into a state like any other.

According to Anatoly Khazanov, who devotes the final chapter of his brilliant book to nomadic statehoods,[40] the emergence of such an entity is dependent on several conditions, including the expansion of the nomads at the expense of the sedentary population, the dimensions of the conquered states (that have to be sufficiently large and stable to accommodate the nomads), and the degree of social differentiation between the nomads and the sedentary population. Nomadic statehoods usually make considerable use of the heritage they inherit from their sedentary predecessors. Khazanov does not refer to many examples for the early stages of nomadic statehoods, nor does he refer to the Seljuks as a good example of such a process. In fact, his model is more applicable to the post-1060s Seljuk state, and therefore to a state that was created during a period of opulence rather than to the state that emerged in Baghdad during the mid 1050s and which had to accommodate the dearth and hunger of those years. Detailed descriptions of the very early stages are totally missing from his model.

[40] Anatoly M. Khazanov, *Nomads and the outside world*, trans. Julia Crookenden, foreword Ernest Gellner, 2nd edn (Madison: University of Wisconsin Press, 1994), pp. 228–302; Tim Ingold, 'Khazanov on nomads', *Current Anthropology* 26.3 (June 1985), 384–7; Peter B. Golden, 'Nomads and sedentary societies in medieval Eurasia', in *Agricultural and pastoral societies in ancient and classical history*, ed. Michael Adas (Philadelphia: Temple University Press, 2001), pp. 71–115.

It seems to me, however, that the detailed descriptions of the events that occurred in Baghdad from 1055 onwards are rare references to the first stages in the creation of a nomadic statehood, when the nomads still relate to the capital and to its institutions as tools that can lead to the acquisition of power and legitimacy. Tughril, who built a palace for himself next to that of the Caliph, was well aware of the importance of this prime location for strengthening his position, but a year later he felt strong enough to abandon the palace and settle on the eastern shore of the Tigris. In order to achieve that, not only did he take his soldiers out of the city but he also destroyed the neighbouring buildings and dismantled the bridges for the fortification of his new camp. Legitimacy and prime location were not as important as separation from the local population.

Social and spatial division between rulers and the ruled are, according to Khazanov, necessary stages in the creation of a nomadic statehood, but in the case of Baghdad we can see that the Seljuks not only preferred living in tents outside the city, they actually referred to the city dwellers as their enemies and to the resources of the city as their building materials, and not as a property belonging to their subjects. During their initial stay in Baghdad, the Seljuks did repair mosques, but they did not bother to build any other public institution or amenity for the benefit of the citizens. Later, they combined their pretence of being the legitimate rulers of the country with their marauding behaviour, pillaging and plundering their own country and their own subjects to provide for their private needs when the whole country suffered from famine and dearth. Similarly, when their tribal coherence was threatened because of the desertion of an important amir or because of the rise of a new contender to the throne, the sultan himself, together with the state's army, acted as if they were still defending their tribal interests, abandoning their official duties and ruling positions to chase the insubordinate member and his followers.

Detailed descriptions of such initial stages in the creation of nomadic statehoods are very rare and they certainly deserve deeper historical and anthropological scrutiny. For the purpose of the present study it is enough to mention that the transition in the behaviour of the Seljuks, from marauding to the running of a state with proper institutions, passed through the embryonic stage of a nomadic statehood. This initial phase lasted a decade – the last and most destructive decade of the dearth in Mesopotamia.

## CULTURAL IMPLICATIONS OF THE CRISIS

To old-school Orientalists and historians of western Europe, it was clear that the cultures that flourished in Iran and Iraq during the tenth and eleventh centuries suffered from a very sharp and abrupt decline, that there was a hiatus in the development of Islamic institutional culture in this region between the late 1020s and the 1060s, and that this hiatus was most discernible in the mid 1050s. For many scholars there was a clear connection between the phenomenon that they described as the 'decline of the Islamic culture in Mesopotamia' and the invasion of the Seljuks. Frederick B. Artz, who wrote standard compilations of the cultural histories of Europe in general and France in particular, said:

> The striking decline that followed this [Islamic] golden age was due to number of causes. In the middle of the eleventh century, the backward Seljuk Turks, lately converted to Mohammedanism, took Baghdād and much of the Near East. The Seljuk authorities were repressive against all who did not agree with the orthodox Muslim theologians . . . The Seljuk . . . brought devastation, depopulations and stagnation. Muslim civilization had, from the eleventh century on, something of the same problem of

being overrun by inferior cultures that the Roman Empire had had in the fifth century. Only in North Africa and in Spain did the old lights of Islamic learning still burn brightly.[41]

Donald E. H. Campbell, a physician who described the development of Muslim medicine in the Middle Ages, similarly accused the Seljuks:

> The increasing ascendancy of Turkish races and their intolerance (a characteristic, it must be acknowledged, of most proselytes) was the first cause of the growth of this inhibitory influence among the Muslims . . . Thus while ethnic philosophy began to find a home in Latin Europe, the orthodox reaction of Islam reduced the Arabic philosophers and physicians to silence.[42]

Eliyahu Ashtor also blames the Seljuks for the decline of the golden age. But unlike his colleagues, he was also aware of the sharp decline of the contemporaneous economy: 'The countless passages where the chronicles speak of the tyranny and the cruelty of the Turkish princes leave no doubt to the plight of Oriental townspeople in the Seljuk age. There must surely have been a general decline of prosperity and as a consequence of misgovernment and poverty there was a decrease of population'.[43]

The claim that Islamic intellectual activity declined during the mid eleventh century ignited anti-Orientalist and post-colonialist criticism,[44] which was directed against the very idea of a cultural

41 Frederick B. Artz, *The mind of the Middle Ages, AD 200–1500: an historical survey*, 3rd and rev. edn (University of Chicago Press, 1980), pp. 175–6.

42 Donald E. H. Campbell, *Arabian medicine and its influence on the Middle Ages* (London: Trübner, 1926), pp. 44–5.

43 Eliyahu Ashtor, *A social and economic history of the Near East in the Middle Ages* (London: Collins, 1976), pp. 214–21. See also Kirti N. Chaudhuri, *Trade and civilisation in the Indian Ocean: an economic history from the rise of Islam to 1750* (Cambridge University Press, 1985), p. 36.

44 See, among many others, George Saliba, *A history of Arabic astronomy: planetary theories during the golden age of Islam* ( New York University Press, 1994), a collection claiming that the period in which Islamic intellectual history was declining was in fact very

decline during the eleventh century and against the assumption that the deeds of the Seljuks, who later developed some of the most important institutions of Islamic learning and governance, were also the reason for the destruction of the culture that preceded them. If there was a decline in this part of the eastern Mediterranean, say the critics, it resulted from the invasions of foreign and 'colonialist' forces such as the Crusaders or the Mongols. The critical approach is at least partially correct. Islamic civilizations continued to flourish after the mid eleventh century and ever later. Polymaths of the calibre of Omar Khayyám – born in Nishapur in AD 1048, towards the end of the climatic disaster, and who died in the same city in AD 1131 – or al-Ghazali (b. 1058, d. 1111) to name but two of the greatest scholars of the period that followed the crisis of the eleventh century, do not mark any intellectual 'decline' and certainly not a 'collapse'.

Similarly, if the time span for the survey of the continuity of Islamic science begins with the rise of the Abbasids in AD 750 and ends with the invasion of the Mongols in AD 1258,[45] or if the geographical setting for the study of this continuity is not specified and includes the entire Mediterranean basin, then the long-term developments can easily mask the serious discontinuities and setbacks that occur during the process. Direct evidence for the connection between climatic disasters, extended hunger or nomadic

productive for astronomy; George Saliba, *Islamic science and the making of the European Renaissance* (Boston, MA: MIT Press, 2007); Sallah E. al-Djazairi, *The golden age and decline of Islamic civilisation* (Manchester: Bayt al-Hikma Press, 2006); Matthew E. Falagas, Effie A. Zarkadoulia and George Samonis, 'Arab science in the golden age (750–1258 CE) and today', *FASEB* (Federation of American Societies for Science after the 11th Century', *Islam and Science* 5.1 (2007), 61–70.

45 William Montgomery Watt, *Islamic philosophy and theology* ( Edinburgh University Press, 1962), who devotes a section to the 'second wave of Hellenism 950–1258' and another to the 'period of darkness 1250–1900'; Donald S. Richards (ed.), *Islamic civilisation, 950–1150: a colloquium published under the auspices of the Near Eastern History Group, Oxford, the Near East Center, University of Pennsylvania* (Oxford: Cassirer, 1973).

invasions and the decline of cultural institutions is very scarce and circumstantial. Concurrence and hypothetical causality can easily be demonstrated but are more difficult to verify.

## DESTRUCTION OF LIBRARIES AND ACADEMIES

Some of the cultural and educational institutions – libraries and academies –that existed and flourished under the Buyid administration in Iran and Iraq in the tenth and early eleventh centuries were totally destroyed during the decades of extended cold and hunger of 1027–60.[46]

An example of such a library is that of the 'house of science [Dāral-ʿIlm]' that was founded in Baghdad by the Buyid vizier Sābūr b. Ardashīr in the early 990s as part of an academy that imitated the functions of the historical 'House of Wisdom' of al-Māʾmūn.[47] The library, which contained more than ten thousand books, some of them models of calligraphy on all scientific subjects, was well endowed and continued to flourish after the death of its founder in 416/ AD 1025–6. The endowment enabled an ample administration of the institution, which was frequented by some of the leading intellectuals of the time. It continued to receive works of contemporary writers until the late 1030s, and was finally burnt down during the 1050s. It was probably burned twice, once in 447/ 1055 during Tughril's first entry into Baghdad and again during his second takeover of the city in December 451/1059. The library was

[46] For an excellent survey, see Youssef Eche, *Les Bibliothèques arabes publiques et semi-publiques en Mésopotamie, en Syrie et en Égypte au Moyen Age* (Damascus: Institut Français de Damas, 1967).

[47] Ruth S. Mackensen, 'Four great libraries of medieval Baghdad', *Library Quarterly* 2.3 (July 1932), 279–99; Yāqūt Ibn ʿAbd Allāh, al-Ḥamawī, *The Irshād al-arīb ilā maʿrifat al-adīb, or dictionary of learned men of Yāqūt*, ed. David S. Margoliouth, 6 vols. (Leiden: E. J. Brill; London: Luzac, 1907–13), vol. VI, p. 358.

sacked after the fire, and the Seljuk vizier ʿAmīd al-Mulk al-Kundurī selected the best remaining books of the collection for his own private library.[48]

The library in Baghdad was only one of many public and semi-public libraries and academies that flourished in the region. Baghdad maintained a long tradition of 'houses of science', beginning with al-Maʾmūn's original 'House of Wisdom', which disappeared in 880.[49] Similar academies, equipped with libraries, are known in Mosul, and they were similarly open to all.[50] The Buyid rulers established libraries in many towns, spreading knowledge during the whole period that is referred to by modern scholars as the 'Shiʿi century' or the 'Islamic Golden Age'.

Al-Muqaddasī visited and enthusiastically described the library that was incorporated into the Buyid palace of Shiraz:

> [The Buyid prince ʿAlī b. Buwayh] built in Shiraz an edifice the like of which I have not seen in the East or in the West . . . the delight and excellence of Paradise. Streams run through it, built domes over it with gardens and trees . . . In the upper part is the library . . . and there was not a book written at that time, of all the various sciences, but happened to be there . . . For every subject there are bookcases, and catalogues in which are the names of the books . . .[51]

Other famous libraries existed in Basra (more than one), Nishapur, Isfahan, Ram Hormuz, Firuzabad, Dhiraz and Rayy. In addition, there were the well-known centres of learning in Ghazna, Bukhara and Syria (where scores of libraries are known in

[48] Ibn al-Athīr, *Kāmil*, vol. X, p. 7; English translation, p. 130; Martinus Th. Houtsma, *Recueil de textes relatifs à l'histoire des Seldjoucides*, vol. II, *Histoire du Seldjucides d'Irāq par al-Bondāri* (Leiden: E. J. Brill, 1889), pp. 1–8.

[49] Yāqūt, *Irshād*, vol. V, pp. 459, 467. [50] Ibid., vol. II, p. 420.

[51] Muqaddasī, Muḥammad Ibn Aḥmad, *The best divisions for knowledge of the regions* [Aḥsan al-Taqāsīm fi Maʿrifat al-Aqālīm], trans. Basil A. Collins (Reading: Garnet, 2001), pp. 363–4.

Damascus, Tripoli and elsewhere).[52] The great viziers of the period also owned private libraries that emphasize the availability of knowledge. One such private library existed in Hamadhan, containing 'one hundred camel-loads of books', with as great an historian as Miskawayh serving as librarian. Another owned no less than 'four hundred camel-loads of books'.[53] The catalogues of the libraries of the time give an idea of the extent of the philosophic content of the period. The *Fihrist* (Catalogue) of Ibn al-Nadīm, which was published for the first time in AD 938 when the Buyids began their ascendancy in Iran, included virtually the entire Aristotelian Corpus and its principal Greek commentaries, many of Plato's writings, pre-Socratic texts translated into Arabic and the works of Euclid and Ptolemy, as well as medical writings ascribed to Hippocrates and the works of Galen.[54]

Many of the libraries still operating during the first quarter of the eleventh century ceased to exist during its second quarter, and many of them did not survive the period of turmoil and dearth between 1027 and 1060. The libraries of Rayy were destroyed in the spring of 1029 when the Buyid ruler of the city asked Maḥmūd of Ghazna to protect him against his own unpaid soldiers. The latter was happy to comply and sacked the city, stoning many people as heretics and

[52] Muqaddasī, *Best divisions*, p. 320; Yāqūt, *Irshād*, vol. II, p. 315; Ibn al-Jawzī, *Muntaẓam*, vol. IX, p. 53; Olga Pinto, 'The libraries of the Arabs', in *Encyclopaedic survey of Islamic culture*, vol. III, *Educational developments in the Muslim world*, ed. Mohamed Taher (New Delhi: Anmol, 1997), pp. 218–46, and [anon.], 'Libraries and academies during the Buwayhid period', pp. 214–17.

[53] Ibn al-Jawzī, *Muntaẓam*, vol. VII, p. 165; Yāqūt, *Irshād*, vol. II, p. 315. See George Makdisi, *The rise of humanism in classical Islam and the Christian West, with special reference to scholasticism* ( Edinburgh University Press, 1990).

[54] Ibn al-Nadīm, Muḥammad Ibn Isḥāq, *The Fihrist of al-Nadīm: a tenth-century survey of Muslim culture*, ed. and trans. Bayard Dodge, *Records of Civilization: Sources and Studies 83* (New York: Columbia University Press, 1970); Franz Rosenthal, *The classical heritage in Islam*, trans. Emile and Jenny Marmorstein (London: Routledge, 1992); Richard R. Walzer, *Greek into Arabic: essays on Islamic philosophy* (Oxford: Cassirer, 1962); Eche, *Bibliothèques arabes*, pp. 315–24.

burning down both the central and private libraries as centres of heterodoxy.[55] The library of Baghdad was burnt twice as a part of the decline of the city, with the books being pillaged by the vizier.

The year 430/1038 is also the last year when the two age-old Jewish Babylonian academies of Sura and Pumbedita are mentioned,[56] marking the dramatic inception of medieval rabbinic culture and the shift in the centre of Jewish cultural and intellectual life westwards from Babylonia to North Africa and Europe. Contemporary sources do not explain this sudden and almost simultaneous disappearance or the ascendancy of Jewish scholarship elsewhere.[57] In any event, the disappearance of Jewish scholarship from Mesopotamia was not gradual. The academies of Babylon were still active and prestigious during the second quarter of the eleventh century; the Gaon of Jerusalem mentioned that his own son studied in Babylon in the Academy of R. Hai Gaon.[58]

## THE 1060S: THE RECOVERY OF BAGHDAD

Under the tolerant Buyid rule of Iraq and western Iran the thriving Islamic societies of the East reached some of their highest cultural and intellectual achievements. The Islamic civilization of the time was described by Giorgio Levi de la Vida as 'more cosmopolitan

55 Ibn al-Athīr, *Kāmil*, vol. IX, pp. 371–2; ʿAbd al-Ḥayy Gardīzī, *Tārīkh-i Gardīzī*, ed. ʿAbd al-Ḥayy Ḥabībī (Teheran: Dunyā-yi Kitāb, 1984 or 1985), p. 193.

56 Jacob Mann, 'The last Geonim of Sura', *Jewish Quarterly Review* 11 (1921), 409–22.

57 Abraham Ibn Daud, *A critical edition with a translation and notes of the Book of Tradition* [Sefer ha-qabbalah], ed. Gerson D. Cohen (Philadelphia: Jewish Publication Society of America, 1967), pp. 58–62.

58 Robert Brody, *Readings in Geonic literature* (Tel Aviv: Hakkibutz Hameuchad, 1998), p. 35 (Hebrew); Jacob Mann, *The Jews in Egypt and in Palestine under the Fatimid caliphs*, 2 vols. (New York: Ktav, 1970; reprinted Oxford University Press, 1920–2), vol. II, pp. 133–5; Moshe Gil, *Palestine during the first Muslim period*, 3 vols. (Tel Aviv University Press, 1983), vol. II, p. 93 (Hebrew).

[than] the Hellenistic and Roman world had ever been', and by Adam Mez as 'the Renaissance of Islam'.[59]

The new institutions of learning that emerged in Baghdad and elsewhere during the second half of the eleventh century no longer gave the same preference to Hellenistic traditions in philosophy and in sciences as their pre-crisis predecessors, and the intellectual shift led to the abandonment of some of the attributes of former intellectual activity. The change was described by many as a 'decline' or even a 'collapse' of Hellenistic traditions in the East, or as a transformation of intellectual interests by those who did not necessarily accept the superiority of the earlier traditions. The fact that new institutional learning was established in Baghdad during the 1060s, basing the training of future administrators on different types of curricular knowledge, is more consensual and avoids the trap of ranking cultures into those that are 'declining superior' or 'rising formerly inferior'. Baghdad underwent a tremendous cultural and governmental change between the late 1020s and the 1060s and more precisely between 1050 and 1065.

The new period that commenced at the beginning of 1060 was a time of relative peace, calm and prosperity.[60] Immediately after resuming power in January 1060, the Seljuks began to restore order, to appoint provincial governors and to reconstruct marketplaces and former governmental residences for their own use.[61] Even the

[59] Adam Mez, *The Renaissance of Islam*, trans. Salahuddin Khuda Bukhsh and David S. Margoliouth (London: Luzac, 1937); Joel L. Kraemer, *Humanism in the renaissance of Islam: the cultural revival during the Buyid age*, 2nd edn (Leiden: E. J. Brill, 1993), p. 5; Hamilton A. R. Gibb, 'An interpretation of Islamic history', in Joel L. Kraemer, *Studies on the civilization of Islam* (Boston, MA: Beacon Press and London: Routledge, 1962), pp. 5–15.

[60] Reuben Levy, *A Baghdad chronicle* (Cambridge University Press, 1929), pp. 185–203.

[61] For the rebuilding of Baghdād during the early 1060s, see Ibn al-Jawzī, *Muntaẓam*, vol. VIII, p. 216; Sibṭ Ibn al-Jawzī, *Mir'at* (Ankara edition), p. 74; George Makdisi, 'The topography of eleventh-century Baghdād', *Arabica* 6 (1959), 178–97; Guy Le Strange, *Baghdad during the Abbasid caliphate* (Oxford: Clarendon Press, 1900), pp. 178, 233, 243.

library of Baghdad, which was burnt twice during the 1050s, was reconstructed, and 1,000 of the 10,000 volumes that it possessed in the past were returned.[62]

The new period of relative abundance and calm is also characterized by a pacification of many of the past division lines that tore society apart during the years of the crisis. The traditional clashes between the Sunnis and the Shiʿis were abated and an historic settlement was reached in 488/1095 allowing people living in the rival quarters, which were kept locked for decades, 'to exchange visits, to trust each other, and to drink in each other's company'.[63] Even the petty Bedouin and Kurdish dynasties of the Jazira stopped interfering with the grain trade.

The great prosperity, which followed decades of extreme dearth, was felt in the provinces as well. In 1060 the ruler of Diyar Bakr, for example, adopted practices towards wildlife that were simply impossible several years earlier: 'During his reign prices were low and people made great display of their wealth . . . He heard that in the winter the birds came out of the mountains into the villages, where they were hunted. He ordered grain from the granaries he possessed to be scattered for them, and they continued to be his guests in this way all his life.'[64]

Improved conditions and the reconstruction of Baghdad affected the attitudes of the chroniclers towards the deeds of the Seljuks themselves. Ibn al-Athīr, for example, no longer presents them as marauders and violent nomads, as he had done while describing their activities during the crisis; rather they were now retired warriors who contemplate the rebuilding of the lands they

[62] Ibn al-Jawzī, *Muntaẓam*, vol. VIII, p. 216.

[63] Ibn al-Jawzī, *Muntaẓam*, vol. IX, p. 87, and compare Ibn al-Athīr, *Kāmil*, vol. X, p. 7; English translation, p. 130.

[64] Ibn al-Athīr, *Kāmil*, vol. X, p. 18; English translation, p. 136.

destroyed. He records a dialogue between Tugril Beg and his brother Chaghril Beg, which ostensibly took place in 452/1060–1 and in which both express repentance for the ruin they have been spreading. 'I have heard', says Chagril, 'that you are ruining the lands you have conquered and taken, whose inhabitants have fled them. This is manifestly in opposition to what God Almighty orders'. Tughril Beg retorts:

My brother, you took Khurasan as a flourishing land, and you have ruined it, although . . . it was your duty to make it flourish. I have come to a land ruined by those who preceded me and destroyed by those before me . . . Necessity leads armies to tramp through it and it is impossible to stop them harming it.[65]

The more agreeable climate, however, was limited to the more eastern regions of Mesopotamia, the Jazira, Iran and Khurasan. The centre of the cold, which shifted westwards during the 1050s, was looming over Anatolia and the shores of the Black Sea, also affecting Armenia and Azerbaijan. The victorious Seljuks gradually adopted proper codes of Islamic behaviour and refrained from attacking Muslim centres. This did not deter them, however, from pillaging the less fortunate Christian provinces, settlements and communities, and from committing mass murder.[66]

The Christian chroniclers noted the shift in the destructive activities of the Seljuks and emphasize the results of their raids. In 1060–1, writes Matthew of Edessa,

[The Turks] became stirred up and . . . went forth with a very large army . . . against the Armenian faithful. Many districts were devastated by the sword and enslaved by . . . the impious beasts who had come forth from

[65] Ibn al-Athīr, *Kāmil*, vol. X, pp. 6–7; English translation, pp. 129–30.
[66] Matthew of Edessa, *Armenia and the Crusades*, 2.11, p. 94.

> the court of the sultan Tughril . . . they reached the populous and renowned city of Sebastia . . .[67]

Concerning the attack of 1062–3 against the Armenian territories of Paghin, T'lkhum and Arkni in Armenia, he says that '[like] bloodthirsty wolves . . . they attacked the entire region . . . The vast plain was filled with blood, captives, and merciless slaughter – something we are not able to relate'.[68] In 1064–5 Alp Arslān, the nephew and heir to Tughrul Beg, 'went forth and reached Armenia . . . subjecting it to the sword and enslavement, killing many Christians that no one is able to relate . . . this disaster to the Christian faithful'.[69] Finally, Alp Arslān captured Ani,

> a city that previously contained 1,001 churches . . . The infidels entered the city, occupied with sharp swords, three swords each, one in each arm and one held by their teeth . . . They massacred the believers heaping their bodies like heaps of stones, fetching the big cross from the dome of the cathedral and using it later as a threshold of their mosque . . . for them to trample.[70]

Ibn al-Athīr and Sibṭ Ibn al-Jawzī also refer to the destruction of Ani and the mass murder of the Christians there, but they prefer to emphasize the meticulously planned attack on the town and the work on the first Islamic madrasa of Baghdad that began a year later.[71]

The extended activities of the Seljuks in the western provinces were noticed by earlier scholars. Says Speros Vryonis, Jr: 'The years between 1058 and the battle of Manzikert were characterized by a financial, administrative and military collapse of the Byzantine presence in Anatolia. The Turks, on the other hand

[67] Ibid., 2.12, p. 96. [68] Ibid., 2.15, p. 97. [69] Ibid., 2.20, p. 101.
[70] Ibid., 2.21, p. 102.
[71] Ibn al Athīr, *Kāmil*, vol. X, pp. 37–40, 49; Sibṭ Ibn al-Jawzī, *Mir'at al-zamān*, pp. 117–18. At p. 124, lines 9–10 he dates the beginning of the works to November 1065.

were raiding the country almost without hindrance, pillaging, almost systematically, all the urban centers of Eastern Asia Minor'.[72]

Vryonis does not explain the reasons for the 'financial, administrative and military collapse of the Byzantine presence in Anatolia', but Eastern chroniclers were aware of the intensification of the cold in the west that resulted in the attacks by the nomads along the Danube frontier as well as along the eastern frontier. Matthew of Edessa reports that in 1065–6 the emperor was defeated in a battle with the Uzes on that frontier.[73] In 1065–6 the Seljuks attacked the castle of T'lkhum, raiding Edessa a year later and concluding with an attack on Nisibis, where 'Many monasteries and villages were burned to the ground, and their traces are still evident today'.[74]

The period of calm that began in 1060 and the renewed accumulation of wealth in Baghdad stand in sharp contrast to the hunger and misery that prevailed in Egypt in the late 1060s. In 452/1069, when there was a severe famine in Egypt and the people were reduced to cannibalism, some were deserting Egypt and moving to Baghdad to escape the hunger. 'Merchants came with the Egyptian ruler's textiles and products, which hunger had made them steal'. Ibn al-Faḍl even praises the Caliph of Baghdad in an ode which mentions hunger ('the years of Joseph') and plague ('the plague of ʿImwās') as the rebellious army of the Fatimid caliph, threatening the latter's own life.[75]

[72] Speros Vryonis, Jr, *The decline of medieval Hellenism in Asia Minor and the process of Islamization from the eleventh through the fifteenth century* (Berkeley: University of California Press, 1971), pp. 85–96.

[73] Matthew of Edessa, *Armenia and the Crusades*, 2.24, p. 105. [74] Ibid., 2.27, p. 107.

[75] Ibn al-Athīr, *Kāmil*, vol. X, pp. 61–2; Ibn al-Jawzī, *Muntaẓam*, vol. VIII, p. 257.

## THE INTRODUCTION OF THE MADRASA (LAW COLLEGE)

The decision to construct the first madrasas of Baghdad during the mid 1060s is probably one of the most important and historically influential institutional and educational reforms carried out by the great Seljuks and their able viziers. The madrasas were about to transform the nature of Islamic education and hasten the Islamization of state machineries.[76]

The construction of madrasas in Baghdad began during the mid 1060s with the Madrasa al-Niẓāmiyya and continued during the late eleventh century with the construction of no less than twenty-four institutions, all located along the east bank of the Tigris, in marketplaces and along the main streets and thoroughfares of the cities. Many were privately endowed by Seljuk officials and by the sultans themselves, and they offered different types of education and training for new officials and administrators.

Daphna Ephrat, who studied the development of Baghdadi learned society in the eleventh century, says:

> The madrasas were established principally for the study and transmission of the purely Islamic sciences (to the exclusion of the so-called foreign or ancient sciences inherited from the Hellenistic world). The advent and spread of the madrasa marked an important phase in the movement toward conformity and uniformity . . . The new madrasas, in other words, represented an attempt to organize Islamic education to a degree hitherto

[76] See Ephrat, *Learned society*; George Makdisi, 'Muslim institutions of learning in eleventh-century Baghdad', *Bulletin of the School of Oriental and African Studies* 24.1 (1961), 1–56; George Makdisi, 'Law and traditionalism in the institutions of learning of medieval Islam', in *Theology and law in Islam*, ed. Gustave E. von Grunebaum (Wiesbaden: Harrassowitz, 1971), pp. 75–88; Gary Leiseer, 'The madrasa and the Islamization of the Middle East: the case of Egypt', *Journal of the American Research Center in Egypt* 22 (1985), 29–47; Abdul Latif Tibawi, 'Origins and character of al-Madrasa', *Bulletin of the School of Oriental and African Studies* 25 (1962), 225–38.

unknown in its history, and to define the boundaries of religious knowledge.[77]

After the mid eleventh century most chancery secretaries had a madrasa education, but what they had studied was *fiqh* and related sciences, not how to draw up a decree or diploma of investiture, let alone a tax register. They obtained the knowledge they needed for governance on the job, as subordinates to senior ministers, but they all arrived in post equipped with a similar education, which they acquired in the madrasas. George Makdisi, who was even more radical in his approach to eleventh-century madrasa learning, maintained in his various writings on the subject that the instruction in these new schools was restricted to Islamic religious law and the subjects elementary to religious education.[78]

Ephrat notes further that 'Several historians have concluded that madrasas served as centers for the recruitment of jurists and bureaucrats, thereby planting the seeds for the creation of a religious establishment incorporated into the state bureaucracy and dependent upon the military ruling elite.' In her view the madrasas are 'instruments of state power, intended to control institutions of learning, which would grant the political rulers influence over the *ʿulamāʾ*. However,

> contrary to this accepted view, this study asserts that the *ʿulamāʾ* of Baghdād enjoyed an autonomous role in the city's public sphere throughout the Seljuk period. They acted independently of the political authorities in courts and madrasas and were reluctant to become involved or assume positions in the official sphere. Moreover, the political rulers avoided the internal affairs of the *ʿulamāʾ* and were careful not to meddle in religious matters in general.

[77] Ephrat, *Learned society*, p. 2.
[78] See above. For earlier origins of the madrasa, see Tibawi, 'Origins'.

The introduction of the madrasa as a central institution of learning, like all the other deeds of the Seljuks in Baghdad following the return of opulence, cannot be labelled a 'decline'. The cadre of teachers and scholars, the curriculum and the training of jurists were transformed and the emphasis shifted from teaching and studying the Hellenistic tradition to Islamic law and theology. But although the term 'decline' in this context is doubtful, it is certain that the golden age of the Hellenistic tradition in this part of the world was over, to be replaced by a different intellectual agenda.

One of the most amazing results of the period that followed the return of opulence is the speed with which formerly coarse and illiterate leaders of dislocated tribes were transformed and able to create an empire. Their empire, based on the employment of able viziers who were trained under the Persian monarchical and governmental tradition (such as Niẓām al-Mulk) and their genuine tribal and nomadic organization of a 'family federation',[79] assigning domains to the leading member of the leading family, facilitated the establishment of an empire extending over Iran, Iraq, Anatolia, parts of Central Asia and Afghanistan. The transformation was accompanied by a revolutionary change in institutional education and governmental practices – and even in the arts. The speed of the transformation is demonstrated by the fact that it took only two years for Niẓām al-Mulk, who served as vizier of Alp Arslān (1063–72), to begin the construction of the famous Madrasa al-Niẓāmiyya (and only five years since the end of the crisis and the victory of the Seljuks), and another two years to complete this revolutionary institution. This course of events sheds new light on ideas concerning collapse and resilience.

[79] Andre Wink, *Al-Hind, the making of the Indo-Islamic world*, vol. I, *Early medieval India and the expansion of Islam, 7th–11th centuries*, 3rd edn (Leiden : E. J. Brill, 1996), pp. 9–10.

CHAPTER SIX

# A crumbling empire: the Pechenegs and the decimation of Byzantium

Michael Angold describes the abrupt decline of the Byzantine Empire during the mid eleventh century in the following words:

> Basil II died in December 1025 after a reign of almost fifty years. He left Byzantium the dominant power of the Balkans and Middle East, with apparently secure frontiers along the Danube, in the Armenian highlands and beyond the Euphrates. Fifty years later Byzantium was struggling for its existence. All its frontiers were breached. Its Anatolian heartland was being settled by Turkish nomads; its Danubian provinces were occupied by another nomad people, the Pechengs; while its southern Italian bridgehead was swept away by Norman adventurers. It was an astonishing reversal of fortunes.[1]

Emperor Basil II was an able warrior and a talented administrator, who led the empire to some of its greatest political and military achievements. During a reign of forty-nine years he succeeded in extending the borders of the empire to their greatest territorial extent since the Muslim conquest, four centuries earlier. His tremendous successes mark the highlight of the Byzantine revival of

[1] Michael Angold, 'Belle époque or crisis? (1025–1118)', in *The Cambridge history of the Byzantine Empire, c. 500–1492*, ed. Jonathan Shepard (Cambridge University Press, 2008), pp. 583–626, p. 583. For a similar description written in the mid 1950s, see Peter Charanis, 'The Byzantine Empire in the eleventh century', in *A history of the Crusades*, gen. ed. Kenneth M. Setton, 6 vols. (Madison: University of Wisconsin Press, 1955–89), vol. I, *The first three hundred years*, ed. Marshal W. Baldin (1955), pp. 177–219, quote on p. 178.

the ninth and tenth centuries,[2] refuting Gibbon's assumption that the Byzantine Empire was, throughout its entire existence, in a state of decline. When Basil II died, in 1025, the empire was certainly not in a state of decline.

Basil II, however, died two years before the beginning of the cold spells of the late 1020s, which were followed by sixty years of territorial, political and economic disasters. It is almost impossible to overestimate the significance of the transformation that the empire underwent during this comparatively short time. In the mid 1080s almost the entire area of the Balkans was ruled by nomads of Oghuz origin or by Norman newcomers, most of Asia Minor was ruled by the Seljuks or the Banū Danishmand, the economy was in ruins, the army was a pale shadow of the past, and the capital itself was threatened. The wave of calamities attained one of its most disastrous peaks during the first half of the 1050s, when southern Italy was lost, the currency devalued and the decaying Macedonian dynasty was replaced by a new line of rulers following a coup d'état. The empire continued to suffer defeats during the late 1050s and 1060s, until the catastrophe of the Battle of Manzikert of 1071, when the Emperor Romanos IV was taken captive and the central Byzantine government abandoned the eastern frontier. During the same year, 1071, the city of Bari, the last Byzantine stronghold in southern Italy, was ceded to the Normans. Even the comparative recovery that followed the ascendance of the Komnenoi (a dynasty that ruled over the Byzantine Empire for over a century between *c.* 1081 and *c.* 1185) was only partial. The empire never returned to its

[2] Alexander. P. Kazhdan and Ann Wharton Epstein, *Change in Byzantine culture in the eleventh and twelfth centuries* (Berkeley: University of California Press, 1990), pp. 11–23; Mark Whittow, *The making of Byzantium, 600–1025* (Berkeley: University of California Press, 1996), chapter 9, 'The age of reconquest, 863–976', and 10, 'The reign of Basil II, 976–1025'.

pre-crisis dimensions, opulence and might. Even the city of Constantinople, which attained its greatest population of perhaps a million people at the beginning of the eleventh century, was decimated, according to Charanis, to fewer than 75,000 inhabitants less than two hundred years later. Charanis' estimations are certainly exaggerated. More recent publications, however, assess the population of Constantinople at the beginning of the eleventh century to vary between 200,000 and 400,000 people and to grow until the crisis of 1204.[3]

The Byzantine Empire, therefore, was not in a steady state of decline, as Gibbon asserted. The late tenth century and the beginning of the eleventh century were periods of prosperity, recovery and success, whereas the period between 1027 and 1084 (and especially the decades between 1046 and 1071) was one marked by disastrous collapse that lasted until the mid 1080s.

The appearance of Oghuz tribes in the Balkans at about the same time that similar dislocated pastoralists of Oghuz origin appeared in the East was no coincidence. The same periods of freeze that initiated the aggressive forays of the Seljuks and led to the collapse of Iran and Iraq, led the formerly peaceful nomadic groups of the Pechenegs, of the Uzes (the Oghuz and the Uzes are the same ethnic group) and of the Cumans to invade the Balkans, to reach the very shores of the Bosphorus, and to set off the collapse of the Byzantine Empire. Similarly, the same cold spell that caused the Tigris to freeze in Baghdad caused the Danube to be

3 Peter Charanis, 'A note on the population and cities of the Byzantine empire in the thirteenth century', in *The Joshua Starr memorial volume*, Jewish Social Studies 5 (New York: Conference on Jewish Relations, 1953), pp. 137–9; David Jacoby, 'La Population de Constantinople à l'époque byzantine: un problème de démographie urbaine', *Byzantion* 31 (1961), 81–109, totally discards these highly exaggerated estimations; Paul Magdalino, 'The Komnenoi (1118–1204)', in Shepard (ed.), *History of the Byzantine Empire*, pp. 627–63, p. 654.

covered by ice, facilitating the migration of the nomads to the south. The Pechenegs – or Patzinaks (as they were known by the Byzantines) – were the first among these groups to invade the empire. They lived in peace with the Byzantines until the end of the tenth century, occupying the plains extending from the north of the lower Danube to the shores of the Dnieper River and preventing the Russians and the Magyars from invading the empire. Their economy was predominantly pastoral and the spatial distribution of their sites indicates a seasonal migration from winter abodes in the lowlands near the Danube and the Black Sea to northern tributaries of the middle and upper Danube in the summer. Most rivers along the steppe corridor in which they used to seasonally migrate still bear Turkic names, indicating a possible Pecheneg origin.[4]

Following the extended cold spells of 1027–30, the Pechenegs were transformed into a violent tribe, attacking their former allies.[5] They crossed the Danube and caused considerable damage, which compelled Emperor Constantine VIII (reigned 1025–8) to launch a

[4] Florin Curta, *Southeastern Europe in the Middle Ages, 500–1250* (Cambridge University Press, 2006), pp. 183–5; I. Conea and I. Donat, 'Contribution à l'étude de la toponymie pétchénègue-couman de la plaine roumaine de Bas-Danube', in *Contributions onomastiques. Publiés à l'occasion du VIe Congrès international des sciences onomastiques à Munich du 24 au 28 Août 1956*, ed. Emil Petrovici (Bucharest: Académie de la République Populaire Roumaine, 1958), pp. 139–69.

[5] For a detailed description of the Pechenegs, their social and political organization in the steppe, and their relations with the Byzantine emperor, see Constantine Porphyrogenitus, *De administrando imperio*, ed. Gyula Moravcsik, trans. Romily J. H. Jenkins, new, rev. edn (Washington, DC: Dumbarton Oaks Center for Byzantine Studies, 1967; 2006 printing), pp. 48–56; Omeljan Pritsak, 'The Pechenegs: a case of social and economic transformation', *Archivum Eurasiae Medii Aevi* 1 (1975), 211–236; Omeljan Pritsak, 'Two migratory movements in the Eurasian steppe in the 9th–11th centuries', in *Proceedings of the 26th International Congress of Orientalists*, ed. Ramchandra N. Dandekar (New Delhi, 1964), vol. II, pp. 157–63. Elisabeth Malamut, 'L'Image byzantine des Petchénègues', *Byzantinische Zeitschrift* 88 (1995), 105–47 and especially 109–12; Alexander A. Vasiliev, *History of the Byzantine Empire, 324–1453* (Oxford: Basil Blackwell, 1952), vol. I, pp. 300–74.

counter-attack.[6] Similarly, following the freeze of 1032–3 they initiated an additional wave of raids on Bulgaria. The simultaneity of violent attacks of dislocated pastoralists in both the Balkans and in Iran and Khurasan, and the concurrency of these events with the peaks of the cold spells, is especially apparent during the reigns of Romanos III (1028–34) and Michael IV (1034–41), when the Pechenegs launched four more invasions,[7] corresponding to the attacks of the Seljuks during the cold spells of 1034–5 and 1036–8 respectively. In 1036 they also invaded Rus' and were defeated by Iraoslav the Wise in Kiev.[8]

The nomadic invasions of the 1030s and 1040s did not endanger the empire. The generals successfully withstood the attacks and suppressed uprisings in provinces as important as southern Italy. The threat to the empire increased and the invasions became more devastating during the cold spells of 1046–50, however, and especially during the extended freezes of the early 1050s when the attacks developed into an imminent danger to the stability of the Byzantine Empire itself.[9]

V. G. Vasilievskii was the first to acknowledge the historical significance of the invasions of the Pechenegs for the future of the empire. As early as 1872 he devoted a 173-page-long essay to their history and referred to their unremitting pressure during the 1050s and 1060s in the following words:

[6] Ioannes Scylitzes, *Synopsis historiarum*, ed. Joannes Thurn, Corpus Fontium Historiae Byzantinae, Series Berolinensis 5 (Berlin: De Gruyter, 1973), Constantine VIII, chapter 2, p. 373.

[7] Ibid., Romanos III Argyros, chapter 10, p. 385, Michael IV the Paphlagonian, chapter 6, p. 397 and chapters 9–10, p. 399.

[8] *The Russian primary chronicle*, trans. and ed. Samuel Hazzard Cross and Olgerd P. Shobowitz-Wetzor (Cambridge, MA: Mediaeval Academy of America, 1953), AM 6542–6544, English translation, pp. 136–7.

[9] The cold spell of the late 1040s was so severe that it led to the desertion of most (although not all) of the inhabited sites south and east of the Carpathian Mountains, regions which had flourished during the tenth century; Curta, *Southeastern Europe*, p. 304.

> This event [the advance of the Pechenegs into Byzantine territory] which has escaped the attention of all modern historical works had enormous significance for the history of humanity. In its consequences it was almost as important as the crossing of the Danube by the western Goths, which initiated the so-called migration of nations.[10]

The Byzantine emperors, like their counterparts in Baghdad, Iran and Khurasan, believed it was possible to appease the cold- and hunger-driven nomads by granting them permission to settle or by showering honours upon them. The Pechenegs accepted the honours, but were not appeased and continued their raids across the Danube. They first crossed the frozen Danube in the winter of 1046 and did so again in December 1048, during the extreme freeze of 1047–8, simultaneously with Seljuk attacks on Armenia in the east. A huge army of nomads (Cedrenus speaks of 800,000 men) deserted the regions north of the Danube, where their herds had died of the cold, crossed the solidly frozen Danube, spreading terror and death everywhere.[11] They were soon decimated by hunger and pestilence, from which they were by no means immune, and their strength diminished. The Byzantines were temporarily able to defeat them, assigning them the defence of the empire against their kinsmen on the north side of the Danube. Shortly thereafter they were joined by other nomads from the north, who similarly had abandoned the northern provinces. They reneged on their oaths and brought the

[10] As translated by Vasiliev, *History*, p. 325, from Vasilii. G. Vasilievskii, 'Vizantija I Pečenegi (1048–1094)' [Byzantium and the Patzinaks], *Trudy* (St Petersburg, 1908), vol. I, pp. 1–117, pp. 7–8 (Russian; originally published in 1872). See Petre Diaconu, 'The Petchenegs on the lower Danube', in *Relations between the autochthonous population and the migratory populations on the territory of Romania: a collection of studies*, ed. Miron Constantinescu, Stefan Pascu and Petre Diaconu (Bucharest: Editura Academiei Republicii Socialiste România, 1975), pp. 235–40, quote on p. 238; Paul Stephenson, *Byzantium's Balkan frontier: a political study of the northern Balkans, 900–1204* (Cambridge University Press, 2000), pp. 80–117.

[11] Georgius Cedrenus, *Compendium historiarum, I. Scylitzae ope*, supplemented and emended by Immanuel Bekker, 2 vols. (Bonn, 1838–9), vol. II, p. 585.

country from the Danube to Adrianople to their mercy. Matthew of Edessa writes:

In the following years [1050–1] the country of the Byzantines was shaken by violent disorders and many provinces were devastated by the ... rapacious and wickedly abominable nation of the Pechenegs, those ... beasts ... pushed against the Magyars and the Magyars in turn pushed against the Uzes and the Pechenegs; then the latter two ... brought much affliction upon Constantinople ... I am unable to relate the sorrowful calamities ... for the Pechenegs savagely and mercilessly enslaved the nation of the Greeks ...[12]

And, indeed, in 1050 the nomads continued plundering the country at their will, to such an extent that Emperor Constantine IX (reigned 1042–55) was forced to transfer his eastern army and create one joint Byzantine army to push them back, enrolling a huge number of mercenaries to ensure victory.[13] The combined army, however, was defeated twice by the nomads, once in 1049 and again, near Adrianople, in June 1050. 'In a terrible night of slaughter the crushed Byzantine regiments were destroyed by the barbarians almost without any resistance; only a small number of them escaped somehow and reached Adrianople. All the gains of former victories were lost.'[14] The diversion of the eastern army to the west and the huge expenditure on mercenaries resulted in bankruptcy and in a tremendous weakening of the empire.[15]

[12] Matthew of Edessa, *Armenia and the Crusades, tenth to twelfth centuries: the chronicle of Matthew of Edessa*, trans. Ara E. Dostourian (Lanham, MD: University Press of America, 1993), 1.95, pp. 79–80.

[13] Louis Bréhier, *Vie et mort de Byzance* (Paris: Albin Michel, 1947), p. 257; Scylitzes, *Synopsis historiarum*, Constantine Monomachos, chapter 28, p. 475.

[14] Stephenson, *Byzantium's Balkan frontier*, pp. 89–93; citation originally in Russian by Vasilievskii, 'Vizantija I Pečenegi (1048–1094)', p. 24, as translated by Vasiliev, *History*, p. 326.

[15] Stephenson, *Byzantium's Balkan frontier* , p. 92.

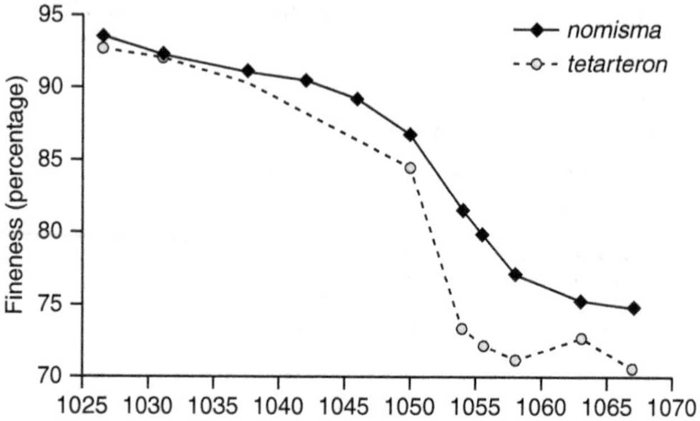


Fig. 6.1 Debasement of the Byzantine gold coins between 1025 and 1067 (after Kaplanis).

The victorious nomads continued ravaging the country in 1051 and 1052, and although the Byzantines succeeded in uprooting three of their detachments, they were again defeated by the nomads in 1053 near the Bulgarian city of Preslav near the Danube. Constantine IX was forced to buy peace at a heavy price: he had to pledge to pay tribute to the nomads in the future.[16]

Political humiliation and military defeats were not the only results of the failure. The recurring defeats led to the deterioration of the Byzantine economy and devaluation of the Byzantine nomisma, which had retained its stability for seven centuries.[17]

The nomisma, dubbed by Roberto Lopez 'The Dollar of the Middle Ages',[18] lost much of its value within a very short time. Costas Kaplanis has pointed to the correlation between the attacks

[16] Michael Attaleiates, *Historia*, ed. Immanuel Bekker, Corpus Scriptorum Historiae Byzantinae 36 (Bonn: Weber, 1853), p. 43 ; Diaconu, 'Petchenegs', p. 238; Vasiliev, *History*, p. 325.

[17] Costas Kaplanis, 'The debasement of the "dollar of the Middle Ages"', *Journal of Economic History* 63 (2003), 768–801.

[18] Robert S. Lopez, 'The dollar of the Middle Ages', *Journal of Economic History* 11 (1951), 209–34; Robert S. Lopez, 'La Crise du besant au Xe siècle et la date du Livre du Préfet', in *Mélanges Henri Grégoire (Annuaire de l'Institut de Philologie et d'Histoire Orientales et Slaves* 10.2) (Brussels: Sécretariat des Éditions de l'Institut, 1950), pp. 403–18.

of the Pechenegs and the debasement of the Byzantine gold coin during the reign of Constantine IX. In the last issue by Basil II (976–1025), the nomisma was still minted in pure gold (94.9 per cent). It was debased slightly to 90–94 per cent under Constantine VIII and Michael IV, but contained a mere 81.5 per cent when Constantine IX died in 1055.[19] The debasement, says Kaplanis, was a desperate attempt to finance the increasing expenditure on wars and mercenaries.[20] Byzantine gold coins, however, continued to be debased after the death of Constantine IX, reaching a nadir of 75 per cent gold content for the nomisma and 70 per cent for the tetarteron during the late 1060s.

Students of Byzantine history who were not aware of the climatic disasters and the sharp and constant devaluation of the nomisma between the 1030s and the 1070s, believed that the emperors of the mid eleventh century prevented the army from receiving the funds it needed because of political reasons, ignoring the actual miserable state of the empire. Peter Charanis wrote:

> [C]ertain emperors of the eleventh century, notably Constantine IX Monomachus (1042–1055), Michael VI (1056–1057), and Constantine X Dukas (1059–1067), tried to ... weaken the military organization by reducing the size of the army, thus depriving the aristocracy of its military commands. The great military triumphs of the tenth century ... created a sense of security and the feeling that the maintenance of a powerful army was no longer necessary. With Constantine IX, peace became the keynote

19 Cécile Morrison, et al., *L'Or monnayé*, vol. I, *Purification et altérations de Rome à Byzance*, Cahiers Ernest-Babelon (Paris: CNRS, 1985); Philip Grierson, 'The debasement of the Bezant in the eleventh century', *Byzantinische Zeitschrift* 47 (1954), 379–94; Philip Grierson, 'Notes on the fineness of the Byzantine solidus', *Byzantinische Zeitschrift* 54 (1961), 91–7; Cécile Morrison, 'La Dévaluation de la monnaie Byzantine au XIe siècle: essai d'interprétation', *Travaux et Mémoires* 6 (1976), 6–48.

20 See also John F. Haldon, *Recruitment and conscription in the Byzantine army c. 550–950: a study on the origins of the Stratiotika Ktemata* (Vienna: Österreichischen Akademie der Wissenschaften, 1979); Warren T. Treadgold, *Byzantium and its army, 284–1081* (Stanford University Press, 1995).

of the imperial foreign policy, and there began a systematic elimination of the aristocracy from the army ... at a time when new and formidable enemies were making their appearance, both in the East and in the West. But the most serious result of the imperial policy was the deterioration of the army and the depression of the enrolled soldiers.[21]

In view of the repeated and humiliating defeats and the evident financial and economic crisis, it is superfluous to claim that Constantine IX Monomachus or any other emperor of the eleventh century deprived his own defeated army of the funds it urgently needed in order to repel the marauders simply because of his personal and political dispositions towards the military aristocracy. Political tension between the two parties, therefore, was certainly not the main reason for the weakening of the army.

The accumulative effect of incessant attacks, cold spells, reduced crops and reduced income, on the one hand, and ever-growing and unavoidable military expenses, on the other, provides a better explanation for the difficulties the emperors faced in strengthening the army or even sustaining it. The necessary budgetary cuts were interpreted, however, as a struggle between the 'bureaucrats' who lived in the comparative safety of Constantinople and who were allegedly unaware of the situation in the provinces.[22]

Tensions between the impoverished Anatolian army and the 'bureaucrats' who were not able to finance it led the former to revolt and march on Constantinople, under the command of Isaac Comnenus, to meet the army of the west in a bloody battle outside Nicaea in 1057 and to topple the Macedonian dynasty.[23] Isaac Comnenus was enthroned as a soldier-emperor and was expected

[21] Peter Charanis, 'Economic factors in the decline of the Byzantine Empire', *Journal of Economic History* 13.4 (1953), 412–24, quote on 417–18.

[22] Michael Psellos, *Chronographia*, ed. and French trans. E. Renauld, 2 vols. (Paris, 1926–8), I.28, p. 17.

[23] Charanis, 'Byzantine empire', 197–8, Attaleiates, *Historia*, pp. 54–6.

to be more attentive to the needs of his army than his predecessors had been. His reign, however, did not yield additional budgets for the army. Isaac Comnenus practised the strictest economy: he attempted to carefully collect all the taxes, annulled land grants and confiscated property belonging to the monasteries, but even he was not able to dramatically change the situation.[24] The overwhelming effect of events deteriorated the economy to such an extent that maintenance of the army was simply too great a challenge for the impoverished empire. The dangers continued to loom and it was impossible to better equip the army or even provide it with adequate food, armour and weapons.

The situation of the eastern Byzantine army remained unchanged even when the empire was ruled by other professional soldiers. Later descriptions also testify to the impoverishment and the inability to finance the only regular Christian army at the time.[25] The army deteriorated to incompetence, wrote Attaleiates, 'because [it was] unarmed and uneager as a result of the deprivation of its provisions. The better soldiers were removed from military service by reason of the greater rank and salary [involved]'.[26]

Scylitzes Continuatus referred to the Byzantine forces defending Melitene in 1058 in the following words: 'being in want of their salary and deprived of the provisions usually supplied to them, they were in an abased and deprived state'.[27] When the Seljuks raided the city of Ani in 1064, pillaging the neighborhood of Antioch, the hastily recruited Byzantine army was 'unexperienced in war,

[24] Attaleiates, *Historia*, pp. 60–2; Psellos, *Chronographia*, VII.60, p. 120.

[25] Attaleiates, *Historia*, pp. 55, 69. [26] Ibid., pp. 78–9.

[27] Scylitzes Continuatus, in Cedrenus, *Compendium historiarum, I. Scylitzae ope*, vol. II, p. 660. The identity of this author is as yet uncertain. Several scholars believe this to be the work of Scylitzes himself, while others reject this view. See Jean-Claude Cheynet, 'Introduction: John Scylitzes, the author and his family', in John Scylitzes, *A Synopsis of Byzantine History: 811–1057*, trans. John Wortley (Cambridge University Press, 2010), pp. ix–xi, p. x.

without horses, nearly unarmed, naked and lacking even the daily bread'.[28]

The same author describes the Byzantine army in 1068, on the eve of the Battle of Manzikert:

> The renowned champions of the Romans who had reduced into subjection all of the east and the west now numbered only a few and these were bowed down by poverty and ill treatment. They lacked in weapons, swords ... javelins and scythes ... They lacked also in cavalry and other equipment, for the emperor had not taken the field for a long time.[29]

## THE END OF BYZANTINE DOMINION IN SOUTHERN ITALY

It is perhaps no mere coincidence that the year 1053–4, following two years in which the nomisma lost 12 per cent of its value, became a landmark for both the decline of Byzantine dominion and the ascent of Norman power in southern Italy. It seems that the inability of the empire to maintain its army was also reflected in its inability to maintain its domains.

Norman immigrants had begun settling in southern Italy around the beginning of the eleventh century, serving as mercenary warriors and adopting Roman rites. In 1009–11 they rebelled for the first time against their Byzantine and Lombard overlords. The second and better documented uprising was conducted in 1017 and was preceded by an 'unprecedented' cold spell that was described by William of Apulia: 'At this time the Italians were astounded by the fall of an extraordinary and up to then

[28] Ibid., p. 662.

[29] Scylitzes Continuatus, in Cedrenus, *Compendium historiarum, I. Scylitzae ope*, vol. II, p. 668. See also Marius Canard, 'La Campagne arménienne du sultan salğuqide Alp Arslān et la prise d'Ani en 1064', *Revue des Études Arménienne* 2 (1965), 239–59.

unprecedented quantity of snow, which killed the bulk of the wild animals and cut down trees, never to grow again'.[30]

The earlier uprising occurred during the cold spell and drought that hit other parts of the eastern Mediterranean, but we do not have direct evidence for a freeze hitting southern Italy at the same time. The rebellion of 1017, however, was suppressed by Basil Boioannes, one of the ablest Byzantine generals of the time, who was successfully entrusted by the Emperor Basil II to reimpose law and order and to re-establish Byzantine rule in the region. The reconquest of southern Italy led the region into more than two decades of prosperity and success. The Byzantines founded new cities and castles and initiated the plantation of mulberry trees that transformed the region into one of the most important centres for the production of silk and other luxury goods in the Mediterranean.

The Normans began acquiring landed property around Naples in 1030 and became more audacious and violent after the arrival from Normandy of more refugees between 1027 and 1035. Their attacks became increasingly persistent from the mid 1040s onwards, compelling the Byzantine governor of the region, Marianos Argyros

[30] Guillaume de Pouille, *La Geste de Robert Guiscard*, ed. Marguerite Mathieu (Palermo: Istituto Siciliano di Studi Bizantini e Neoellenici, 1961), c. 1, pp. 100–2, 4–51. Cedrenus, discussing the revolt of 1009, does not mention the Normans at all: Cedrenus, *Compendium historiarum*, vol. II, pp. 456–7. For a description of the events, see Gay Jules, *L'Italie meridionale et l'empire byzantin depuis l'avènement de Basil Ie jusqu'à la prise de Bari par les Normands (867–1071)* (Paris: Fontemoing, 1904), pp. 366–75; Ferdinand Chalandon, *Histoire de la domination normande en Italie et en Sicile*, 2 vols. (Paris: Librairie Picard, 1907), vol. I, pp. 48–54; Charles H. Haskins, *The Normans in European history* (Boston and New York: Houghton Mifflin, 1915), pp. 197–8; Einar Joranson, 'The inception of the career of the Normans in Italy – legend and history', *Speculum* 23.3 (July 1948), 353–96; Grahm A. Loud, 'Southern Italy in the eleventh century', *The new Cambridge medieval history*, vol. IV, *c. 1024–c. 1198*, ed.. David Luscombe and Jonathan Riley-Smith (Cambridge University Press, 2004), part 2, pp. 94–119; David Luscombe and Jonathan Riley-Smith, 'Byzantine Italy and the Normans', in *Conquerors and churchmen in Norman Italy*, Variorum Collected Studies 658 (Aldershot: Ashgate, 1999), essay 3, pp. 215–33; Gordon S. Brown, *The Norman conquest of southern Italy and Sicily* (Jefferson, NC: McFarland, 2003).

(who was the son of the leader of the rebellion of 1017) to turn in 1053 to Pope Leo IX in a desperate appeal for help. Argyros begged the Pope to prevent the Normans from pursuing their forays in the region and 'to force that wicked people, who are pressing Apulia under their yoke, to leave'.[31]

It is evident that in 1053 the empire collapsed under the weight of an enormous financial and economic crisis and was not able to provide the important province of southern Italy with adequate help. Pope Leo IX set out against the Normans with an army of Italians and Swabian mercenaries, but was defeated at the Battle of Civitate on 15 June 1053 and was held hostage for ten months (June 1053 to March 1054) at Benevento until he acknowledged the Normans' conquests in Calabria and Apulia. He died soon afterwards, on 19 April 1054.[32]

The sudden collapse of the Byzantines in southern Italy is not easy to explain. Vera von Falkenhausen has pointed to the enigma:

> Apparently, something went wrong, for less than fifty years after Basil's death, the Byzantines were driven out of Italy, and the Normans accomplished the Christian conquest of Sicily. Why were the Byzantines so rapidly swept away from Southern Italy after their impressive performances during the last decade of Basil II's regin? What undermined Basil's achievements?[33]

The traditional explanations relate the collapse of the Byzantines in southern Italy to the swift ascendance of the Normans, but this is certainly only a partial explanation. The number of Normans in

[31] Guillaume de Pouille, *Geste*, c. 2, 70–5, pp. 136–7.
[32] Huguette Taviani-Carozzi, 'Léon IX et les Normands d'Italie du Sud', in *Léon IX et son temps*, ed. Georges Bischoff and Benoît-Michel Tock (Turnhout: Brepols, 2006), pp. 299–329.
[33] Vera von Falkenhausen, 'Between two empires: Byzantine Italy in the reign of Basil II', in *Byzantium in the year 1000*, ed. Paul Magdalino, Medieval Mediterranean 45 (Leiden: E. J. Brill, 2003), pp. 135–60.

southern Italy was limited, and with such a limited force they could not have conquered such an important region if the empire was at the zenith of its power (as it was during the rebellion of 1017). It seems, therefore, that the reasons for the collapse should not be sought only in the ascendance of the Normans but also in the deterioration of the imperial power in Constantinople itself and in its provinces. The Normans entered a power vacuum and were able to pursue the weakness of Byzantium until the crisis was over and the powers were stabilized (although without resuming the previous power) sometime in the late 1080s and early 1090s.

## THE GREAT SCHISM OF 1054

The events in southern Italy in 1053–4 might provide a different and probably also a better explanation for another major event – the great schism – that followed the collapse of Byzantine rule in southern Italy and involved the same Emperor Constantine IX Monomachus and the same pope (at least in the earlier phases of the crisis).

The great schism is usually interpreted as a political and theological event reflecting different attitudes between East and West. It was Edward Gibbon, however, who claimed, centuries ago, that this highly important event needed to be analyzed in wider political, cultural and psychological contexts. Gibbon, however, emphasized the psychological aspects of the schism and Greeks' feelings of cultural and religious superiority over the Latins. The Byzantines, he wrote, were not able to accept the supremacy of the West because 'they had first received Christianity; they had pronounced the decrees of the seven general councils, they alone possessed the language of Scripture and philosophy; nor should barbarians, immersed in the darkness of the West presume to argue on the high and mysterious questions of theological science'.[34] The common reading of the events that preceded the schism is of a political event that reflects the cultural divergence of the two churches and which got out of hand.[35]

The event was indeed political. During the summer of 1053, while Leo IX was concluding his Papal–Byzantine anti-Norman alliance, he already nourished plans for a more comprehensive alliance with the Byzantines in which the Pope would play the leading role. A letter (now lost) from the Patriarch of Constantinople (Cerullarius) suggested such a religious and political rapprochement. But the Patriarch considered himself equal to the Pope and offered no compromise on the Pope's expectation of subordination of Constantinople to Rome.[36] The Pope, on the other hand, did not hesitate to cite, in his correspondence with the Patriarch, an extensive section from the forged document known as the *Donation of Constantine*, assuring the Patriarch that the document (which he used for the first time in diplomatic history) was genuine and therefore that the Pope, the legitimate successor to Peter, was also the rightful head of the whole Church.[37] Despite

34 Edward Gibbon, *History of the decline and fall of the Roman Empire*, ed. John B. Bury (London: Methuen & Co., 1909), vol. VI, ch. 60, pp. 366–9; Deno J. Geanakoplos, 'Edward Gibbon and Byzantine ecclesiastical history', *Church History* 35.2 (1966), 170–85.

35 See Louis Bréhier, *Le Schisme oriental du XIe siècle* (Paris: Leroux, 1899); Richard Mayne, 'East and West in 1054', *Cambridge Historical Journal* 11.2 (1954), 133–48; Steven Runciman, *The eastern schism* (Oxford: Clarendon Press, 1955); Yves Congar, *After nine hundred years* (New York: Fordham University Press, 1959); Aidan Nichols, *Rome and the Eastern churches: a study in schism* (Edinburgh: T. & T. Clark, 1992). For a different view of the schism, claiming it was not a full-scale schism but 'an unsuccessful attempt to bridge old disagreements in order to achieve the urging political objective of a military alliance', that it 'affected persons, not institutions' and that it gained its importance only two hundred years later, see Evangelos Chrysos, '1054: schism?', *Cristianità d'Occidente et Cristianità d'Oriente (secoli VI–XI)* (Spoleto, 2004), [Centro Italiano di Studi Sull'Alto Medioevo 51], 547–71, 557, 566–7.

36 Cornellius C. J. Will, *Acta et scripta quae de controversiis ecclesiae Graecae et Latinae saeculo undecim composita extant* (Lipsiae, 1861), p. 91.

37 Ibid., pp. 85–9 and 89–92.

these fundamental disagreements, the correspondence paved the way for the arrival of an official delegation in Constantinople. The delegation was hosted by the Emperor, who was probably more aware than the Patriarch of the empire's need of strong allies, in the imperial palace during the winter of 1054. The Patriarch, who was not as eager as the Emperor, was to conclude the alliance with the Pope, avoided meeting his legates throughout their sojourn in Constantinople and encouraged his men to enter into theological debates with them. Finally, on Saturday 16 July 1054, still without a word from the Patriarch, the delegates deposited a bull, excommunicating Cerrularius, on the altar of Santa Sophia, and departed back, after exchanging farewells with the Emperor.[38] Two days later they consented to the requests of the Emperor and returned in the hope of finally meeting with the Patriarch and concluding the expected alliance with the empire. The meeting, however, was cancelled because the Emperor himself was denied his customary right to be present at a meeting.

Public opinion was shocked and angered by the excommunication and by the behaviour of the Emperor. Serious rioting broke out in the city, forcing the emperor to make a formal submission of a confused and humiliating edict in which he consigned to the Patriarch's punishment all those who had collaborated on the bull of excommunication, including the interpreters. Cerullarius pronounced anathema upon the legates and their followers, and this sentence was formally and publicly declared on 24 July, but by then the legates were on their way home.[39]

The events that led to the 'schism' clearly indicate that the Emperor was eager to find new allies in the West and was ready

[38] Latin text in ibid., pp. 151–4.

[39] See ibid., pp. 151–2; for the imperial edicts see ibid., pp. 155–68; Mayne, 'East and West', 135–8.

to ignore straightforward insults and humiliations. The Roman delegates believed they could separate the cause of the Patriarch and his clergy from that of the Emperor and the people and convert Byzantium into part of the Roman Church as a reward for the alliance. When they visited Cerullarius, they were annoyed by the Patriarch's refusal to greet them in the Oriental manner or to bow. It is clear that both the Emperor and the Pope underestimated the opposition of the Patriarch and the inhabitants of Constantinople to such an arrangement.[40]

The estrangement between the Church of Rome and that of Constantinople is often presented as a process of *longue durée* with its beginnings in the Photian Schism, continued by the issue of the *Filioque* (and its possible removal from the creed) and the question of the unleavened bread. But such explanations do not take into consideration the idiosyncratic characteristics of the events of the early 1050s – the incessant attacks of the nomads, the ascendance of the Normans and the economic disaster or the evident difference between the responsibility of the Emperor and that of the Patriarch. The possible connection between the economic and military distress of the mid eleventh century and the great schism was not properly studied.

Vasiliev wrote: 'It was this schism, which, by rendering fruitless all efforts at conciliation between the Empire of Constantinople and the West, paved the way for the fall of the Empire'.[41] I would dare reverse his wording and claim that it was the economic collapse of the empire that paved the way for an attempt at conciliation between Constantinople and the West, and it was the failure of this attempt that led to the schism.

[40] Will, *Acta et scripta*, p. 177. [41] Vasiliev, *History of the Byzantine Empire*, vol. I, p. 339.

## RENEWED ATTACKS BY NOMADS

Tughril Beg resumed his attacks on Byzantium and in 1054 he attacked Armenia, plundered Manzikert and reached Erzerum itself before mounting a retreat because of the harsh winter.[42]

The period that followed lasted for twenty-five years between 1056 and 1081, beginning with the weak Michael VI and the coup d'état of Isaac Comnenus, and was characterized by frequent changes on the throne and by the exertion of power by all the external enemies of the empire: the Normans continued their advance southwards towards Sicily and later eastwards towards the Balkans and Byzantium itself, the Pechenegs and the Uzes moved southwards plundering the Balkans and the outskirts of Constantinople, and the Seljuks intensified their forays in Anatolia in the East.[43]

The years 1058–9 were years of extreme cold. Says Matthew of Edessa:

> In this same year [1059] a severe famine took place throughout the whole land and many perished by a cruel and violent death because of this famine; for because of the abundance of snow, rain did not fall on the land, and thus there was no harvest and many productive areas became sterile. On the other hand at the beginning of the next year there was plenteousness and abundance of all types of foodstuffs, so much that one mod yielded one hundred mod.[44]

[42] ʿIzz al-Dīn Abū al-Ḥasan ʿAlī Ibn al-Athīr, *al-Kāmil fī al-taʾrīkh*, ed. Carl J. Tornberg, 13 vols. (Leiden: E. J. Brill, 1862–71; reprinted Beirut: Dār Ṣāder, Dār Beyrouth, 1965–7), vol. IX, p. 599.

[43] Nicephorus Bryennius, *Comentarii*, ed. Augustus Meinecke, Corpus Scriptorum Historiae Byzantinae (Bonn: Weber, 1836), pp. 31–2; Joannes Zonaras, *Epitomae historiarum*, ed. Moritz Pinder, Corpus Scriptorum Historiae Byzantinae, vols. 29–31 (Bonn: Weber, 1841–97), vol. III, pp. 640–1.

[44] Matthew of Edessa, *Armenia and the Crusades*, 2.11, p. 94.

Cedrenus corroborates this testimony by claiming that in 1059 the Uzes 'crawled out of the caves in which they were hidden' and joined the Hungarians in their attack against the empire. The nomads extended their incursions as far as Sofia, and Emperor Constantine X Ducas, who seized the throne after the abdication of Isaac Comnenus in 1059, had to send an army to fight them. At the same time the city of Sabastiya (Sivas) in Anatolia was pillaged by the Seljuks.[45]

The invasions of the Turkish tribes and the threat of the Oghuz continued to loom over the western provinces for twenty more years, bringing the empire to one of its lowest ebbs, despite the comparative abundance in the east.[46] Some of the incursions against the cities of Anatolia were mounted without the actual participation of Alp Arslān or the other leaders of his court. In the east, Alp Arslān himself besieged Ani in 1065 and continued his unremitting attacks on Edessa and Antioch. In 1067 he ruined Caesarea (Kayseri), the capital of Cappadocia, pillaging its main sanctuary – the Church of Basil the Great – where the relics of the saint were kept.[47]

During the same year, 1065, when Alp Arslān was besieging Ani, another 'race' of nomads called the 'Uzes' (a corruption of Oghuz), which was, according to Scylitzes Continuatus, 'more noble and numerous than the Pechenegs', crossed the Danube, defeating the Byzantine army and taking its generals as captives.[48] The Uzes were estimated by contemporaneous chroniclers to number 600,000 and

45 Vasiliev, *History*, p. 351.

46 See Cahen, Cl. *Pre-Ottoman Turkey: a general survey of the material and spiritual culture and history c. 1071–1330*, translated from the French by J. Jones-Williams (London: Sidgwick & Jackson, 1968); Charanis, 'Byzantine Empire', pp. 184–5.

47 Attaleiates, *Historia*, p. 94; Scylitzes Continuatus in Cedrenus, *Compendium historiarum, I. Scylitzae ope*, vol. II, p. 661.

48 Scylitzes Continuatus in Cedrenus, *Compendium historiarum, I. Scylitzae ope*, vol. II, p. 654.

were divided into three groups. One of these groups plundered northern Greece, spreading destruction and death that forced the local inhabitants to consider emigration.

Attaleiates writes that 'the entire population of Europe was considering the question of emigration'. And Scylitzes Continuatus adds: 'The Ouzes ... with their entire population and domestic belongings, after having crossed the Ister, triumphed at once over the defending soldiers ... and filled all the fields surrounding the Ister, for the people amounted, as those who saw them would confirm, up to 600,000 warlike and bellicose men.'[49] However, the cold and hunger that forced the Uzes to invade the south did not spare the invaders themselves. They were reduced in number and were forced to move northwards, where they were defeated by their fellow Pechenegs and by the Bulgars. The survivors were recruited into the Byzantine army and were settled in Macedonia.

When the Emperor Constantine X Ducas died, in 1067, a capable general and a former professional soldier, Romanus Diogenes, ascended to the throne and reigned until his defeat at the hands of the Seljuks in Manzikert in 1071. During his first two years on the throne Diogenes encountered the Seljuks in half a dozen battles, but soon it became clear that Cappadocia was inundated by various unrelated bands, who were arriving in Asia Minor from different directions, pillaging centres as big as Iconium (Konya), and who did not obey the orders of any central authority. The migration of the nomads was so vast that even Alp Arslān was in no position to prevent them from raiding and pillaging the empire. The Ghazi Danishmends, for example, who were the rivals of the Seljuks during the conquest of Anatolia, roamed north of the area in

[49] Ibid. An identical description is given by Attaleiates, *Historia*, p. 83.

which the Seljuks were moving, attacking and pillaging Christian villages.[50]

Meanwhile the Normans continued their advance into southern Italy. They completed its conquest with the capture of Bari in the spring of 1071, only a few months before the disastrous Byzantine defeat by the Seljuks in Manzikert in August 1071.[51] This defeat marks the end of the reign of Romanus Diogenes and was a deathblow to the Byzantine domination in the East. The Byzantine Empire without eastern Asia Minor, Armenia and Cappadocia, which were lost forever, was no longer the same empire.

The years between the defeat of 1071 and the accession of Alexius Comnenus, in 1081, were a period of internal strife and further penetration of enemies into the heart of the decaying empire.[52] Thus did Attaleiates describe the situation:

> Under this emperor [Michael VII] almost the whole world, on land and sea occupied by the impious barbarism, has been destroyed and has become empty of population, for all Christians have been slain by them and all houses and settlements with their churches have been devastated by them in the whole East, completely crushed and reduced to nothing.[53]

[50] For the Turkish penetration into Asia Minor in the eleventh century, see Speros Vryionis, *The decline of Medieval Hellenism in Asia Minor and the process of Islamization from the eleventh through the fifteenth century* (Berkeley: University of California Press, 1971), pp. 69–117. See also Paul Wittek's lecture, 'Turkish Asia Minor up to the Osmanlis', included in his *The rise of the Ottoman Empire* (London: Royal Asiatic Society, 1938).

[51] The situation in southern Italy is described in a letter written on the 11 November 1064, which was directed to the head of the yeshiva from the great merchant Nehorai b. Nissim, who writes 'on the business, generally that is, the state of the ships and the people arriving on them, and the news from Sicily and the burning of ships and the impoverishment of our people …' Moshe Gil, *Palestine during the first Muslim period*, 3 vols. (Tel Aviv University, 1983), vol. III, no. 500, lines 20ff. (Hebrew).

[52] For the years 1071–81 see Vryionis, *Decline of medieval Hellenism*, pp. 103–13.

[53] Attaleiates, *Historia*, p. 9, Attaleiates was certainly a partisan of Nikephoros III Botaneiates who dethroned his legitimate predecessor Michael VII Doukas and is therefore suspected of presenting the past in darkened colours, but his descriptions in this context are reliable.

The political collapse of the Byzantine Empire continued during the 1070s, when Emperor Michael VII Doukas, who succeeded (or more correctly, usurped) Romanus Diogenes on the throne, signed a marriage alliance with the Norman leader Robert Guiscard. Guiscard attacked the empire after the deposition of Michael in 1078 in order to defend the rights of his daughter, who was married to the son of the Byzantine emperor. On his way, he occupied Corfu and Durazzo (February 1082), after defeating the new Emperor Alexius Comnenus in the Battle of Dyrrhachium (October 1081). But his advance towards Constantinople was interrupted because another ally, Pope Gregory VII, was besieged in Castel Sant'Angelo by Henry IV (June 1083).

The advance of the Normans fits into the larger pattern of the expansion of Europe,[54] but interpreting their advance in the light of European expansion presents us with only half of the picture. The geographical history of Europe during the second half of the eleventh century, and especially during the 1050s and the 1060s, can be divided into two diametrically opposing halves. While the western half enjoyed prosperity and abundance that led to population increase and economic growth and expansion, the eastern half of the Mediterranean suffered from a sharp decline that led to the disintegration of bureaucracies, even those as big as the Byzantine Empire, and also to economic collapse and to decay. This dichotomous picture reflects dichotomous environmental settings: a warmer period in the west, characterized by mild weather and more plentiful yearly crops, leading to plenitude and wealth; and cold spells and periods of freeze, characterized

[54] Robert Bartlett, *The making of Europe: conquest, colonization and cultural change, 950–1350* (Princeton University Press, 1993), pp. 86–90.

by reduced crops, famine, pestilence and incessant attacks of dislocated nomads in the east.

It is difficult to say in which part the weather was more influential on the destiny of the West, but an analysis based on depiction of expansion alone is certainly partial.

CHAPTER SEVEN

# Egypt and its provinces, 1050s–1070s

Egypt and the countries that were its neighbours and who depended on its surplus were seemingly less affected than Mesopotamia by droughts of the late 1040s, but hunger prevailed there nevertheless. Two letters of merchants, written by Benayah b. Mūsā in 1046 and preserved in the Geniza, refer to hunger in the Rīf (the delta of the Nile):

> In the Rīf it is impossible to obtain a slice of bread, nor is it possible in Tinnīs, neither dear nor cheap, so people eat carobs . . . I am extremely weakened and the situation is tough; may God look at me . . . I did not buy anything, because there is famine in the Rīf.[1]

Ibn al-Athīr also records a drought and a plague that began in 440/16 June 1048 'in all countries: in Mecca, Iraq, Mosul, the Jazira (Mesopotamia), al-Shām (Syria, Palestine), Egypt'.[2]

Egypt, however rejoined the severe drought and shortage cycle during the 1050s when the Nile was deficient in 444/1052–3[3] and

[1] Moshe Gil, *A history of Palestine, 634–1099* (Cambridge University Press, 1992), p. 602a, lines 5–7, and 603a, lines 15–16; see also Moshe Gil, 'Institutions and events of the eleventh century mirrored in Geniza letters (part I)', *Bulletin of the School of Oriental and African Studies* 67.2 (2004), 161–2.

[2] ʿIzz al-Dīn Abū al-Ḥasan ʿAlī Ibn al-Athīr, *al-Kāmil fī al-taʾrīkh*, ed. Carl J. Tornberg, 13 vols. (Leiden: E. J. Brill, 1862–71; reprinted Beirut: Dār Ṣāder, Dār Beyrouth, 1965–7), vol. IX, p. 552.

[3] The reason for the famine was 'a failure of the Nile' to rise; see Aḥmad Ibn ʿAlī al-Maqrīzī, *Ighāthat al-umma bi-kashf al-ghumma* (Cairo, 1957), p. 17.

once again for two years in 446–7/1054–6.[4] Ibn Taghrībirdī says that the drought of 1056 was so severe that many people fled Egypt and the majority of the people of Fustat died of hunger or 'ate each other'.[5] Ibn al-Athīr refers to the regional nature of the Egyptian droughts when he says that the drought of 1055/6 was felt in Mecca when bread was sold dearly and later when it was not found at all. The people of Mecca and the pilgrims were about to die, but God sent them locusts, which they ate and were thus saved. He also mentions that the famine was the result of an insufficient rise of the Nile.[6]

The drought of 1054–6 is also mentioned in the letters of the Geniza. Moshe Gil provides a handful of examples. In December 1055 Joseph b. Faraḥ writes from Fustat that the 'city – by God – is in dreadful distress, wheat and bread are gone, things without which we cannot (stay alive)'.[7] Around the same time, Nissīm b. Ḥalfōn describes how difficult it is to find wheat in the Delta: 'I went from city to city, but was unable to do anything. . . . I was unsuccessful'. The hunger of 1056 is also described in the letters of the Geniza described by Gil. In one sent by Ismāʿīl b. Faraḥ on 29 October 1056 from Alexandria, he complains that 'there is famine in the city'. A

[4] Tāj al-Dīn Muḥammad Ibn ʿAlī Ibn Muyassar, *al-Muntaqā min Akhbār miṣr (Choix de passages de la Chronique d'Égypte d'Ibn Muyassar)*, ed. Ayman Fuʾād Sayyid, Textes Arabes et Études Islamiques 18 (Cairo: Institut Français d'Archéologie Orientale du Caire, 1981), p. 15; Aḥmad Ibn ʿAlī al-Maqrīzī, *Ittiʿāẓ al-ḥunafāʾ bi-akhbār al-aʾimma al-fāṭimiyyīn al-khulafāʾ*, ed. Jamāl al-Dīn al-Shayyāl and Muḥammad Ḥilmī Muḥammad Aḥmad, 3 vols. (Cairo: Lajnat Iḥyāʾ al-Turāth al-Islāmī, 1967–73), vol. II, pp. 218, 220, 224–5, 230, 240; al-Maqrīzī, *Ighātha*, pp. 17, 19–20, for translation, see Gaston Wiet, 'Le Traité des famines de Maqrīzī', *Journal of the Economic and Social History of the Orient* 5.1 (1962), 18–24. For the economic crisis under al-Mustanṣir, see Mark R. Cohen, *Jewish self-government in medieval Egypt: the origins of the office of the Head of the Jews* (Princeton University Press, 1980), pp. 54–60.

[5] Abū al-Maḥāsin Yūsuf Ibn Taghrībirdī, *al-Nujūm al-Zāhira fī Mulūk Miṣr wal-Qāhira*, 16 vols. (Cairo: Dār al-Kutub, 1929–72), vol. V, 59.

[6] Ibn al-Athīr, *Kāmil*, vol. IX, p. 614.

[7] Moshe Gil, *Palestine during the first Muslim period*, 3 vols. (Tel Aviv University Press, 1983), vol. III, p. 296 (no. 515b, lines 3–5).

week later, on 6 November 1056, the same Ismāʿīl, still in Alexandria, writes: 'there is nothing more in demand in this city than anything which can be eaten'. In another letter he says that 'whoever goes out of his house . . . dies and is eaten, and if he stays home he will die of hunger'. Peraḥyah b. Sahlān, writing from Alexandria at the same time, mentions how much he had lived in fear throughout the entire month because of 'the matter of the water'.[8]

The Fatimids tried to overcome the crises through rigorous administrative regulations; as a first measure they refrained from purchasing the annual stock for the state granaries, investing the customary 100,000 dīnārs in the acquisition of timber and iron, instead.[9] When the crisis was not over in 446/1054–5, the vizier, al-Yāzūrī, intervened and bought all the grain directly from the merchants, selling it to the hungry people at a fixed price.[10] He was unsuccessful, however, and hunger lingered on in 447/1055 when 'many died in the land of Egypt'. Ibn Taghrībirdī adds that the plague spread in 1056 'all over the world', killing 10,000 people every day.[11]

[8] Moshe Gil, 'Institutions and events of the eleventh century mirrored in Geniza letters (part I)', *Bulletin of the School of Oriental and African Studies* 67.2 (2004), 162–3. The last letter was written in October when the Nile was in its 'plenitude'.

[9] Al-Maqrīzī, *Ittiʿāẓ*, vol. II, p. 225; for the monopoly of grain supply, see al-Maqrīzī, *Ittiʿāẓ*,, vol. III, pp. 72, 86, 165–6, 341; Boaz Shoshan, 'Fatimid grain policy and the post of the *muḥ tasib*', *International Journal of Middle East Studies* 13 (1981), 181–9. This measure was implemented temporarily during periods of shortage. When the Egyptian governments resumed accumulating grain, they were reported to have stored as much as 1 million irdabbs (equivalent to 70,000 tons); see al-Maqrīzī, *Ittiʿāẓ*, vol. III, p. 72. Al-Maqrīzī, however, believes that it was a greedy mistake on the part of the vizier, which made him face the crisis of 446 with empty barns.

[10] Al-Maqrīzī, *Ittiʿāẓ*, vol. II, p. 226; al-Maqrīzī, *Ighātha*, pp. 20–2.

[11] Ibn Muyassar, *al-Muntaqā*, p. 13; for 1056, see Ibn Taghrībirdī, *Nujūm*, vol. V, p. 59; al-Maqrīzī, *Ittiʿāẓ*, vol. II, pp. 230, 240; al-Maqrīzī, *al-Mawāʿiẓ wal-iʿtibār*, ed. Muhammad al-ʿAdawī, 2 vols. (Cairo: al-Būlāq, 1853–4), vol. I, p. 335, for translation, see Wiet, 'Traité', 21; for the economic crisis under al-Mustanṣir, see Cohen, *Jewish self-government*, pp. 54–60.

The Fatimid government requested Byzantine Emperor Constantine IX to intervene and ship grain to Egypt. The emperor, who was in desperate need of acquiring allies, agreed, despite his own wretched economic situation, but died before fulfilling his promise. His wife Theodora (reigned January 1055–September 1056), however, revoked the promise, which was so difficult for her to fulfil.[12] Desperate, the Fatimid caliph reacted by ordering the expulsion of 3,000 local Christians from Jerusalem and the locking of the Church of the Holy Sepulchre and confiscation of all its treasures.[13]

The famine and hunger that hit Egypt from 1052 to 1056, accompanied by a drought in Palestine, were also recorded in Mesopotamia. Bar Hebraeus reports the following:

> In the year 448/1056 sickness and a great famine came upon Baghdad . . . and more than one-third of the population perished. And thus also was it in Syria and in Egypt, and especially in Persia. In the city of Bukhara eighteen thousand biers of the dead went out in one day. And . . . in three months there were a thousand thousand [*sic*] and six hundred and fifty thousand people [dying]. And in Samarkand, within two months, two hundred and thirty-six thousand people died. It was said that from the beginning of the world there never was such a plague as this.[14]

[12] According to Ibn Muyassar, *al-Muntaqā*, p. 13, the emperor promised to send 400,000 irdabbs (32,000 tons) of wheat to Egypt; see also al-Maqrīzī, *Itti'āẓ*, vol. II, pp. 227–9, 230–1; Wolfgang Felix, *Byzanz und die islamische Welt im frühen 11. Jarhundert: Geschichte der politischen Beziehungen von 1001 bis 1055*, Byzantina Vindobonensia 14 (Vienna: Verlag der Österreichischen Akademie der Wissenschaften, 1981), pp. 119–23. Instances of grain import were recorded in 422/1031–32, see al-Maqrīzī, *Itti'āẓ*, vol. II, p. 180; for a ship loaded with grain that arrived from Muslim Spain, see David Wasserstein, *The rise and fall of the party-kings: politics and society in Islamic Spain 1002–1086* (Princeton University Press, 1985), p. 136.

[13] See Gil, *History of Palestine*, p. 380; Abbas Hamdānī, 'Byzantine–Fatimid relations before the Battle of Manzikert', *Byzantine Studies* 3 (1974), 169–79; Felix, *Byzanz und die Islamische Welt*, pp. 80–1. The acts were explained as a reaction to the Byzantine decision to stop the invocation of the name of the Fatimid caliphs during Friday services in the mosque of Constantinople.

[14] Bar Hebraeus (Abū al-Faraj), *The chronography*, translated from the Syriac by Ernest A. Wallis Budge, 2 vols. (Oxford University Press, 1932), p. 209.

According to both Ibn al-Athīr and Ibn al-Qalānisī, the drought and plague were still present in both Iraq and in Egypt in 448/1057; in 449/1058 and even in the following year people were reduced to eating dogs, and the dead were not buried properly.[15] In Egypt, famine continued to take a heavy toll of human life and disrupted the collection of state revenues until the end of the 1050s.[16]

After the execution in 450/1058–9 of vizier al-Yāzūrī, Egypt was thrown into complete havoc: the government lost control of the impoverished provinces;[17] the flow of taxes was halted; and clashes began within the army.[18] In the years that followed the whole system collapsed, leaving the soldiers unpaid and totally unrestrained. The Turkish regiment seized the personal treasure of the Caliph, dividing it among themselves, together with the income of Syria and the provinces.[19]

## 'THE GREAT CALAMITY'

A famine of biblical dimensions and lingering for seven years (457–64/1065–72) led to the destruction of Fustat and the reduction of the country to sheer starvation. Ibn Taghrībirdī specifically notes that the drought persisted for seven years, 'as in the days of Joseph

---

[15] Ibn al-Athīr, *Kāmil*, vol. IX, pp. 631, 636; according to Ibn al-Athīr, a thousand people died every day; Ḥamza Abū Yaʿlā Ibn al-Qalānisī, *Dhayl taʾrīkh dimashq*, ed. Henry F. Amedroz (Beirut and Leiden: E. J. Brill, 1908), p. 8; Ibn al-Dawādārī, *Kanz al-durar wa-jāmiʿ al-ghurar*, ed. Ṣalāḥ al-Dīn al-Munajjid (Cairo, 1961), vol. VI, pp. 369–371, says that every day 10,000 people died as well as many poor people who could not be counted; the price of wheat reached eight dinars for an irdabb.

[16] Ibn Taghrībirdī, *Nujūm*, vol. V, p. 59; Ibn Dawādārī, *Kanz*, vol. VI, p. 371.

[17] Al-Maqrīzī, *Ittiʿāẓ*, vol. II, pp. 257; al-Maqrīzī, *Mawāʿiẓ*, vol. II, p. 335.

[18] Al-Maqrīzī, *Ittiʿāẓ*, vol. II, pp. 199–200, 265–7; Ibn Muyassar, *Muntaqā*, pp. 13–14.

[19] Al-Maqrīzī, *Ittiʿāẓ*, vol. II, p. 275; Ibn Muyassar, *Muntaqā*, p. 32; Ibn al-Athīr, *Kāmil*, vol. X, p. 83; Ibn Taghrībirdī, *Nujūm*, vol. V, p. 81; Ibn al-Qalānisī, *Dhayl*, p. 95. The vizier, however, told the mercenaries that there was no money because the entire income of the provinces was 'farmed out' in *iqtāʿ*.

*al-ṣiddīq* (the biblical Joseph)' and that the worst year was that of 462/1069–70, and that even when the Nile went up and down there was no one to plant the land because people perished and there were conflicts among the governors and their subjects'.[20] The crisis was described by contemporaneous chroniclers using very strong designations such as 'infamous calamity', 'calamity and dearth', 'ordeal' and 'anarchy', or simply 'the great calamity' (*al-shidda al-ʿuẓmā*).[21]

A letter from the Cairo Geniza describes the drought of 1065 in very realistic terms. Nehorai b. Nissīm wrote from Fustat to Yeshuʿa b. Ismāʿīl in Alexandria: 'the city is at a complete standstill. There is no buying or selling, and no one is spending a single dirham. *All the people's eyes are turned toward the Nile. May God in His mercy raise its water*'.[22] In another letter written by Avon b. Sedaqa to the same Nehorai b. Nissim in Fustat, the writer rejoices that God 'summoned' to him two sacks of wheat, that he describes as 'pure gold', for the very high price of three and a quarter dinars.[23]

20 Ibn Taghrībirdī, *al-Nujūm*, vol. V, pp. 3, 83, 84; see Ibn al-Jawzī, Abū al-Faraj ʿAbd al-Raḥmān ibn ʿAlī, *al-Muntaẓam fī ta'rīkh al-mulūk wal-umam*, 11 vols. in 6 vols. (Hyderabad: al-ʿUthmāniyya, 1357–9/1938–40), vol. VIII, pp. 257–8.

21 Ibn Muyassar, *Muntaqā*, p. 34; see also al-Maqrīzī, *Mawāʿiẓ*, vol. I, p. 337; al-Maqrīzī, *Ighātha*, pp. 23–4; Ibn al-Athīr, *Kāmil*, vol. X, p. 61.

22 Gil, *History of Palestine*, p. 241a, lines 22–4; emphasis the present author. The letter is not dated, and Gil dates it to the drought of the mid 1040s. Udovitch, however, dates it to the great disaster of the 1060s; see Abraham L. Udovitch, 'A tale of two cities: commercial relations between Cairo and Alexandria during the second half of the eleventh century', in *The medieval city*, ed. Harry A. Miskimin, David Herlihy and Abraham L. Udovitch (New Haven, CT: Yale University Press, 1977), pp. 143–62, especially p. 153.

23 Moshe Gil, *Palestine during the first Muslim period*, 3 vols. (Tel Aviv University Press, 1983), vol. III, p. 244 (no. 501, lines 19–20) (Hebrew), dated 28 August 1065. The situation in Palestine was better than that in Fustat; see ibid., vol. III, p. 469a, line 21; p. 478b, line 4 about Israel b. Nathan enquiring about the price of wheat in Fustat. For the price of wheat, see Eliyahu Ashtor, *Histoire des prix et des salaires dans l'Orient Medieval* (Paris: Ecole Pratique des Hautes Études, 1969), p. 50. A woman wrote from Fustat to her husband in Alexandria on 26 September 1070 that 'we are under terror and famine'; see Gil, *History of Palestine*, p. 619b, lines 8–9.

The situation became even worse and the monthly expenditure on mercenaries increased from 28,000 to 400,000 dinars. In 460–1/1067–9 the shortage led to clashes between Turkish soldiers who tried to dislodge the black (Sudanese?) regiments from their positions in Upper Egypt.[24] Disorder was widespread and the land was left uncultivated.[25] In 1068 the unpaid Turkish regiment took the palace treasures in lieu of salaries and sold them in the markets of Cairo. Enormous stockpiles of weapons, stables full of riding animals and thousands of books were sold at very low prices.[26] Later that year the vizier himself confiscated twenty-five camel-loads of books, estimated to have a value of 100,000 dinars, in lieu of his salary. We know in detail what the Fatimid treasury contained before and after it was sacked thanks to a fifth/eleventh-century treatise that records the information, and we can only follow – and even regret – the destruction of knowledge caused by the calamity.[27]

The situation continued to deteriorate in 462/1069–70 when all the remaining treasures were looted and sold in the markets or burnt and destroyed. Even the royal family was not spared: the women of the harem died of starvation and members of the royal family fled to Syria and Baghdad, bringing the treasures they looted with them.[28]

[24] Al-Maqrīzī, *Itti'āẓ*, vol. II, pp. 276 and 257; al-Maqrīzī, *Mawā'iẓ*, vol. II, p. 335; Ibn Muyassar, *Muntaqā*, pp. 332–3.

[25] Al-Maqrīzī, *Itti'āẓ*, vol. II, pp. 279; Ibn Taghrībirdī, *Nujūm*, vol. V, p. 3.

[26] Al-Maqrīzī, *Itti'āẓ*, vol. II, pp. 275–6, 280–95; Yaacov Lev, 'Army, regime, and society in Fatimid Egypt, 358–487/968–1094', *International Journal of Middle East Studies* 19 (1987), 363, n. 131; and on the crisis in general, see Yaacov Lev, *State and society in Fatimid Egypt*, Arab History and Civilization 1 (Leiden and New York: E. J. Brill, 1991), pp. 44–6.

[27] Al-Qāḍi al-Rashīd Ibn al-Zubayr, *Book of gifts and rarities: selections compiled in the fifteenth century from an eleventh-century manuscript on gifts and treasures*, translated by Ghāda al-Hijjāwī al-Qaddūmī (Cambridge, MA: Harvard University Press, 1996), pp. 229–41.

[28] Ibn al-Athīr, *Kāmil*, vol. X, pp. 61–2; Ibn al-Jawzī, *al-Muntaẓam*, vol. VIII, p. 257.

Caliph al-Mustanṣir succeeded in coming to a certain agreement with one of the leaders of the Turkish regiment, but the agreement did not hold for long. In 463/1070–1 the Turkish regiment set on fire the grain port in Fustat, and in 464/1071–2 violently took control of the entire city. The Caliph became dependent on the subsidies paid to him.[29] Yāqūt calls this period the 'destruction of Fustat'. The two quarters, the eastern and western sides of the city, he says, were ruined and deserted. People were reduced to cannibalism.[30] Fustat never recovered from this period of decay and part of it remains in ruin to this day.

The calamities that hit the Nile Valley in the second half of the eleventh century can be divided into two main periods. The first calamity period is that of the mid 1050s, which was probably the most widespread of all the calamities of the eleventh century, causing the maximum possible damage. It was felt in Bukhara and in Khurasan, it led to a civil war in Iraq, to the collapse of the Byzantine economy, and it was in the background of the collapse of Byzantine rule in southern Italy and probably in the deepening of the conflict between the Byzantine Empire and the Papacy too. The years between 1050 and 1058 were so disastrous because for the first time the climatic disasters hit three climatic regions at once: there were cold spells in an area spreading from Bukhara to the Balkans, there were extensive droughts in the Levant, and insufficient rising of the Nile in Egypt.

The second period, which began in Egypt in 1065, affected Egypt as well as the Levant and Asia Minor but was not felt in Iran and Khurasan. On the contrary, these years were recorded in the

[29] Al-Maqrīzī, *Itti῾āẓ*, vol. II, pp. 305–7; Ibn Muyassar, *Muntaqā*, p. 38; Ibn al-Athīr, *Kāmil*, vol. X, p. 86; Ibn Taghrībirdī, *Nujūm*, vol. V, pp. 22, 91.

[30] Shihāb al-Dīn Abū ῾Abd Allāh Yāqūt al-Ḥamawī al-Rūmī, *Mu῾jam al-Buldān*, ed. Ferdinand Wüstenfeld (Leipzig: F. A. Brockhaus, 1868), vol. III, p. 900.

northern regions as a period of abundance. It was during the first and more widely affective period that the collapse of another historically famous agricultural province is recorded.

## THE INVASION OF NORTH AFRICA BY THE BANŪ HILĀL AND BANŪ SULAYM

The mass departure of the Bedouin tribes of Banū Hilāl and Banū Sulaym from Egypt during the mid eleventh century has been discussed in many scholarly publications over the past two centuries, although all the writings were based on a handful of written and archaeological evidence, and it seems that the heated debates reflect ideology more than historical research.[31]

[31] Antoine E.-H. Carette, *Recherches sur l'origine et les migrations des principales tribus de l'Afrique septentrionale et particulièrement de l'Algérie, Exploration scientifique de l'Algérie . . . 1840, 1841, 1842* (Paris: Impr. Impériale, 1853); Ernest Mercier, *Histoire de l'établissement des Arabes dans l'Afrique Septentrionale, selon les documents fournis par les auteurs Arabes et notamment par l'Histoire des Berbères, d'Ibn Khaldoun, etc.* (Paris: Challamel, 1875); Georges Marçais, *Les Arabes en Berbérie du XIe au XIVe siècle* (Paris: E. Leroux, 1913); Emile F. Gautier, *Le Passé de l'Afrique du Nord: les siècles obscurs* (Paris: Payot, 1952); Jean Poncet, 'Le mythe de la "catastrophe' hilalienne"', *Annales: Histoire, Sciences Sociales* 22 (1967), 1099–120; Hady R. Idris, 'L'Invasion hilalienne et ses consequences', *Cahiers de Civilisation Médiévale* 11 (1968), 353–69; Hady R. Idris, 'De la réalité de la catastrophe hilalienne', *Annales: Histoire, Sciences Sociales* 23 (1968), 390–6; Claude Cahen, 'Quelques remarques sur les Hilaliens et le nomadisme', *Journal of the Economic and Social History of the Orient (JESHO)* 11 (1968), 130–3; Jacques Berque, 'Les Hilaliens repentis ou l'Algérie rurale au XV siècle d'après un manuscrit jurisprudentiel', *Annales ESC* 5 (1970), 1325–53; Jacques Berque, 'Du Nouveau sur les Banḥ Hilâl?', *Studia Islamica* 36 (1972), 99–113; Douglas L. Johnson, *Jabal al-Akhạr, Cyrenaica: an historical geography of settlement and livelihood* (University of Chicago Press, 1973); Michael Brett, 'Fatimid historiography: a case study – the quarrel with the Zirids, 1048–58', in *Medieval historical writing in the Christian and Islamic worlds*, ed. David O. Morgan (University of London Press, 1982), pp. 47–59; Jacques Thiry, *Le Sahara Libyen dans l'Afrique du Nord médiévale* (Leuven: Peeters, 1995), pp. 210–47; Michael Brett, 'The way of the Nomad', *Bulletin of the School of Oriental and African Studies* 58 (1995), 251–69; Radhi Daghfous, 'Aspects de la situation économique de l'Egypte au milieu du Vè/XIè siècle: contribution à l'étude des conditions de l'immigration des tribus Arabes (Hilāl et Sulaym) en Ifriqiya', *Cahiers de Tunisie* 97–8 (1997), 23–50; Jean-Louis Ballais, 'Conquests and land degradation in the eastern Maghreb', in *The archaeology of drylands: living at the margin*, ed. Graeme Barker and David Gilbertson (London: Routledge, 2000), pp. 125–36.

The invasion was traditionally linked to political motivations of the Fatimid government. Ibn al-Athīr writes:

> The Arabs entered Ifriqiyya because Muʿizz Ibn Badis, the . . . Sultan [of North Africa] had recognized the Abbasid Caliph of Baghdad instead of the Fatimid Caliph of Cairo in 440/1048–89 . . . Al-Yāzūrī [the vizier] incited the caliph . . . to send the Arabs Westwards and gave them presents . . . [that they will] conquer of the land of Ifriqiya.

Al-Muʿizz, relates Ibn al-Athīr, tried to buy peace by showering the nomads with presents, but 'they went back to raiding and destroying', defeating the armies of al-Muʿizz in the Battle of Haydaran in 446/1054–5. The nomads besieged Qayrawan, forcing al-Muʿizz to emigrate to the coast, and in Shaʿabān 449/November 1057 Qayrawan was sacked and destroyed, a disaster from which it never recovered.[32]

Michael Brett has convincingly shown that this explanation is no more than political propaganda composed after the fall of al-Yāzūrī to humiliate him, although the tradition was later copied and spread by Ibn Muyassar, Ibn al-Athīr, al-Nuwayrī and finally even Ibn Khaldūn.[33] Ibn Khaldūn's description of the events is the most detailed. He enumerates the Hilali tribes that went to North Africa,[34] claiming, *a posteriori*, that the Fatimid caliph allotted each of them their own town and province in the form of an anticipatory grant of a domain yet to be conquered. Ibn Khaldūn says that the nomads did not oppose the scheme to go to North Africa and that the following waves were ready to pay two dinars

[32] Ibn al-Athir, *Kāmil*, vol. IX, pp. 566–70, translated by Brett, 'Fatimid historiography' pp. 47–8.

[33] Brett, 'Fatimid historiography'.

[34] Ibn Khaldūn, *Histoire des Berbères et des dynasties musulmanes de l'Afrique septentrionale*, trans. Baron de Slane, 4 vols. (Paris: Geuthner, 1925–56), vol. I, pp. 32–3, 36–9; Thiry, *Sahara*, pp. 211–12.

each to cross the Nile westward.[35] He presents the nomads in the most negative manner, comparing them to a cloud of locusts devastating and destroying everything they encountered on their way.[36]

Many scholars accepted the pejorative descriptions of the medieval authorities, ascribing the invasion of North Africa and the destruction and devastation of the thriving agricultural provinces and flourishing capital city Qayrawan to petty Fatimid considerations and to the destructive nature of the nomads.[37] Other scholars reject these ideas (including Ibn Khaldūn's) as being anti-nomad and even 'Orientalist', claiming that the Banū Hilāl and Banū Sulaym were the symptom rather than a cause of the events.[38]

The Banū Hilāl, maintains Brett, had long been present in Ifriqiya, killing the ruler of Tripoli in 1037–8. He claims that the Banū Hilāl had migrated west of the Nile as early as the end of the tenth century, though it is clear that the massive migration occurred during the famine of the 1050s.[39]

Letters from the Cairo Geniza indicate that North Africa was hit by a drought in the summer of 1045, and that the country and its government were weakened long before the assumed arrival of the Banū Hilāl. Isaac b. David writes from Qayrawan to his Jerusalem business associate in 1045 that the prices of wheat in the 'West' (Maghrib) are rocketing, that the government is unable to stop this rise and the recession that followed it, and that even the army suffers from rising food prices.[40] Another letter sent from Qayrawan in

[35] Ibn Khaldūn, *Histoire*, vol. I, p. 33; Ibn ʿIdarī, *Histoire de l'Afrique et de l'Espagne intitulée Al-Bayano'l-Mogrib*, trans. Edmond Fagnan, 2 vols. (Alger: P. Fontana, 1901–4), vol. II, p. 441.

[36] Ibn Khaldūn, *Histoire* vol. I, pp. 33–4.

[37] Idriss, 'Invasion'; Idriss, 'De la réalité'.

[38] Especially Poncet, Daghfous, Johnson and Thiry.

[39] Michael Brett, 'The Zughba at Tripoli, 429H (1037–8 AD)', *Society for Libyan Studies, Sixth Annual Report* (1974/5), 41–7.

[40] Gil, *Palestine*, vol. III, p. 181 (no. 485); on p. 178 Gil assumes the letter's date to be *c.* 1045.

August 1052 indicates that the situation was already very serious when the Banū Hilāl were only supposed to have departed from Egypt.[41] Geomorphological studies conducted in Cyrenaica during the late 1990s have showed that the process of desertification began there before the 'destructive invasion' of the Bedouins.[42]

It is therefore clear that the Banū Hilāl began migrating westward before the assumed treaty with al-Yāzūrī, although it is also possible to assume that the Fatimids of Egypt were supportive of this move, trying to rid themselves of the nomads before the situation in Egypt got out of hand. North Africa is, therefore, another victim of the ecological disaster of the mid 1050s.

## NOMADIZATION IN PALESTINE AND NORTH AFRICA

Christian sources describe the destruction inflicted by North African nomads (the Lawata tribes) on the cultivated lands of Lower Egypt that they had overrun. Sāwīrūs Ibn al-Muqaffaʿ says that their very presence (40,000 horsemen with their families) imposed a heavy burden upon the population on which they preyed. Cultivation of the land was neglected together with the irrigation works and the payment of taxes to the government. One of the oldest functioning bureaucracies was on the verge of a total collapse.[43]

41 Cambridge University Library, Taylor-Schechter Geniza Collection, 13 J 26, fol. 9, Nahray 227.

42 Ballais, 'Conquests'.

43 Sāwīrūs Ibn al-Muqaffaʿ, *History of the patriarchs of the Egyptian Church: known as the history of the Holy Church*, vol. II, part 2, *Khael III – Shenouti II (AD 880–1066)*, translated and annotated by Aziz Suryal Atiya, Yassa ʿAbd al-Masīḥ and Oswald H. E. Burmester, Publications de la Société d'Archéologie Copte, 3–5, 11–5, Textes et Documents (Cairo: Société d'Archéologie Copte, 1948–59), vol. II, part 2, pp. 203–4; Kosei Morimoto, *The fiscal administration of Egypt in the early Islamic period* (Kyoto: Dohosha, 1981), pp. 252–3; Cohen, *Jewish self-government*, pp. 58, 61–3.

Sāwīrūs b. al-Muqaffaʿ describes cruel attacks on Christian communities in Upper Egypt, including the systematic destruction of Christian farmhouses and monasteries and the massacre of monks.[44] The extended period of hunger and the lack of security led to the final decline and desertion of the sages of the Jerusalem Academy, which was apparently the last remnant of the great academies of the east. The Academy moved on to Tyre sometime during 'the great calamity', when the Jewish community in Jerusalem was depleted. The desertion of the Jerusalem Academy, like the desertion of the Babylonian academies several years earlier, is another aspect of the collapse of institutions transmitting classical traditions in the eastern Mediterranean during the mid eleventh century.

[44] Sāwīrūs, *History* (Cairo), vol. II, part 3, pp. 314–15.

# PART THREE

# *Cities and minorities*

CHAPTER EIGHT

# Jerusalem and the decline of Classical cities

In the previous chapters I briefly narrated the fate of some important centres in the eastern Mediterranean that were founded (Baghdad, Qayrawan, Fustat) or flourished (Constantinople) during the period that corresponds in western Europe to the 'Early' or the 'High' Middle Ages, a period that is usually associated with urban decline and stagnation. These eastern Mediterranean metropolitan centres, however, underwent a very sharp decline during the mid eleventh century, most notably during the 1050s, a period that corresponds to the recovery of cities in the West. Many of the cities that declined during the eleventh century did not regain their previous grandeur and for centuries remained pale shadows of their own glorious past. The giant scale of the eastern centres in the period that preceded the decline is misleading. The population of Constantinople in the pre-crisis period was estimated as being close to one million. Although this figure was probably reduced considerably during the eleventh century, nevertheless as a figure of two hundred thousand inhabitants is still three or four times higher than the population of any western European city of the time.

The numbers chroniclers provide of citizens who died during the famines and pestilences, or of other people who deserted their hunger-stricken abodes, are probably exaggerated, but the destruction of Qayrawan and Fustat or the decline or desertion of suburbs in Baghdad and Constantinople in the eleventh century is independently attested by archaeological excavation and by written testimonies. The severity of the decline of the important urban centres of the eastern Mediterranean was indeed unprecedented.

The urban decline, however, was not limited to the big agglomerations: provincial centres also underwent a similar and at times even more discernible collapse. Extensive excavations conducted at medieval sites in Israel and Jordan during the last two decades provide us with data which was not available previously and show quite clearly that many of the regional centres of these regions, those which had already been established during the Classical periods and those which were founded by the Muslims, declined and were sometimes even deserted during the eleventh century. A detailed and comparative reading of the archaeological as well as the historical evidence indicates that the decline was limited mainly to two short periods when the crisis was most acute: the first during the late 1020s; the second divided into two – during the 1050s and again in the late 1060s.

New archaeological evidence is so abundant and testifies so clearly to an urban decline during the eleventh century that a reassessment of the previous model that pointed at a different mechanism and different dating of urban decline in this region is required.

## THE DECLINE OF CLASSICAL URBANISM IN THE EASTERN MEDITERRANEAN: THE PIRENNE THESIS

Until the beginning of the 1980s it was customary to assume that the Muslim conquest of the eastern and southern Mediterranean led to the end of a millennium-long development and expansion of cities that had already been established in those regions during the Hellenistic and Roman periods. It was widely assumed that the continuous evolution and growth of these cities was interrupted abruptly by the Muslim conquest in the seventh century, that the structure of those cities underwent a fundamental transformation during the period that followed this conquest, and that the new entities that replaced the previous Classical cities followed an altogether different urban pattern and were therefore entitled 'Islamic Cities'. A model was established to differentiate between the archetypical pattern of this newly created 'Islamic City' and its contemporaneous 'Medieval City' in the West. It emphasized the introduction of central mosques, central markets, public baths, ethnic segregation and the specialization of trades in the 'Islamic City', and the absence of these from the 'Western Medieval City'.[1]

The archetypical development of the 'Western Medieval City' was defined by the Belgian scholar Henri Pirenne (1862–1935) in the late nineteenth century. In three masterly articles published in the *Revue Historique* in 1893 and 1895, Pirenne provided for a new

[1] Gustav E. Von Grunebaum, 'The structure of the Muslim town', in *Islam: essays in the nature and growth of a cultural tradition*, American Anthropological Association Memoirs 81 (Ann Arbor, MI: American Anthropological Associaton, 1955), pp. 141–58. See also Ira Lapidus (ed.), *Middle Eastern cities* (Berkeley: University of California Press, 1969); Ira Lapidus, 'Evolution of early Muslim urban society', *Comparative Studies in Society and History* 15 (1973), 21–50. For an overview and criticism, see Janet L. Abu Lughod, 'The Islamic city – historic myth, Islamic essence, and contemporary relevance', *International Journal of Middle Eastern Studies* 19 (1987), 155–76; André Raymond, 'Islamic city, Arab city: orientalist myths and recent view', *British Journal of Middle Eastern Studies* 21.1 (1994), 3–18. For the model itself, see William Marçais, 'L'Islamisme et la vie urbaine', in *Comptes rendus de l'Académie des Inscriptions et Belles Lettres* (Paris: Boccard, 1928), pp. 86–100; George Marçais, 'L'Urbanisme Musulmane', in *Vème Congrès de la Fédération des Sociétés Savantes de l'Afrique du Nord, Tunis* (Algiers, 1940), pp. 31–48; William Marçais, 'La Conception des villes dans l'Islām', *Revue d'Alger* 2 (1945), 517–33. Roger Le Tourneau extended the model by adding the example of Fez; see Roger Le Tourneau, *Fès avant le protectorat: Étude économique et sociale d'une ville de l'occident musulman* (Casablanca: Mesnil, 1949); Roger Le Tourneau, *Les Villes Musulmanes de l'Afrique du nord* (Algiers: Maison des Livres, 1957). For the development of cities in North Africa and Syria, see Jean Sauvaget, *Alep, essai sur le développement d'une grande ville syrienne: des origines au milieu du XIXe siècle* (Paris: Geuthner, 1941); Jean Sauvaget, 'Le Plan antique de Damas', *Syria* 26 (1949), 314–58.

reading of European urban history and created a historical paradigm that is still relevant today. Medieval towns, he maintained, were distinct from those of previous periods and especially from the remains, physical and institutional, of the Roman *civitates*. 'The "new" (i.e. medieval) towns,' he argued, 'had nothing in common with their Roman or early medieval predecessors, except their names and locations.'[2]

Pirenne's new synthesis emanated from his own empiric work,[3] but it was dependent to a great extent on the pioneering works of a French school which was very active at the time and which emphasized the importance of the material contained in the rich archives of provincial cities for the reconstruction of urban history. Pirenne, who spent a post-doctoral year in Paris, became acquainted with their works[4] and attempted to provide an explanation for a repeating phenomenon that appeared in many of them; the almost complete absence of written archival documents or built monuments that can be dated to the period between the seventh and the mid

[2] Henri Pirenne, 'L'Origine des constitutions urbaines au Moyen Âge', *Revue Historique* 53 (1893), 52–83; Henri Pirenne, 'L'Origine des constitutions urbaines au Moyen Âge (Suite 1)', *Revue Historique* 57 (1895), 57–98 and 'L'Origine des constitutions urbaines au Moyen Âge (Suite 2)', *Revue Historique* 57 (1895), 293–327; see also Henri Pirenne, 'Villes, marchés et marchands au Moyen Âge', *Revue Historique* 67 (1898), 59–70.

[3] Henri Pirenne, *Histoire de la constitution de la ville de Dinant au Moyen-Âge*, Université de Gand, Recueil de Travaux Publisés par la Faculté de Philosophie et Lettres (Gand: Clemm, 1889).

[4] For a contemporary summary of the new ideas, see Achile Luchaire, *Les communes françaises à l'époque des Capétiens directs* (Paris: Hachette, 1890). See also Abel Lefranc, *Histoire de la ville de Noyon et de ses institutions, jusqu'à la fin du XIIIe siècle* (Paris: École Pratiques des Hautes Études, 1869); Arthur Giry, *Histoire de la ville de Saint-Omer et de ses institutions jusqu'au XIVe siècle* (Paris: École Pratiques des Hautes Études, 1877); Arthur Giry, *Les Établissements de Rouen: études sur l'histoire des institutions municipales de Rouen, Falaise, Pont-Audemer, Verneuil, La Rochelle, Saintes, Oleron, Bayonne, Tours, Niort, Cognac, Sain-Jean-d'Angély, Angoulême, Poitiers, etc.* (Paris: École Pratiques des Hautes Études, 1883); Arthur Giry and André Réville, *Emancipation of the medieval towns*, trans. and ed. F.G. Bates and P.E. Titsworth (New York: Henry Holt, 1907); Jules Flammermont, *Histoire des institutions municipales de Senlis* (Paris: F. Vieweg, 1881).

tenth centuries.[5] Pirenne suggested, therefore, a new interpretation of urban history that was based on precisely this cultural hiatus. He assumed that both the silence of the documents and the lack of physical evidence were the results of a general urban decay or even of a total disappearance of urban life in western Europe at the time. He therefore devoted most of his seminal urban articles to the rebutting of previous models that suggested an undisturbed economic/legal/institutional continuum between the Roman period and the Middle Ages. Finally he concluded that 'Nowhere in western Europe, except perhaps in Italy, did any Roman town survive [this period of decay] and provides the basis for the renewed urban life in the eleventh and twelfth centuries.'[6]

Pirenne suggested a tripartite model for the 'European towns': a Classical (or Roman) period that lasted until the sixth or seventh century AD; a period of decay between the seventh and ninth centuries AD when the ancient *civitates* lost their characteristics and the vestiges of the Classical cities ceased to exist; and a third period that began in the tenth century when a new type of 'medieval town' emerged and continued to develop until modern times. Pirenne's urban history became a standard which is still used to explain the development of cities in many parts of western Europe. In his later publications, however, he suggested a comprehensive interpretation, based on his tripartite revolutionary (rather than evolutionary) paradigm for the decline of the Classical (or Roman) world. This paradigm, which later became known as the Pirenne Thesis, was the first attempt to replace the standard

[5] In 1890 Achille Luchaire wrote: 'Il faut se résigner à constater un fait, contre lequel on ne peut faire rien, l'absence de documents relatifs à la constitution municipale des cités et des bourges pendant quatre cents ans, du VIIe siècle au XIe. Selon toute apparence, cet énorme hiatus ne sera jamais comblé.' Luchaire, *Communes françaises*, p. 11.

[6] Pirenne, 'Origine des constitutions urbaines (Suite 1)', 70.

interpretation that had prevailed since the Renaissance and which was rephrased by Edward Gibbon to explain the decline and fall of the Roman Empire. Pirenne maintained that the decline of the Classical world was the result of the Muslim conquest of the southern Mediterranean and not the result of the rise of the Catholic Church or the invasions of the Germanic tribes. Similarly, he asserted that the recovery of the tenth and eleventh centuries was the result of the renewed vitality of European commerce in the regions known today as central western Europe.

The Pirenne Thesis was later rejected by many scholars, especially by those who were more acquainted with the history of the Mediterranean and of the Islamic world,[7] but the theory explaining the alleged decline of the Classical cities of the eastern and southern Mediterranean during the seventh century and the rise of 'Islamic towns' in their stead is a tacit acceptance of the Pirenne Thesis or of the urban theory that preceded it.

## 'FROM POLIS TO MADINA' AND BEYOND

The assumption that the conquest of the eastern and southern Mediterranean by the Muslims led to an immediate and sharp decline of the urban culture that existed in these regions was also abandoned, at least partially, following the publication of the seminal article of Hugh Kennedy in 1985. Kennedy maintained that the decline of Classical urbanism in the region was a long-term process

[7] For a collection of articles criticizing the thesis, see Alfred F. Havighurst (ed.), *The Pirenne thesis: analysis, criticism and revision* (Boston, MA: D. C. Heath, 1969), and especially Robert S. Lopez, 'Mohammed and Charlemagne: a revision', *Speculum* 18 (1943), 14–38s. See also Eliyahu Ashtor, 'Quelques observations d'un Orientaliste sur la thèse de Pirenne', *Journal of the Economic and Social History of the Orient* 13 (1970), 166–94.

that had begun in the sixth century, well before the rise of Islam, and which lasted for half a millennium thereafter.

> [U]rban change in the Middle East took place over a number of centuries and . . . was a long drawn out process of evolution. Many of the features which are often associated with the coming of Islam, the decay of the monumental buildings and the changes in the classical street plan, are in evidence long before the Muslim conquest. We should perhaps think in terms of a half millennium of transition.[8]

Kennedy's evolutionary rather than revolutionary paradigm, which emphasized the lengthy process of decline that started in the sixth century and which continued during the entire Early Muslim period, has become standard over the last twenty-five years. However, his model has been recently reviewed by Gideon Avni, who maintains that the theory of a slow and continuous decline of Classical urbanism in the eastern Mediterranean is not supported by the results of recent archaeological excavations and should therefore be abandoned or at least extensively revised.[9]

During the same 'early Muslim period' of alleged decline, says Avni, there were cities that enjoyed unprecedented growth and prosperity; other cities underwent initial periods of decline and recovered and expanded thereafter; while a few other urban centres, especially in areas bordering on the desert, collapsed and ceased to exist as living entities forever. And many of the cities that continued

8 Hugh Kennedy, 'From Polis to Madina – urban change in Late Antique and early Islamic Syria', *Past and Present* 106 (1985), 3–27, especially 17.

9 See Gideon Avni, '"From Polis to Madina" revisited – urban change in Byzantine and early Islamic Palestine', *Journal of the Royal Asiatic Society*, 3rd series, 21 (2011), 301–29; see also Yoram Tsafrir and Gideon Foerster, 'Urbanism at Scythopolis – Beth Shean in the fourth to seventh centuries', *Dumbarton Oaks Papers* 51 (1997), 85–146: 'There is a certain stage in the process of change when we are obliged to use terms such as "decline" or "deterioration" of the city. We believe that this arrived when the streets were narrowed to lanes', 141.

to exist and to flourish at the time then declined abruptly during the late tenth or mid eleventh centuries.

Avni's paradigm relies heavily on the results of intensive archaeological excavations conducted in Israel during the last two decades, and is therefore more substantiated than that of his predecessors. He analyzes the fate of cities and provincial centres in Palestine, pointing to the cities that flourished until the tenth century and declined during the middle of the century that followed. Tiberias, for example, occupied an area that was twice as big in the early eleventh century than it was in the heyday of the Byzantine period, in the sixth century. The city collapsed abruptly and without any apparent reason during the second half of the eleventh century, however.

But the most obvious example, at least from the archaeological point of view, is Ramla, which was probably the biggest city in Palestine during the early eleventh century. It declined abruptly from the 1020s onwards until it was virtually decimated and by the time of the Crusader conquest it was no more than a tiny stronghold with a handful of inhabitants when it was abandoned, in June 1099.

Avni, however, supports his claim with archaeological evidence only, and does not suggest any explanation for the above collapses. Yet his claim is that the Islamization of the country was certainly not the reason for an urban collapse: the reasons for the collapse of the cities should be sought elsewhere. Much of his argumentation is based on the archaeological excavations conducted in Jerusalem, and while summarizing the results of those excavations he repeats his main conclusion:

The archaeological evidence does not support claims for constant decline in Jerusalem during the Early Islamic period. It rather points to a clear pattern of continuity between the Byzantine to the Early Islamic period, with a very slow and gradual process of change. The only urban area in which a dramatic change occurred was the Temple Mount – Ḥaram el-Sharīf – and its surroundings. Other parts of the city remained practically unchanged, with Christian institutions still dominating the urban landscape. It seems that Christian religious institutions still flourished for few centuries following the Islamic conquest.[10]

The archaeological evidence, it is true, shows quite clearly that most of the decline of Christian Jerusalem occurred during the later tenth or the eleventh centuries. The archaeologists do not possess enough data to precisely date the collapse, but it is clear that Christian churches and monasteries of the fifth and sixth centuries continued to function within and without the walls of the old city, and that they did so under the Islamic regime of the eighth, ninth and tenth centuries. The extensive excavations to the north of Damascus Gate demonstrate that there was no interruption in the activity of Christian institutions during the early Muslim period, and that these institutions continued to flourish despite the evident Islamization in the other parts of the city, especially in the surroundings of the Temple Mount.

The physical decline of the tenth and eleventh centuries was not limited to neighbourhoods occupied solely by the Christian communities. Although the exact location of the neighbourhhoods occupied by the Jewish and Muslim communities of the city is still not a matter of consensus, Islamic monuments, including the Ummayad palaces of the Ḥaram al-Sharīf, were totally abandoned during the same period.[11] In short, it was the urban fabric of the city

[10] Avni, '"From Polis to Madina" Revisited'; Thaddée J. Milik, 'La Topographie de Jérusalem à la fin de l'époque byzantine', *Mélanges de l'Université Saint-Joseph de Beyrouth* 37 (1960/1), 125–89.

[11] Benjamin Mazar, 'The excavations in the Old City of Jerusalem', *Eretz Israel* 9 (W. F. Albright volume) (1969), 161–74 (in Hebrew), especially 170–4, noted that the hoard of coins dated to 1063 is the last sign of life in the palaces.

of Jerusalem and not that of a certain community that underwent a sharp decline during the mid eleventh century.

Jerusalem is probably one of the best documented cities in the eastern Mediterranean, and is certainly more documented than any other provincial city in the region. Many dozens of well-dated letters, which were sent from Jerusalem and kept in the Cairo Geniza, contain precious data about daily life in the city and about its economy. A comprehensive reading of these documents, together with the results of archaeological excavations, is therefore essential for the provision of a more accurate reconstruction of the collapse of this urban centre, and probably for the decay of Levantine urbanism in general.

In the following two chapters I will attempt to show that the details of the decline are recorded in the archaeological and historical evidence, and that an integrated reading of the abundant historical material together with analysis of the accumulative archaeological data is the key for reconstruction of the decline. From the economic point of view, however, Jerusalem was no different than any other city in the region, and the processes that affected it are the same processes that affected other provincial centres. Jerusalem will serve, therefore, as a case study of such urban processes in the cities of the Levant.

## JERUSALEM DURING THE ELEVENTH CENTURY

Many of the letters sent from Jerusalem during the eleventh century describe distress, pestilence and hunger, and many mention phenomena that usually accompany such periods of distress: the collapse of public authority, attacks of dislocated nomads, persecution of minorities, an excess of taxes, immigration, and even the desertion of cities. Instances of dearth and descriptions of its results are mentioned, however, almost exclusively in letters sent from Jerusalem in three specific periods: between 1007 and 1013, between 1023 and 1030, and between 1052 and the early 1070s. It is probably no coincidence that these years correspond to the periods in which famine and pestilence prevailed in Egypt and elsewhere. It is clear from these letters that every period of a regional extended shortage led to a rise in taxes, to violent activities by nomads, to persecutions of minorities, and to the desertion of the urban centres. Very few letters – if any – dealing with dearth, distress or their common results were sent during any of the other periods.

The fact that dearth is mentioned only in periods of dearth is probably not as obvious as it seems at first glance, and the letters reflect the cultural and spatial effects of seemingly short and supposedly ephemeral periods of hunger on the topography, demography and sociology of cities. Such effects, needless to say, are still very poorly studied and their enormous effects hint at a phenomenon that is anything but trivial.

## PERIODS OF DEARTH

The Christian community of Jerusalem had already suffered during the famine of the 960s from the declining ability of the central government to impose law and order and from the inter-religious tension that came in its wake. The tension led to open attacks on Christians that erupted in May 966, one of the most painful years of the hunger. The rioters sacked the Church of the Holy Sepulchre, set its dome on fire, killed the patriarch, tied his body to a pillar and burnt it. They also pillaged the Church of Holy Zion, which remained in ruins, at least partially, until the beginning of the twelfth century.[12]

The next outbreak of anti-minority tension occurred in Jerusalem and elsewhere in 1009, during the reign (and upon the order) of the Egyptian caliph al-Ḥākim and when there was a severe hunger, the last of five years of continuous hunger that prevailed in Egypt between 1004–9.[13] The destruction of the Church of the Resurrection marked the beginning of acts of oppression against the Christian population, which extended even to forced conversion to Islam. In Fustat, al-Ḥākim ordered the destruction of two other churches standing near the Church of St Mark, one belonging to the Copts and the other to the Nestorians.[14]

The drought in the Levantine coastal area probably lasted longer than the one prevailing in Egypt, and Palestine suffered from turbulences until 1014. Letters written by members of the Jewish community in Jerusalem complain about the deeds of the coalition, which included the Bedouins and the local Christian community,

[12] Yaḥyā Ibn Saʿīd al-Anṭākī, *Histoire de Yaḥyā Ibn Saʿid d'Antioche*, ed. and trans. Ignace Kratchkovsky and Alexander Vasiliev, *Patrologia Orientalis* 18.5 (Turnhout: Brepols, 1924), pp. 101–4. The Church of the Resurrection was also sacked in 325/937, with no connection to climatic dearth. See Moshe Gil, *A history of Palestine, 634–1099* (Cambridge University Press, 1992), p. 324.

[13] Yaḥyā Ibn Saʿīd al-Anṭākī dates the order to destroy the church to Tuesday 5 Ṣafar 400/ 28 September 1009; *Histoire de Yaḥyā Ibn Saʿid d'Antioch*, facsimile 2, *Patrologia Orientalis*, 23.3, pp. 283–4. Cedrenus provides the same date, although he erroneously ascribes the order to al-ʿAzīz; see Cedrenus Georgius, *Compendium historiarium, I. Scylitzae ope*, supplemented and emended by Immanuel Bekker, 2 vols. (Bonn, 1838–9), vol. II, p. 456. The date provided by William of Tyre is not accurate; neither are those given by Muslim sources. Gil, *History*, pp. 373–6.

[14] ʿIzz al-Dīn Abū al-Ḥasan ʿAlī Ibn al-Athīr, *Al-Kāmil fī al-taʾrīkh*, ed. Carl J. Tornberg, 13 vols. (Leiden: E. J. Brill, 1862–71; reprinted Beirut: Dār Ṣāder, Dār Beyrouth, 1965–7), vol. IX, pp. 208–9; Yaḥyā ibn Saʿīd al-Anṭākī, *Eutychii Patriarchae Alexadtrini Annales, II*, Corpus Scriptorum Christianorum Orientalium, 51 (Scriptores Arabici, 7), ed. Louis Cheikho et al. (Louvain: Secrétariat du Corpus SCO, 1960), p. 186; Ibn al-Jawzī, Abū al-Faraj ʿAbd al-Raḥmān ibn ʿĀlī, *al-Muntaẓam fī taʾrīkh al-mulūk wal-umam*, 11 vols. in 6 vols. (Hyderabad: al-ʿUthmāniyya , 1357–9/1938–40), vol. VII, pp. 239–40.

against the Jews and their Fatimid patrons. But the dearth and the nomads did not spare the Christian urban communities either. Yaḥyā Ibn Saʿīd al-Anṭākī asserts that many of the Christians living in Palestine emigrated to Byzantium, most settling in Antioch.[15]

The dearth of the mid 1020s is even better documented than the previous ones. The number of Bedouin attacks on cities and villages increased considerably, and places bordering on the desert, such as Aylah, al-Arish, and Farama were repeatedly pillaged.[16] The lingering hunger was associated with the extension of the Bedouin raids until they succeeded in occupying places as central as Ramla, killing many of its inhabitants, pillaging, violating women and leading to a partial desertion of the city by many of its inhabitants.[17]

The provincial Fatimid governor of Jerusalem, in constant need of funding for his struggle against the nomads, imposed new and considerable taxes on the Jewish population. The heads of the community warned the governor that the additional tax would lead to the desertion of the city by at least half the Jewish population, but the governor refused to listen. Later, when it became clear that many of the Jews were unable to pay the new tax, many of them were imprisoned or forced to sell or mortgage their houses and property,[18] and many others left or died in the plague that followed the dearth.[19]

[15] Yaḥyā Ibn Saʿīd, *Histoire* (*Patrologia Orientalis* edition), p. 297; see also above, Chapter 3.

[16] ʿIzz al-Mulk Muḥammad Musabbiḥī, *Al-Juzʾ al-arbaʿūn min akhbār miṣr*, edited by Ayman Fuʾād Sayyid and Thierry Bianquis, 2 vols. (Cairo: Institut Français d'Archéologie Orientale du Caire, 1978–84), vol. I, pp. 34–5, 52, 76.

[17] Ibid., vol. I, pp. 47–51, 57–8, 83–4, 89, 98.

[18] Moshe Gil, *Palestine during the first Muslim period*, 3 vols. ( Tel Aviv University Press, 1983), vol. II, pp. 83–4 (no. 49).

[19] See Jacob Mann, *The Jews in Egypt and in Palestine under the Fatimid caliphs*, 2 vols. (New York: Ktav, 1970; reprinted Oxford University Press, 1920–2), vol. I, p. 106; see also Chapter 3 and Gil, *Palestine*, vol. II, pp. 97–8 (no. 57).

## DELINEATING NEW WALLS

The dearth of the second half of the 1020s was followed by two decades of relative abundance beginning in the early 1030s and ended during the early 1050s. The urban population of Jerusalem, however, did not recover so easily from the lingering period of famine and pestilence, and several of the city's neighbourhoods were virtually deserted. The relative prosperity enabled the reconstruction of the city walls and repair of the Islamic shrines of the Ḥaram, but the new walls were delineated to match the diminished population of the city, which was too small to fill the space encircled by the ancient walls. The former fortifications were constructed during the fifth century, when the population was several times larger than during the mid eleventh century. Eleventh-century Jerusalem was unable to defend such a long delineation.

The exact outline of the walls is not known, and so far they have not been discovered archaeologically. The exact date of construction is still a matter of debate, but it is commonly agreed that new walls that were constructed in Jerusalem during the later tenth or eleventh centuries encircled a considerably reduced area, leaving Mount Zion and the lower hill known today as the 'City of David' outside their perimeter.

Some scholars have suggested that the southern sections of the city were abandoned by the end of the tenth century, but these assumptions are not supported by any written testimony.[20] The first

[20] Dan Bahat, 'The physical infrastructure', in *The history of Jerusalem – the early Muslim period (638–1099)*, ed. Joshua Prawer and Haggai Ben-Shammai (Jerusalem: Yad Ben Zvi, 1996), pp. 38–101, especially pp. 37–41. Vincent and Tsafrir believe that the southern walls were abandoned as early as the second half of the tenth century, ascribing their new alignment to the reign of the Fatimid caliph al-Muʿizz; see Louis-Hugues Vincent and Félix-Marie Abel, *Jérusalem nouvelle* (Paris: J. Gabalda, 1912–26), vol. II, p. 942; Yoram Tsafrir, 'Muqaddasi's gates of Jerusalem: a new identification based on Byzantine sources', *Israel Exploration Journal* 27 (1977), 152–61. Ben Dov delays the date of deserting the Byzantine southern wall to the second half of the

direct evidence for the rebuilding of the walls is supplied by Yaḥyā Ibn Sa'īd al-Antākī, who clearly claims that the reconstruction of the new wall began in early 1033, using stones taken from the churches of Mount Zion, which were sacked and probably also abandoned during the riots of 966.

> [The Fatimid caliph] Al-Ẓāhir (1021–1036) began in this year (424/1033) to build the wall of the noble city of Jerusalem ... [T]hose in charge of building [the wall] destroyed many churches in the vicinity of the town and took their stones for the wall; and they also intended to destroy the church of Zion and other churches in order to take their stones for the wall.

But the works were interrupted because of

> a terrible earthquake ... the likes of which had never been known, at the end of Thursday, 10 Safar 425/ 4 January 1034 [the correct date should be 5 December 1033]. The earthquake caused ... part of the chief mosque of Jerusalem and monasteries and churches in the region [to] collapse.[21]

Ibn al-Athīr supports Yaḥyā al-Antākī's assertion by claiming that the works in the Ḥaram (he speaks about the repair of the collapse of the Dome of the Rock that occurred in 407/1016–17)[22] had begun in 423/1032, a year before the earthquake.[23] The documents of the Geniza provide us with yet another description that clearly indicates that there was no connection between the earthquake and the rebuilding of Jerusalem. A letter written by the Gaon Solomon b. Judah attests that on the first day of Passover 1034 (7 April 1034), some four months after the earthquake itself, a stretch about nine

eleventh century; see Meir Ben Dov, *Historical atlas of Jerusalem* (New York: Continuum, 2002), pp. 187–92.

[21] Yaḥyā ibn Sa'īd al-Antākī, *Eutychii Patriarchae Alexadtrini*, ed. Cheikho et al., p. 272.

[22] For the earthquake of 20 Rabī' I 407/ 27 August 1016, see Ibn al-Jawzī, *Muntaẓam*, vol. VII, p. 283; Ibn al-Athīr, *Kāmil*, vol. IX, p. 295.

[23] Mujīr al-Din, *Histoire de Jérusalem et de Hébron*, ed. Heni Sauvaire (Paris: Leroux, 1876), pp. 68–9; Max van Berchem, *Matériaux pour un Corpus Inscriptionum Arabicarum*, part 2, *Syrie du Sud. Jérusalem "Ḥaram"*, 2 vols. (Cairo: Institut Français d'Archéologie Orientale, 1925–7), vol. I (1925), nos. 220–2, pp. 261–74.

and half meters long (15 cubits) and some twenty or more layers wide of the wall collapsed. Other letters sent by the same Gaon detail the clearing of the debris from the road and the beginning of the works themselves, including the means necessary for them. The collapse damaged the 'cave' – the synagogue – which was situated in one of the Herodian gates of the Temple Mount itself.[24] The chronological discrepancy clearly shows that the works were well under way when the earthquake hit the country, in December 1033.[25] Therefore, the works were not repairing sudden and urgent damage caused by the earthquake because they preceded it.[26]

Construction and reconstruction of city walls are major public works characterizing periods of prosperity. The works were initiated because there was a need to renew the 600-year-old walls that were far too extensive for the reduced population of Jerusalem. The earthquake, however, probably interrupted the works, forced the person in charge to reallocate some of the funds

[24] Gil, *Palestine*, vol. II, p. 140 (no. 79, lines 27–9); for the restoration works see ibid., vol. II, pp. 216–17 (no. 119), and ibid., vol. II, pp. 218–19 (no. 120).

[25] Ibn al-Jawzī, *Muntaẓam*, vol. VIII, p. 77. The quite extensive works on the Temple Mount led Oleg Grabar to propose that the Fatimids attempted to renew the holiness of Jerusalem. See Oleg Grabar, 'Al-Ḳuds: B. Monuments', *Encyclopedia of Islam*, 2nd edn, ed. Peri J. Bearman, Thierry Bianquis, Clifford E. Bosworth, Emeri van Donzel and Wolfhart P. Heinrichs (Leiden: E. J. Brill, 2010), vol. V, p. 342. Matthew of Edessa, *Armenia and the Crusades, tenth to twelfth centuries: the chronicle of Matthew of Edessa*, trans. Ara E. Dostourian (Lanham, MD: University Press of America, 1993), 1.60, p. 55 locates the centre of the damage in the north:

> one half of the city of Balash fell down. And the earth swallowed up many villages in Syria with their inhabitants . . . *and portions of the walls of the Temple of Jerusalem fell down*, and a minaret of the Arabs in Ascalon, and the top of a minaret in Gaza, and a half of the city of Acre. And the sea retreated three parasangs, and men went into it to collect fish and shell-fish; but the waters returned and drowned some of them. (Emphasis mine.)

[26] Joshua Prawer, 'The Jerusalem the Crusader captured: a contribution to the medieval topography of the city', in *Crusade and settlement: papers read at the first conference of the Society of the Study of the Crusades and the Latin East*, ed. Peter W. Edbury (Cardiff College Press, 1985), pp. 1–14, especially p. 2; Gil, *Palestine*, vol. II, p. 400.

and efforts to the more urgent task of repairing the damage that threatened the walls of the Ḥaram, and may even have caused a serious delay.

Rebuilding of the city walls was resumed during the mid 1040s and, according to the Latin chronicler William of Tyre – the most important source for these events – the decision was taken by the Egyptian government when the Fatimid kingdom was at the summit of its might, wealth and wisdom.

> The Caliph, desiring to enlarge the limits of his empire and expand his sovereignty far and wide . . . sent his armies and seized by force the whole of Syria . . . Appointing governors over all the cities, establishing taxes and making the whole region tributary to him. *Moreover he ordered each city to rebuild its walls and raise strong towers round about.*

The recent discovery of the Fatimid city wall of Caesarea Maritima sheds new light on this testimony, and, despite our inability to locate the Fatimid wall of Jerusalem archaeologically, we can assume that it was as strongly built as the one discovered in Caesarea Maritima. 'The citizens', William says,

> were compelled to finance this endeavor and . . . a fourth part of this work was assigned to the wretched Christians who were living at Jerusalem. But . . . the wealth of their entire community was scarcely sufficient to enable them to restore even one or two of these towers.

The Christian community of Jerusalem appealed to the Byzantine emperor, explaining to him the pretexts by 'which their enemies were seeking to destroy the pitiful people'. Emperor Constantine IX Monomachus agreed to finance the rebuilding of the walls of Jerusalem, but he conditioned that 'they could obtain a promise from the lord of the land that none but Christians should be permitted to dwell within the circuit of the wall which they proposed to erect by means of the imperial donation'.[27]

William of Tyre's description leaves a very short period of time in which both the Fatimid caliph al-Mustanṣir (who ascended the throne as a 6-year-old minor in 1036) and Monomachus (reigned 1042–55) were strong enough to initiate such an endeavour (al-Mustanṣir) or finance it (Monomachus). During the early 1050s both were faced with a financial, economic and military crisis and both were probably unable to pursue the project.

An earlier truce between an Egyptian caliph and a Byzantine emperor was concluded during the second half of the 1030s (between 1036 and 1038). In this earlier event it was the regent of the minor al-Mustanṣir who agreed that Michael IV (1034–41) would rebuild the Church of the Holy Sepulchre at his own expense; that the Byzantine emperor would appoint the Patriarch of Jerusalem. Moreover, the Christians were permitted to rebuild all the churches that were destroyed during their own rule. According to William of Tyre, the reconstruction of the Church of the Resurrection was completed in 1048. The itinerary of Naṣīr-i-Khusraw in 1047 indicates that this assertion is accurate and that most of the works were already concluded by then.[28] Naṣīr-i-Khusraw describes the church as being complete, including 'Byzantine brocades' and detailed paintings.[29]

[27] *Willelmi Tyrensis Archiepiscopi Chronicon*, ed. R. B. C. Huygens, Corpus Christianorum Continuatio Mediaevalis 63–63a (Turnhout: Brepols, 1986), 9.18, pp. 443–5.

[28] According to Yaḥyā ibn Sa'īd al-Antākī the truce was signed during the reign of al-Ẓāhir in 428/1036, Yaḥyā Ibn Sa'īd al-Antākī, *Eutychii Patriarchae Alexadtrini*, ed. Cheikho et al., p. 270; Ibn al-Athīr believes that it was signed during the reign of al-Mustanṣir in 429, Ibn al-Athīr, *Kāmil*, vol. IX, p. 460; Bar Hebraeus, however, dates it to 427/1035 while al-Ẓāhir was still Caliph, but says that it was signed by al-Mustanṣir. Bar Hebraeus (Abū al-Faraj), *The chronography*, translated from the Syriac by Ernest A. Wallis Budge, 2 vols. ( Oxford University Press, 1932), vol. I, p. 196; *Willelmi Tyrensis Archiepiscopi Chronicon*, 9.18 (pp. 443–5).

[29] Guy Le Strange, *Palestine under the Moslems* (London: Palestine Exploration Fund, 1890), pp. 204–6.

It is reasonable, therefore, to assume that the agreement to finance the reconstruction of the inner walls of the Christian quarter of Jerusalem was signed between Monomachus' ascendance to the throne (1042) and the completion of works on the Church of the Holy Sepulchre, more probably towards the end of the works there, between 1045 and 1048. Reconstruction of the wall was probably suspended again during the crisis of the 1050s and was not completed before 1063, which was another intermediate year between two periods of dearth.[30]

The decline of Jerusalem during the eleventh century was not uniform. The Christian quarter on the upper hill continued to exist as before and was even strengthened and fortified by the new wall, whereas the southern part of the city and the lower Tyropoeon Valley were abandoned during the late tenth century and certainly during the great crisis of the 1020s and that of the 1050s.

According to a Jewish chronicle which was written most probably during the eleventh century, the southern part of the city, where the Jewish quarter was built, was covererd with the ruins of many generations and it is the Jews who undertook to restore the area. The Jews established a market and built their houses in the same neighbourhood, using building materials they found among the ruins.[31]

Excavations held in the lower Tyropoeon Valley in the 1920s do not support the claim that during the eleventh century the southern part of the city was ruined for many generations. The excavations show that the residential quarters in the valley continued to be occupied without interruption until the late tenth century and were

[30] See also Moshe Gil, 'The Jewish quarters of Jerusalem during the Early Muslim Period', *Shalem* 2 (1976), 19–40 – Gil maintains that the Byzantine walls of Jerusalem still existed in 1063; Bahat, 'Physical infrastructure', p. 45.

[31] Gil, *Palestine*, vol. I, pp. 1–3 (no. 1, lines 1–18.)

abandoned thereafter. Similar results were obtained in very recent extensive excavations of the Western Wall Plaza and the Giv'ati parking lot. The excavations clearly demonstrate that this part of the city was deserted by its previous inhabitants during the late tenth century or the first part of the eleventh century, and that the Jewish community of seventy families (as attested by the document) was the only remaining community.[32] An additional letter written in 1057 maintains that the obligations of the Jews who settled in that part of the city still included catering for the cleanliness and repairs and to guard the wall in their area.[33] A hoard discovered in the ruins of the seventh- and eighth-century Ummayad palaces south of the Temple Mount/al-Ḥaram al-Sharīf reveals that the palaces were finally deserted during the reign of al-Mustanṣir, in 1063.[34]

## THE TYROPOEON VALLEY AND THE GATES OF THE TEMPLE MOUNT

The desertion of the Tyropoeon Valley during the eleventh century can possibly explain the smaller number of gates connecting the Ḥaram with the Tyropoeon Valley, below it, during the later tenth and the early eleventh centuries. The two Herodian gates that are

[32] John W. Crowfoot and Gerald M. Fitzgerald, 'Excavations in the Tyropoeon Valley, Jerusalem, 1927', *Annual of the Palestine Exploration Fund* 5 (1929), 58–60; Robert A. S. Macalister and John G. Duncan, 'Excavations on the Hill of Ophel, Jerusalem 1923–1925', *Annual of the Palestine Exploration Fund* 4 (1926), 137–45; Jodi Magness, 'Re-examination of the archaeological evidence for the Sassanian Persian destruction of the Tyropoeon Valley', *Bulletin of the American School of Oriental Research* 287 (1992), 67–74; Shlomit Weksler-Bdolah, Alexander Onn, Brigitte Ouahnouna and Shua Kisilevitz, 'Jerusalem, the Western Wall plaza excavations, 2005–2009 – a preliminary report', *Hadashot Arkheologiyot* 121 (2009); Doron Ben Ami and Yana Tchehanovetz, 'Jerusalem, Giv'ati parking lot', *Hadashot Arkheologiyot* 120 (2008); Doron Ben Ami and Yana Tchehanovetz, 'Jerusalem, Giv'ati parking lot, preliminary report', *Hadashot Arkheologiyot* 122 (April 2010).

[33] Gil, *Palestine*, vol. III, p. 17 (no. 420, lines 34–6).

[34] See note 11 above.

known today as Warren's Gate and Barclay's Gate, after the archaeologists who discovered them, were still in use during the visits of Ibn al-Faqīh in 903, of Ibn ʿAbd Rabbihi in 913, and of al-Muqaddasī in 985. The two gates, however, ceased to function and were probably blocked sometime between al-Muqaddasī's visit and that of Naṣīr-i-Khusraw in 1047.[35] Naṣīr-i-Khusraw mentions only one opening in the western wall in addition to the Bāb Dāwūd (the modern Gate of the Chain), which led to the top of the bridge connecting the Ḥaram with the upper city. Apparently the two Herodian gates leading directly from the Tyropoeon Valley into the Ḥaram were abandoned during the late 1020s. Several scholars put this down to the earthquake of 1033 that allegedly caused the destruction of the walls and the blocking of the gates. Overestimation of the results of the earthquake of 1033 has been dealt with above, and here too it is not in accordance with archaeology or the written documents. The massive Herodian gates are still fairly intact. The lintels of both Barclay's Gate (the southern of the two) and Warren's Gate are seemingly original, and there is no sign that they were affected very severely by any of the earthquakes that hit Jerusalem from the eleventh century onwards.[36] At least one of the gates, Warren's Gate, was probably used as the synagogue known as al-Maghāra (the Cave) during the period that preceded the arrival of the Crusaders. According to letters written by Gaon Solomon b. Judah, mentioned above, the synagogue was not affected directly by the earthquake, and it was several months after the seism, during the first day of Passover, that part of the wall collapsed and the debris blocked the passage. The collapse caused damage to the synagogue, but nobody was hurt. According

[35] See also Ibn al-Faqīh, trans. Le Strange, *Palestine* pp. 162–3.

[36] Meir Ben-Dov, *Jerusalem's fortifications: the city walls, the gates and the Temple Mount* (Tel Aviv: Zemorah, Bitan, 1983), p. 144 (Hebrew).

to the same writer, the wall was soon reconstructed by the Jews themselves, and the synagogue continued to function as before.[37] Gates are functional elements that remain in use until their *raison d'être* ceases to exist. The gradual desertion of the valley beneath the walls of the Ḥaram, which had already begun in the late tenth century and was completed during the late 1020s, is a process that stripped the gates of their purpose and could explain the blocking of the two gates that led to the Ḥaram and the transformation of one of them into a synagogue. In any event, the construction of the synagogue preceded the earthquake and it continued to exist after the repair of the wall.[38]

In order to better understand the effect of the gradual desertion of the Tyropoeon Valley, a three-dimensional representation of the city is needed. Based on a reconstruction of twelfth-century Jerusalem made by Dan Bahat, Figure 8.1 clearly shows that medieval Jerusalem was divided into two separate urban fabrics – a Christian city in the upper hill and the Temple Mount, which is visually conceived as an acropolis – forming a huge wall that towered over the valley beneath like a citadel. This visual differentiation might explain, at least partially, the separate histories of the Temple Mount and of the city itself during the twelfth and

[37] See note 24 above.

[38] Dan Bahat, 'Identification of the gates of the Temple Mount and the "Cave" in the early Muslim period', *Cathedra* 106 (2002), 61–86 (Hebrew); Michael H. Burgoyne, 'The gates of the Haram al-Sharif', in *Bayt Al Maqdis*, Oxford Studies in Islamic Art 9, ed. Julian Raby and Jeremy Johns (Oxford University Press, 1992), pp. 105–24, especially pp. 116–18; Shimon Gibson and David M. Jacobson, *Below the Temple Mount* (Oxford: Tempus Repartum, 1996), pp. 80–3. Warren's Gate was probably still known during the Crusader period as an indirect entry to the Temple Mount, see Theodericus in Robert B. C. Huygens (ed.), *Peregrinationes tres*, Corpus Christianorum Continuatio Mediaevalis 39 (Turnholt: Brepols, 1994), pp. 158–9, lines 503–10. See Charles Clermont Ganneau, *Archaeological researches in Palestine during the years 1873–1874*, 2 vols. (London: Palestine Exploration Fund, 1896–8), vol. I, pp. 165–6; see also Benzion Dinburg, '"A house of prayer and Learning" for Jews in the Temple Mount in the days of the Arabs', *Me'asef Zion* no. III (5689 [1929]), 55 (in Hebrew).

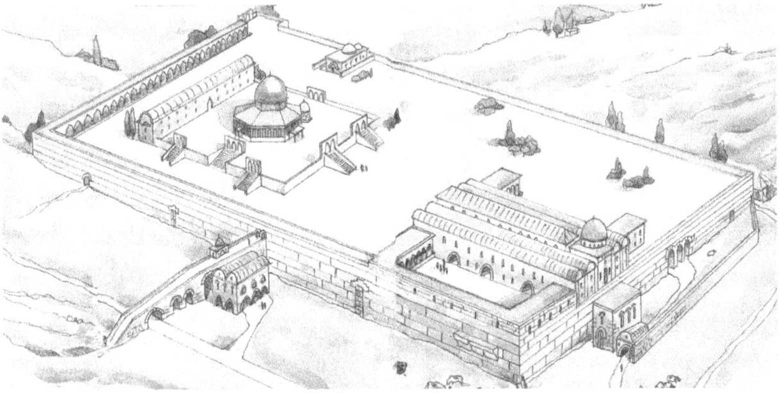

Fig. 8.1 The western wall of the Temple Mount, the deserted Tyropoeon Valley and the two blocked Herodian gates – Barclay's Gate (*right*) and Warren's Gate (*left*). The only gate that continued to serve uninterruptedly is the Chain Gate over the bridge.

thirteenth centuries. The Temple Mount resisted longer than the city itself during the Frankish siege of 1099, and the physical separation enabled the signing of a treaty between the Ayyubids of Egypt and Frederick II in 1229 in which Jerusalem was physically divided between the Muslims, who continued to govern the Temple Mount, and the Latins, who governed the Christian city on the upper hill.

Dan Bahat (see Fig. 8.1) in his doctoral thesis and Michael Burgoyne in his monumental treatise on Mamluk Jerusalem have maintained that the valley separating the Temple Mount and the upper hill on which the Christian quarter is located was at least partially deserted during the Frankish period and that the area 'immediately to the west of the Ḥaram wall in this vicinity remained largely undeveloped until the Ayyubid and Mamluk periods'.[39] The gradual decline of Jerusalem since the 960s and following several

[39] Dan Bahat, 'The topography and toponomy of Crusader Jerusalem', PhD thesis, Hebrew University of Jerusalem, 1991; Michael B. Burgoyne, *Mamluk Jerusalem: an architectural study* (London: British School of Archaeology in Jerusalem, 1991).

Fig. 8.2 The current height of the walls of the Temple Mount as they tower today in the southeastern corner of the Ḥaram al-Sheriff.

cycles of famine, hunger and emigration is probably the reason for the desertion of the lower Tyropoeon Valley.

## DROUGHTS AND HUNGER DURING THE SECOND HALF OF THE ELEVENTH CENTURY

Dearth, famine and an excess of taxes, as well as the inability of the government to impose law and order, reappear in letters sent from

Jerusalem between 1052 and 1058 after more than two decades during which dearth was virtually not mentioned. The difficulties in Jerusalem correspond to the period of hunger that prevailed throughout the eastern Mediterranean during these years. This was the second period (after the hunger of the second half of the 1020s), in which the crisis was felt everywhere in the region.

One of these letters, an early one sent in 1052, refers to Jerusalem as a place unsuitable for living. The agitations, it reports, and the armed gangs that rule the country prevent anybody from opening shops or building houses: 'The Land is dead and its inhabitants are poor dead, especially Jerusalem ... [which] is very cold for a very long period'.[40] Another letter depicts the poverty of Jerusalem's community in the winter of 1053 using dozens of negative adjectives. The writer, Joseph ha-Kohen b. Solomon Gaon, describes the distress of the people of Jerusalem at the time: 'eaten by swallowers ... devoured by the insolent ... the poor, the destitute ... squeezed and mortgaged ... that have also to suffer the noise of the Edomite masses [the Christians]'.[41] Another letter, depicting the hardships caused by the armed Muslim bands, is a response to a question asking whether it is worth settling in Jerusalem. The author, Abraham b. Isaac al-Andalusī, answers in the negative, warning his partner not to send shipments of clothes to be sold in Palestine because 'the country is full of armed troops and no one dares to open a shop or to wear new clothes'. He further explains the difficulties in carrying on with proper Jewish life and of earning a living in such a place: 'Cattle are not slaughtered, not on a

[40] Written by the Andalusian, Abraham b. Isaac; see Gil, *Palestine*, vol. III, pp. 258–9 (no. 504, especially lines 19ff.); Gil, *History of Palestine*, p. 401; Bernard Chapira, 'Document provenant de la gueniza du Caire', *Revue des Études Juives* 56 (1908), 234–7.

[41] Written by Joseph ha-Kohen b. Salomon Gaon; see Gil, *Palestine*, vol. II, pp. 761–2 (no. 411).

weekday nor on the Sabbath, fowl is not to be had, and it is cold in the city for a long period of time.' Other letters and documents written in 1054 testify to unpaid debts and to the inability of merchants to make a profit from their merchandise.[42]

Such documents can be interpreted as customary letters of request by a Jewish community, but the fact that similar letters were not sent before the renewal of dearth or after its abatement enhance their value as indications of the real dearth that prevailed in the city. A further collaboration for the poor state of Palestine and of the Levant during this period is provided by Sibṭ Ibn al-Jawzī, while describing the rise of the Seljuks in Baghdad:

> 'in June 1056 the sultan [Tughril Beg] ordered his troops to equip themselves and send for their tents, their children and households, to be . . . ready to depart for Syria. They [refused and] said, "This is a ruined land. There are no supplies or fodder there."'[43]

The direct persecution of the Christian community of Jerusalem culminated when an order was issued by the Fatimid caliph in 1056 to expel 3,000 local Christians from Jerusalem, to lock the Church of the Holy Sepulchre and to confiscate its treasures.[44] The reason for this aggression was probably the refusal (or, more accurately, the inability) of the Byzantine authorities to supply Egypt with grain. The Egyptians were probably not aware of the poverty of

[42] Gil, *Palestine*, vol. III, pp. 257–61 (no. 504); Gil, *History of Palestine*, p. 211.

[43] Sibṭ ibn al-Jawzī (Yūsuf ibn Qazughlī), *Mirʾat al-zamān fī taʾrīkh al-aʿyān: al-ḥiqba 345–447 H*, ed. Janān Jalīl Muḥammad al-Ḥamawundī (Baghdad: al-Dār al-Wataniyya, 1990), p. 5.

[44] See Gil, *History of Palestine*, p. 380, Abbas Hamdānī, 'Byzantine–Fatimid relations before the Battle of Manzikert', *Byzantine Studies* 3 (1974), 169–79; Wolfgang Felix, *Byzanz und die islamische Welt im frühen 11. Jarhundert: Geschichte der politischen Beziehungen von 1001 bis 1055*, Byzantina Vindobonensia 14 (Vienna: Verlag der Österreichischen Akademie der Wissenschaften, 1981), pp. 80–1. The acts were explained as a reaction to the Byzantine decision to stop the invocation of the name of the Fatimid caliphs during Friday services in the mosque of Constantinople.

Constantinople and the collapse of the currency. In any event, the pillage of the treasures of the church was probably profitable for the Egyptian government in the short run, but it was destructive for Jerusalem in the long run. The expulsion of 3,000 inhabitants came on top of previous desertions, famines and pestilences and the inability of the central government to govern, further weakening the city.[45]

The situation of the Jewish community at the time was no better. A letter written by Elijah ha-Kohen b. Solomon Gaon in the autumn of 1057 says that 'few remained in Jerusalem',[46] and later on in the same letter it states: 'life in big cities is hard, even more so in Jerusalem, where a curse prevails, its nourishments come from afar and livelihood is scarce; many who came to the city were impoverished and demeaned'.[47]

The fragile state of security is attested again and again. The author of a letter written in Tyre on 14 January 1058 and sent to Fustat mentions a lack of security caused by hunger and the payments due to the guards – an eighth dinar for a camel load – telling his addressee: 'You are not unfamiliar with the security situation in Damascus and the whole of Syria.'[48]

Despite their own miserable situation, the Jews who lived in Jerusalem were concerned about the famine in Egypt and about the 'condition' of the Nile, about which they enquired on several

[45] Maurice Canard, 'La Destruction de l'église de la Résurrection', *Byzantion* 35 (1965), 16–43; Ibn Muyassar, *al-Muntaqā min taʾrīkh miṣr*, ed. Henri Massé (Cairo: Institut Français d'Archéologie Orientale, 1919), p. 7; Aḥmad Ibn ʿAlī al-Maqrīzī, *al-Mawāʿiẓ wal-iʿtibār*, ed. Muhammad al-ʿAdawī, 2 vols. (Cairo: Būlāq, 1853–4), vol. II, p. 127 (sub anno 447/1055–6): 'al-Mustanṣir had sent his men to [the Church of Holy Sepulchre] in Jerusalem to confiscate whatever they have found there, a great quantity of Christian property'.

[46] Gil, *Palestine*, vol. II, pp. 15–16 (no. 420b). [47] Ibid., vol. II, p. 17 (no. 420c).

[48] Solomon D. Goitein, *Letters of medieval Jewish traders* (Princeton University Press, 1973), p. 92; Gil, *Palestine*, vol. III, p. 301 (no. 517, line 6).

occasions.[49] From 1059 onwards the condition of Jerusalem was considered to be slightly better than that of Fustat, and there were people who preferred staying in Jerusalem to returning to Fustat. A letter from Jerusalem to Fustat sent in 1059 explains a decision to remain in Jerusalem, 'because of the shortage prevailing in Egypt', and enquires about 'the price of wheat and bread [in Fustat], and about news from the Maghrib'.[50] In another section of a letter from the same correspondence (sent in 1060) the writer, Israel b. Nathan, enquires once again about the price of wheat in Fustat and says he is ready to enter the grain market and invest a certain sum in buying wheat and exporting it to Fustat.[51] Hunger was soon to hit Jerusalem again. In a letter written on 31 December 1061, Israel b. Nathan complains that 'in Jerusalem there is starvation. A qafiz of flour sells for 3 to 31/2 dinars due to the additional cost of sifting it . . . God save us and the poor creatures'.[52] Another letter written in 1060 demanded specifically: 'Please inform me about the situation of the water [of the Nile] and the prices and if you need anything'.[53] Three letters written in about 1060 by the head of the Jewish community in Jerusalem, ʿEli ha-Kohen b. Ezekiel, mention a special tax of 7 dinars, which was imposed on shops in Jerusalem. ʿEli attempted to reduce the tax, even by two dinars, but failed.[54]

The difference between the famine in Egypt and the famine in Palestine, and the fact that people preferred spending the difficult

[49] A letter of 'Eli ha-Kohen b. Ezekiel; see Gil, *Palestine*, vol. III, p. 56 (no. 442r, line 21); the Nile is also mentioned in another piece written by the same author, ibid., vol. III, p. 57 (no. 444r, line 8).

[50] Israel b. Nathan to Nahray b. Nissim, ibid., vol. III, pp. 137–8 (no. 469, 137, lines 21–2 and p. 138, lines 6–7), October 1159.

[51] Ibid., vol. III, p. 159v (no. 478, lines 1 and 4).

[52] Gil, *History of Palestine*, p. 278; Gil, *Palestine*, vol. III, p. 167v (no. 480, line 5).

[53] A letter of by 'Eli ha-Kohen b. Ezekiel, Gil, *Palestine*, vol. III, p. 79 (452r, line 8).

[54] Ibid., vol. III, pp. 65–7 (no. 447, lines, 6–15); ibid., vol. III, p. 71 (no. 449, line 19), the governor of Jerusalem is described as being in trouble.

years in Palestine rather than in Egypt, despite the droughts that prevailed in both of them, exemplify the difference between the two. A year in which the Nile does not rise is doomed to end in hunger and eventually in pestilence too. Hunger does not spare anybody, in the Delta or in Upper Egypt. A drought in Palestine, however, is never so absolute. It will certainly lead to a rise in prices and to hunger among the poor. A severe drought can cause the migration of dislocated pastoralists from the south to the north, but the precipitation in the north of the country will always be enough to cultivate grain.

The consequence of the hunger of the late 1060s was another blow to the weakened and decimated communities of the Holy City. The inability of the authorities to impose law and order on the nomads and the anarchy that became the lot of Palestine in such periods of shortage was apparent again in 1065. The attack launched by Bedouin tribes against a caravan of German pilgrims that made its way to Jerusalem through Nablus was mentioned in chapter 7. Only 2,000 of the 7,000 pilgrims in the convoy were saved.[55]

The dearth continued to loom over Jerusalem and food was scarce. In a letter sent from Jerusalem in August 1065, the Maghribi merchant Avon b. Ṣedaqa reported to his commercial partner Nahray b. Nissīm in Fustat that he had succeeded in finding a sack of excellent grain, which he describes as 'pure gold', but for an exaggerated price.[56] In a later letter sent from Jerusalem in October 1065, the same author asserts that the initial hunger was

[55] Claude Cahen, 'La Chronique abrégée d'Al-ʿAẓīmī', *Journal Asiatique* 230 (1938), 353–448, especially 368.

[56] Gil, *Palestine*, vol. III, p. 244 (no. 501, lines 19–20), 28 August 1065. For the regular price of wheat, see Eliyahu Ashtor, *Histoire des prix et des salaires dans l'Orient Medieval* (Paris: École Pratique des Hautes Études, 1969), p. 50.

followed by floods and heavy rains that probably destroyed the next year's harvest.[57]

The disastrous economic crisis that struck both Jerusalem and the Fatimid caliphate during the late 1060s and early 1070s might explain the construction of three new Latin Christian establishments: two hospices – one for men and one for women – and a church dedicated to St Mary (known later as the monastery of Latina) 'a stone's throw' away from the doors of the Holy Sepulchre. The construction of these establishments is mentioned only in Latin sources, the main source being the Chronicle of William of Tyre. William relates the construction of the establishments by merchants arriving from Amalfi, men who used to trade with the East and were concerned about the needs of the pilgrims visiting the Holy Places. Amatus of Montecassino adds that the hospital in Jerusalem was built by an Amalfitan family headed by a certain Maurus, who died in 1071. William maintains that the permission was granted by the Fatimid caliph al-Mustanṣir himself, and therefore before the city was conquered by the Seljuks in 1073. These two testimonies determine the date of the construction to the most severe years of the famine: between the later 1060s and the very early 1070s.[58] In any event, according to John the Archbishop of Amalfi (*c.* 1070–82), he was received in Jerusalem by his fellow citizens, who had earlier built the three establishments that were supported by alms sent from Amalfi.[59]

57 Gil, *Palestine*, vol. III, p. 502, margin 1–5; Gil, *History of Palestine*, p. 401.

58 *Willelmi Tyrensis Archiepiscopi Chronicon*, 18.4–5, pp. 814–17; Amatus de' Monte Cassino, *Storia de' Normanni*, ed. Vicenzo de Bartholomaeis, Fonti per la Storia d'Italia 76 (Rome: Tipografia del Senato in Roma, 1935), pp. 341–2; Jonathan S. C. Riley-Smith, *The Knights of St John in Jerusalem and Cyprus, c. 1050–1310* (London: Macmillan, 1967), p. 36.

59 Rudolf Hiestand, 'Die Anfänge der Johanniter', in *Die Geistlichen Ritterorden Europas*, ed. Joseph Fleckenstein and Manfred Hellman (Sigmaringen: Thorbecke, 1980), p. 34, n. 17; *Willelmi Tyrensis Archiepiscopi Chronicon*, 18.4–5, pp. 814–17.

Although the altar in the hospital was no more than a 'modest chapel' (*oratorium modicum*) and despite the fact that a Latin hospice, whose foundation is usually attributed to Charlemagne, already existed in Jerusalem in the 860s, permission to build new monastic institutions in Jerusalem deserves more attention. Students of the history of the Jerusalem hospital tend to follow William of Tyre and to emphasize the commercial and political importance of the Amalfitans to the welfare of the Fatimid caliphate, but Jerusalem was not a port-city and the institutions had nothing to do with commercial activities. Moreover the hunger-stricken Fatimids of the later 1060s and the beginning of the 1070s were not involved in serious activities of international commerce, and in any event they had never allowed – even during the heyday of their kingdom – the construction of religious institutions in Cairo, Alexandria, or in any other port-city of the eastern Mediterranean. An Amalfitan community did exist in Cairo in the tenth century, and 200 merchants were massacred in Cairo in the later tenth century, but no commercial or religious institution was built by those merchants in any of the major cities of the region.[60]

The atmosphere in the late 1060s was different: Cairo and Fustat were cut off from supplies, the low level of the Nile continued from 1065 to 1072, and the famine forced the citizens of Cairo to eat dogs, cats and horses; tales of cannibalism are also recorded.[61] There is no doubt that the caliph and his entourage were far more susceptible to being bribed during this period of political and economic decay. Furthermore, political reasoning should not be excluded. But the

[60] Claude Cahen, 'Un Texte peu connu relatif au commerce oriental d'Amalfi au Xe siècle', *Archivo Storico per le Province Napoletane* 34 (1953/4), 1–8; Claude Cahen, 'Le Commerce d'Amalfi avant, pendant et après la croisade', *Comptes-rendus de l'Académie des Inscriptions et Belles-lettres* (Paris, 1977), pp. 291–301.

[61] Stanley Lane-Poole, *A history of Egypt in the Middle Ages*, 2nd edn (London: Methuen, 1914), pp. 145–7.

fact that the permission is not mentioned in any of the Arabic documents at the time testifies towards the illicit option, and that is perhaps why the Benedictines of Saint Maure describe the origin of the Amalfitan establishment in Jerusalem as being acquired 'by means of donatives . . . "varias merces, easque insolitas et Turcis gratissimas" . . . the Amalphitans of Egypt obtained from Ramansor Mustesaph (al-Mustanṣir), Caliph of Egypt a permission to allow them to build a church, a monastery, a hospital and two hostels, one for male and one for female pilgrims'.[62] A possible excuse is provided by William of Tyre, who says that the people of Amalfi were the 'friends and carriers of useful articles' for the Fatimid kingdom and therefore an ample area was designated at their request, at 'that part of the city occupied by the Christians'; there 'they were to erect any building they desired'. The only restriction was, therefore, to construct their institutions in the quasi-autonomous Greek quarter of the city.[63]

The decline of Jerusalem between the 1020s and the 1070s was not the result of a single political event or of a spectacular and singular natural disaster such as an earthquake; it was, rather, the result of a long and continuous series of calamities that commenced with a regional and unprecedented dearth and famine, was followed by pestilence that cost the lives of many, and continued with many political disturbances (rebellions and invasions of nomads, for example), from the weakness of the central governments to impose law and order, and from the persecution of the minorities, who were probably the absolute majority at the beginning of the eleventh century. The rate of decline of the Jewish and Christian communities was not identical. The Jewish community was more dynamic

[62] Jean Mabillon, *Annales ordinis S. Benedicti occidentalium monachorum patriarchae* (Luca, 1739–45), cap. XIII, p. 402.

[63] *Willelmi Tyrensis Archiepiscopi Chronicon*, 18.5, pp. 815–17.

economically and intellectually, and tended to cooperate with the Fatimid rulers of Fustat (where a sister Jewish community flourished) and with the Muslim inhabitants of the city. The Jews were persecuted by the Christians whenever the latter had the opportunity to harass them, and due to their more intense international commercial activity the Jews were more vulnerable to the difficulties raised by economic crises. The Jewish leadership deserted the city when it became clear that life had become unbearable and that the Fatimid government was no longer able to impose law and order. The desertion of the Jewish Academy to Tyre, which followed the desertion of the academies of Baghdad thirty years earlier, was a death blow not only to the Jewish community in Jerusalem but to Jewish intellectual activity in the East. The next generations of Jewish wisdom would be nourished elsewhere.

When the Crusader warriors conquered Jerusalem at the end of the eleventh century, says Solomon D. Goitein, they destroyed an already destroyed city.[64]

[64] Shelomo Dov Goitein, *Palestinian Jewry in early Islamic and Crusader times in the light of the genizah documents* (Jerusalem: Yad Izhak Ben-Zvi, 1980), p. 229 (Hebrew).

CHAPTER NINE

# Water supply, declining cities and deserted villages

Research for this book did not begin with an attempt to write a 'grand theory'. On the contrary, I was attempting to solve very local issues that bothered me at the time: why did the aqueducts, leading fresh water to the city of Jerusalem, cease to function during the mid-eleventh century? Later it became clear that the aqueducts of Jerusalem were not the only water system that ceased to function at the time, and that the neglect of water systems was associated with a more general decay of urban centres and with a concurrent collapse of administrations, economies, and cultures. In this chapter I will examine the water supply of Jerusalem and propose a possible explanation for the neglect of fresh water aqueducts, associating it with the sharp decrease in the discharge of the springs that fed these aqueducts that followed the climatic crisis.

## AQUEDUCTS AND CITIES

Jerusalem, like many other Classical cities, had an aqueduct system supplying it with running water. The aqueduct was built in the first century BC (at the latest) when the Second Temple was still functioning, enabling the gathering of the multitudes in the Temple and the sacrifice of animals.[1]

[1] Amihai Mazar, 'A survey of the aqueducts to Jerusalem', in *The aqueducts of Israel*, ed. David Amit, Joseph Patrich and Yizhar Hirschfeld (Portsmouth, RI: Journal of Roman Archaeology, 2002), pp. 210–44. According to Josephus, the 'Lower Conduit' was built

The most important part of this system, the aqueduct, known as the 'Lower Aqueduct', was still functioning in the late tenth century. Al-Muqaddasī (*c.* 985) claims that the city contains plenty of water, stored in underground cisterns and open pools, and that spring-water is collected in two reservoirs, 'from [where] there is a channel that brings the water to the city'.[2] The situation, however, was altered considerably before the mid eleventh century. When Nāsir-i Khusraw visited Jerusalem in 1047, he states clearly that '[Jerusalem] is situated on top of a hill and has no source of water save rain. The villages on the other hand, have springs, but there are more inside the city.'[3]

When the Crusaders captured the city in 1099 it had no aqueduct of running water at all. No Frankish chronicler, no visitor to the city, not even one legal document issued in it during the next two centuries refers to an aqueduct supplying the city with running water. The ruins of the ancient Roman aqueducts are not mentioned. The situation became even worse because many of the springs, except the Siloam, dried out. '[Jerusalem]', writes the Russian Abbot Daniel in 1108, is a place 'absolutely destitute of water; one finds neither river, nor wells, *nor springs near Jerusalem*, with the exception of the Pool of Siloam. The inhabitants of the town, and cattle, have therefore nothing but rain-water for their use'.[4]

by Pontius Pilatus (AD 26–36); Josephus Flavius, *Antiquities of the Jews* 18.3.2–3. There are archaeological considerations that support the assumption that the aqueduct was built even earlier; see also Charles Clermont-Ganneau, 'Roman inscriptions on a Jerusalem aqueduct', *PEFQSt* 33 (1901), 118–22; Charles Wilson, 'Centurial inscriptions on the syphon of the high-level aqueduct at Jerusalem', *Palestine Exploration Fund Quarterly Statements* 37 (1905), 75–7.

[2] Muqqadasī, *Aḥsan al-taqāsīm fī maʿrifat al-aqālīm*, ed. Michael J. de Goeje (Leiden: E. J. Brill, 1906), p. 168.

[3] Nāṣir-i Khusraw, *Nāṣer-e Khosraw's book of travels* (Safarnāma), trans., introduction and annotation William M. Thackston, Jr (Albany, NY: Bibliotheca Persica, 1986), p. 21.

[4] *Vie et pèlerinage de Daniel*, in *Itinéraires russes en orient*, traduit pour la Société de l'Orient Latin par Mme B. de Khitrovo (Geneva, 1889), p. 18; *The pilgrimage of the Russian Abbot Daniel to the Holy Land, 1106–1107*, annotated by Charles W. Wilson, *Library of the Palestine Pilgrims Text Society 4* [no. 3] (London: Palestine Exploration Fund, 1895),

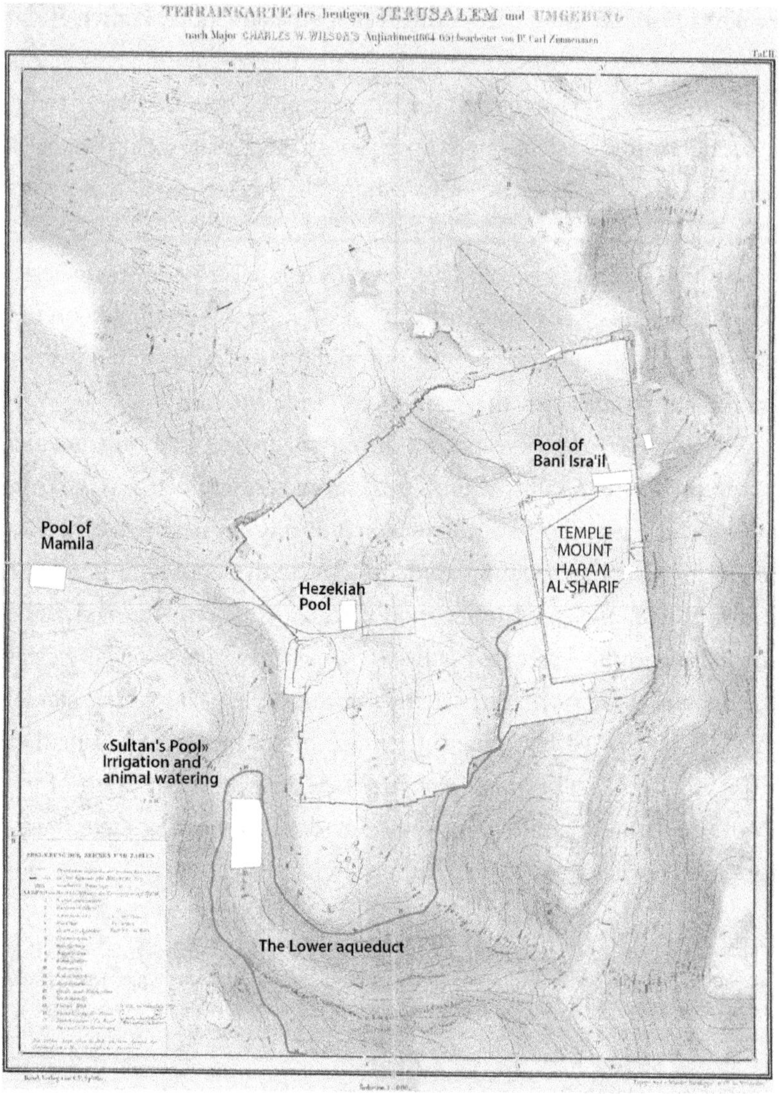


Fig. 9.1 Aqueducts and storage pools in Jerusalem: 1. the 'Lower Aqueduct' leading running water from the sources of the al-ʿArrūb some 20 km south of Jerusalem via local winter aqueducts; 2. local aqueduct leading water from the Mamīlā Pool; 3. local aqueduct collecting water from the northern part of the Tyropoeon Valley; 4. local aqueduct collecting water from the northeast.

William of Tyre, who unlike Daniel was born and educated in Jerusalem and who lived there for many years, is the most explicit source. In his chronicle, completed in the early 1180s, he writes: 'The city lies in arid surroundings, entirely lacking in water. There are no streams, no springs or rivers and the people depend upon rain-water only. They collect rain-water in the numerous cisterns that are spread throughout the city during the winter season and use it during the whole year.' The situation, he says, was never any better. He even blames Solinus for not telling the truth while maintaining that 'Judea is renowned for its waters'.[5] Otherwise, William writes, 'the face of the earth was changed considerably since Solinus' time'. In any event, both native-born William and the Russian pilgrim Daniel refer to the absence of springs in the vicinity of Jerusalem.[6]

In his description of the 1099 conquest of the Temple Mount, Albert of Aachen mentions a huge reservoir, which he calls the 'royal cistern'. Into this reservoir, which 'held water in its cavern the extent and great capacity of a lake', many of the Saracens were chased by the Franks. Some of them were even drowned in the water: 'Many Christians and Saracens fell headlong through the openings in the roof of the cistern and were drowned.' 'Throughout the siege,' he writes, 'the water of this royal cistern used to be measured out to needy citizens and soldiers to water horses, flocks and herds, and for every necessary use.' The cistern, however, was filled only by rain-water. 'Every time rain fell,' wrote Albert of

pp. 25–6, emphasis the present author. In the early 1170s Rabbi Benjamin of Tudela wrote: 'The people of Jerusalem . . . drink . . . rain-water, which they collect in cisterns in their houses'. *The itinerary of Benjamin of Tudela*, ed. and trans. Marcus N. Adler (London: H. Frowde, 1907), p. 23.

[5] *Willelmi Tyrensis Archiepiscopi Chronicon*, ed. Robert B. C. Huygens, Corpus Christianorum Continuatio Mediaevalis 63–63a (Turnhout: Bepols, 1986), 8.4, pp. 388–9, lines 24–34.

[6] Ibid., 8.4, p. 389. William even blames the former Muslim inhabitants of the city for blocking up the springs and reservoirs around the city 'as far as five or six miles away' in an attempt to compel the Franks to abandon the siege.

Aachen, 'this cistern was filled with water flowing from the roofs of the palace and from gutters and from the arched roof to the Lord's Temple and from the roofs of many buildings, serving all the inhabitants plentifully through all the seasons of the year with cold and healthy water'.[7] Similar description is provided by Nāṣir-i Khusraw more than fifty years earlier, who, while describing the roofs of the Aqsa Mosque, writes that 'no water is allowed to escape and go to waste, since it all drains into cisterns'.[8]

The ancient aqueduct that supplied the city with fresh drinking water since the Roman period no longer functioned, but the cisterns were full of fresh water and there was enough drinking water, even during the siege. Is it possible to assume that the ancient aqueduct was no longer necessary?

William of Tyre resolves the enigma by mentioning the short local aqueducts collecting winter rain-water from streets and gutters that existed before the siege of 1099 and led winter floods from dry streams outside the city wall into the pools located to the north of the Temple Mount and into the cisterns of the Temple Mount itself. These short-distance temporary aqueducts were kept tidy and repaired regularly. 'Conduits,' reports William (who is referring to them), 'brought in water . . . into two immense pools located just outside the temple precincts but within the city limits'.[9] Both pools were located north of the Temple Mount, part of the city that was not connected by gravity to any source of water and therefore had never been provided with running water or supplied by aqueducts. The amount of rain-water collected from the roofs through gutters

[7] *Historia Ierosolimitana*, 6.22; Albert of Aachen, *Historia Ierosolimitana – History of the journey to Jerusalem*, ed. and trans. Susan B. Edgington (Oxford: Clarendon Press, 2007), pp. 430–1.

[8] Nāṣir-i Khusraw, *Nāṣer-e Khosraw*, p. 27.

[9] *Willelmi Tyrensis Archiepiscopi Chronicon*, 8.4, p. 390.

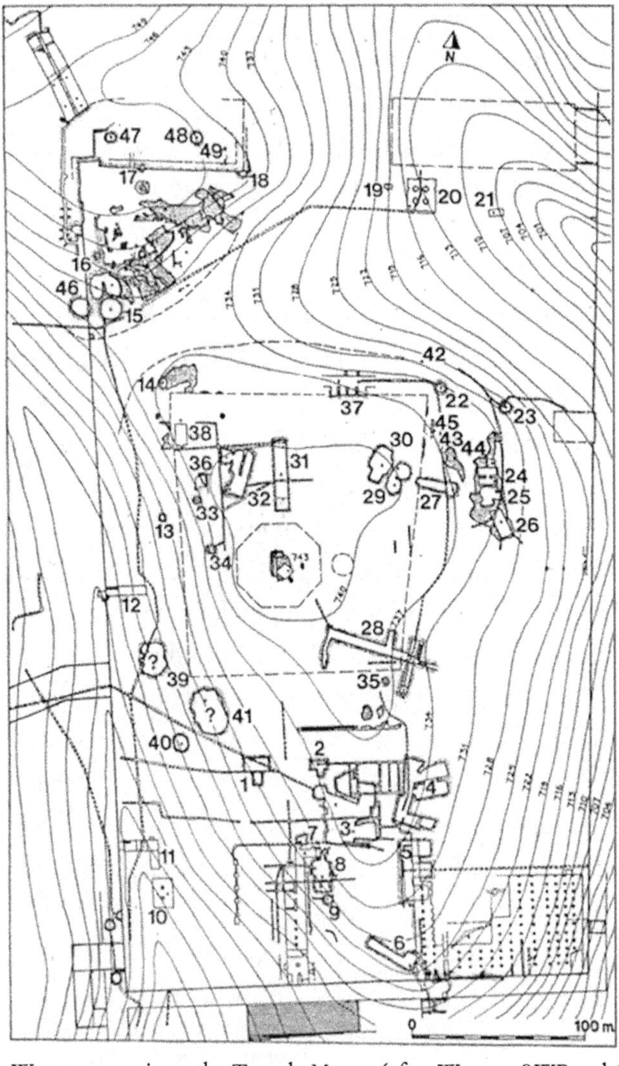


Fig. 9.2 Water reservoir on the Temple Mount (after Warren *SWP* and Gibson).

and by the local short temporary aqueducts was enough to fill the reservoirs.

The common explanation for the disappearance of long-distance fresh water aqueducts from medieval townscapes is that the governance skills needed for their regular upkeep and repair were simply lost in the Middle Ages. 'In former days,' says Peter Llewellyn when referring to the deterioration of the urban landscape in *eleventh-century Rome*, 'a large and complex organization had maintained the aqueducts, the drainage of the city and the retaining walls of the Tiber banks [but] that organization had now vanished'.[10] The effect of the alleged eleventh-century neglect of the aqueducts cannot be underestimated. The line of Aqua Virgo, for example, the only aqueduct that still functioned in the late eleventh century, determined the settlement of Rome's population. The city had contracted during the mid eleventh century into the low-lying Tiber-bend quarter, later known as the *abitato*, where it was easier to obtain water, abandoning settlement on the hills.[11]

An alternative explanation is provided by other scholars who maintain that the daily needs of populations could have been met from other resources such as wells, rivers and private cisterns, and that aqueducts supplying running water were not really necessary.[12] '[I]t must be understood that water consumption has more to do with culture than physical necessity', says Cyril Mango. 'The amount of water we drink is relatively small, whereas bathing is a matter of social custom.'[13] Bryan Ward-Perkins, however, rightly

[10] Peter Llewellyn, *Rome in the Dark Ages* (London: Faber, 1971), p. 97.

[11] Bryan Ward-Perkins, *From classical Antiquity to the Middle Ages: urban public building in northern and central Italy, AD 300–850* (Oxford: Clarendon Press, 1984), p. 125; Robert Coates-Stephens, 'The walls and aqueducts of Rome in the early Middle Ages, AD 500–1000', *Journal of Roman Studies* 88 (1998), 166–78.

[12] Harry B. Evans, 'Water distribution: *quorsum et cui bono*', in *Future currents in aqueduct studies*, ed. A. Trevor Hodge (Leeds: F. Cairns, 1991), pp. 21–7; A. Trevor Hodge, *Water distribution in ancient Rome: the evidence of Frontinus* (Ann Arbor: University of Michigan Press, 1994), pp. 135–6.

[13] Cyril Mango, 'The water supply of Constantinople', in *Constantinople and its hinterland*, ed. Cyril Mango and Gilbert Dagron (Aldershot: Variorum, 1995), pp. 9–18, quote on p. 9.

believes that the prosperity of the Classical cities was dependent to a great extent on the availability of running water.

> The prosperity of the Classical cities was conditioned by their ability to . . . supply the citizens with ample distribution of water. Aqueducts . . . [enabled] the construction of . . . latrines . . . fountains, palaces and other public amenities. In fourth century Rome . . . there were eleven major aqueducts that supplied eleven large bath-buildings, 856 smaller ones, 1,352 public water cisterns, and 144 public lavatories with water.[14]

According to this approach, the 'social customs' conducted in the bath-houses, fountain-clad streets and latrines were the very essence of 'urban culture', and they were made possible by the continuous supply of running water. In the case of Classical Jerusalem, the very existence of sacrifice rituals was totally dependent on a continuous supply of running water for the purification of the priests and cleansing of the whole area. The installations revealed in the vicinity of the Temple Mount of Jerusalem and on the Temple Mount itself testify to the abundance of water supply.

Is it possible to assume that the aqueducts ceased to function because of the loss of the skills for their repair? In the case of Jerusalem, the answer is in the negative: it is hard to believe that the Frankish rulers of the city, who mastered the skills needed for the construction and maintenance of the aqueducts leading the water of winter floods into the city and for construction of sophisticated castles containing complicated water systems, lost the skills needed for the repair of the existing bigger ones. The skills are not that different. William of Tyre claims that the aqueducts were truncated at the time of the siege of 1099, but Nāṣir-i Khusraw clearly shows that they stopped running and stopped supplying the city with fresh water during the first half of the eleventh century.

[14] Ward-Perkins, *Classical Antiquity*, p. 121.

The alternative claim, that 'the daily needs of populations could have been met from other resources', is certainly correct, if the citizens of the cities would have given up their craving for a luxurious way of life and adopted an austere regime which would cater only to their basic needs in smaller and poorer cities. In short, the abandonment of water systems meant giving up the very essence of urban life.

It is true, however, that the provision of a minimal amount of water to Classical cities was not dependent solely on aqueduct-borne running water. If we calculate the amount supplied directly by rains, wells and springs without the delivery of water through aqueducts, we can even calculate how many citizens could have lived in a certain city. The case of Jerusalem, a medium-sized city with a walled area of about 80 hectares and an average rainfall of 540 millimetres per year, shows that even the arithmetic is easy.

The average amount of rainfall within the walled area of Jerusalem is about 432,000 $m^3$ (800,000 $m^2$ × 0.54 m). If the city succeeds in creating sufficient storage space and in storing every drop of rain-water, without any evaporation or pollution, then the population that can permanently dwell there is of about 23,500 people.[15] Such assumptions are certainly superfluous: it is absolutely unfeasible to catch and store 100 per cent of the rainfall – it is definitely impossible to avoid evaporation, certainly in the Mediterranean climate and in open reservoirs – and it is very difficult to avoid stagnation and pollution.

The measured ratio between rainfall and run-off from paved roofs and small watersheds does not exceed 2 : 1, which means

[15] The minimal average consumption per capita is calculated on the basis of the UN Water Poverty Index (WPI, approximately 50 litres per capita/per diem, i.e., 18.250 $m^3$ per annum, including the amount needed for irrigation and for the watering of household animals). For the calculation of WPI, see Caroline A. Sullivan et al., 'The Water Poverty Index: development and application at the community scale', *Natural Resources* 27 (2003), 189–99.

that only 65 per cent or 280,500 $m^3$ of the rainfall can be stored.[16] The fact that the whole of Jerusalem was unpaved, together with evaporation and pollution, probably reduced the amount of the collectible run-off to at least 50 per cent (i.e., 216,000 $m^3$), an amount that together with the flow of the Siloam can supply the very basic needs of less than 12,000 inhabitants.

Another, more difficult, method of calculating the dependence of the city on rain-water is to reckon the capacity of the city's pools and cisterns. The three open pools of medieval Jerusalem (Mamilla, Hezekiah and Banū Isrāʾīl) did not exceed 140,000 $m^3$, and most of the water evaporated or became polluted during the hot season. It is easy to show that together with the big underground cisterns of the Temple Mount, the Church of the Holy Sepulchre, the Muristan (and so on), and in addition to the private cisterns, water storage space in medieval Jerusalem was greater than the annual amount of collectible run-off.[17]

Digging more underground cisterns could probably at least partially solve the problem of evaporation, but such an endeavour was too expensive and too complicated for most cities of the East, and certainly for Jerusalem. Therefore, the city continued to depend on the cisterns created in Antiquity (those of the Temple Mount) or during the Byzantine period (those of the Church of the Holy Sepulchre and of the Muristan) and on water stored in private cisterns.[18]

[16] Aharon Yair and Raphael Garti, 'The water supply of ancient Arad', in *Early Arad II: the Chalcolithic and Early Bronze IB settlements and the Early Bronze II city: architecture and town planning: sixth to eighteenth seasons of excavations, 1971–1978, 1980–1984*, ed. Ruth Amiran and Orrit Ilan (Jerusalem: Israel Museum and Israel Exploration Society, 1996), pp. 127–38.

[17] The maximum capacity of Hezekiah's Pool was 37,531$m^3$; that of Mamilla Pool was 41,613$m^3$ and the pool of Banū Isrāʾīl 27,527.5 $m^3$ (since this pool has been filled up since 1934, the calculation is according to the position of the drain). Altogether, the quantity of the three pools is 101,015 $m^3$.

[18] An additional cistern created during the reign of Justinian under the 'new church' of Mary (the Nea) and supplied by the aqueduct was abandoned before the twelfth century; see Nahman Avigad, 'A building inscription of the Emperor Justinian and the Nea in Jerusalem', *Israel Exploration Journal* 27 (1977), 145–51.

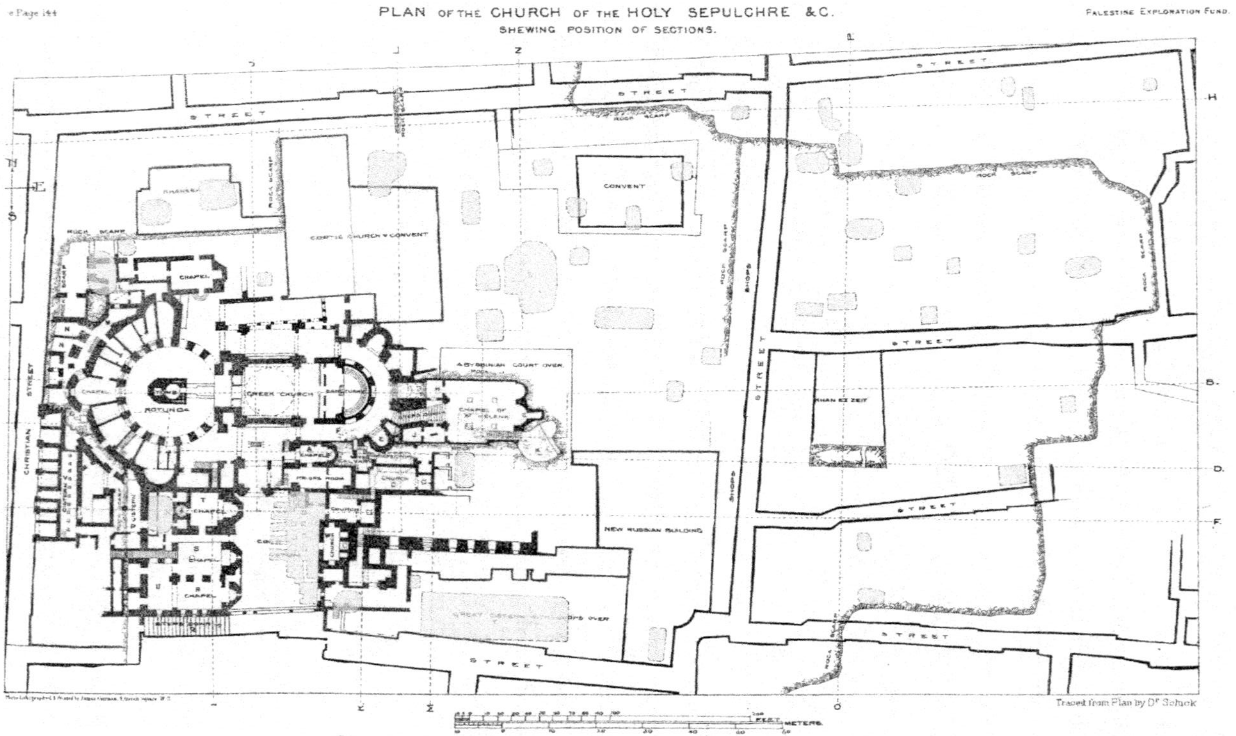


Fig. 9.3 Water reservoirs in the vicinity of the Church of the Holy Sepulchre (after Schlick).

The example of the additional covered cistern, which was built by Justinian in Constantinople during the 530s, demonstrates how complicated it was to construct such a storage space. Justinian demolished one of the wings of the open courtyard of the prestigious basilica – a building constructed by Constantine – in order to dig the cistern and provide a solution to the acute need for water. In commenting on this enterprise, which was intended to store the overflow of the aqueduct of Valence and provide water for the Great Palace, Procopius says explicitly that the cistern was meant to remedy the shortage of water during the *summer months* and enable a steady supply of water to the palace, regardless of the season.[19] The fact that even the aqueduct of Valence, which supplied the palace of Constantinople with water, could not be relied upon during summertime hints at a possible reason for the desertion of the aqueducts. Most of the springs of the eastern Mediterranean are not fed by huge underground perennial aquifers, but depend on local aquifers that are liable to be reduced considerably or even to dry up entirely during the dry season, if droughts recur. Three or four years of recurring drought are usually enough for a medium-sized and even a large-size spring to dry up during the summer.

In average years a city like Jerusalem could have filled all its storage space with rain-water only, but sole dependence on rain-water limits the growth and prosperity of a city, preventing any possible fluctuation. The situation is further deteriorated in years of drought. Deficiency of one standard deviation in the annual average rainfall (corresponding to a decrease of 150 mm per year in the case of Jerusalem) would have resulted in a further decline of the population, and certainly in their standard of living. An additional permanent supply of running water is needed in order to maintain the urban culture of a city, and this was even crucial during the early

[19] Procopius, *De Aed.*, 1.11.10–15.

Roman period, when the Temple was still functioning. Small places, desert palaces and monasteries could have sufficed with rain-water and the water collected in dry riverbeds,[20] but for Jerusalem, like any other Classical city in the eastern Mediterranean, permanent springs or aqueducts were vital for refilling the cisterns during the late dry summers. An additional supply of water could not only have doubled the permanent population or brought many more pilgrims to the city, but actually enabled more sophisticated lifestyles for the citizenship. The 'social customs' referred to by Mango – bathhouses, water sports, sophisticated latrines and fountains – were actually the essence of Classical urban culture and their disappearance transformed urban life.

The fact that the aqueducts leading running water to Jerusalem and Rome were abandoned during the eleventh century, and the fact that many other aqueducts supplying urban centres in the eastern Mediterranean with running water were also abandoned (at an as yet unknown date), calls for a more thorough look for the reason for these phenomena and for the local affects of the droughts during the relevant period.

## SPRINGS, PROVINCIAL CITIES AND HINTERLANDS: THE CASE OF JERUSALEM

The long-term mean annual rainfall in Jerusalem (1847–2000) is 554 mm/yr, but the fluctuation between an extremely rainy year (such as the 1,188 mm/yr in 1991/2), a moderately dry year (464 mm in 1969/70) and an extremely dry year (218 mm in 1959/60) is of more

[20] For classical desert sites, depending entirely on such occasional floods, see Patricia Hidiroglou and Claude Grenache, 'Aqueducts, basins, and cisterns: the water systems at Qumran', *Near Eastern Archaeology* 63.3 [*Qumran and the Dead Sea scrolls: discoveries, debates, the scrolls and the Bible*] (2000), 138–9; Leigh-Ann Bedal, 'Desert oasis: water consumption and display in the Nabataean capital', *Near Eastern Archaeology* 65.4 [*Petra: a royal city unearthed*] (2002), 225–34.

than two standard deviations from the average. All the springs in the Judean Hills, and most of the springs in the mountainous areas of the Levant, are perched springs that depend solely on the annual amount of rain-water. Recent studies show that the yearly fluctuation between 1920 and 2002 ranges between 360 mm/yr to 700 mm/yr, which is only one standard deviation of the average.[21]

The discharge of springs, as well as the capacity of hinterlands to provide cities with agricultural products, is also dependent on the annual rainfall. The number of springs (in the Judean Hills there are 160 perched springs, discharging between 3,400 $m^3$/yr and 49,500 $m^3$/yr)[22] determines the map of potential agriculture and irrigation, and fluctuations in rainfall lead to corresponding changes in the discharge of springs. A comparison between the annual rainfall and the discharge of springs in the Judean Hills over the last twenty years clearly shows that while the measured fluctuation rainfall was of ±30 per cent, the fluctuation of the discharge of the springs was between ±60 per cent and ±80 per cent.

Several years of moderate drought (of less than half a standard deviation from the average) will lead to a considerable decline in the discharge of the springs and to serious difficulties in dry farming and husbandry. Severe droughts, however, can be catastrophic for spring-dependent settlements and can lead to their total desertion.

When summarizing the recent study on seasonal fluctuation in comparatively small perched springs in the mountainous parts of Palestine, Peleg and colleagues say:

[21] Nadav Peleg and Haim Gvirtzman, 'Groundwater flow modeling of two-levels perched karstic leaking aquifers as a tool for estimating recharge and hydraulic parameters', *Journal of Hydrology* 388 (2010), 13–27; Nadav Peleg, Efrat Morin, Haim Gvirtzman and Yehouda Enzel, 'Changes in spring discharge as potential amplifiers of societal response to rainfall series in the Eastern Mediterranean' (forthcoming): I would like to thank the authors for sharing with me the results before they were published.

[22] Israel Hydrological Service, *Development and status of Israel's water resources as of fall 2006* (Jerusalem: Office of National Infrastructure, 2008), p. 438.

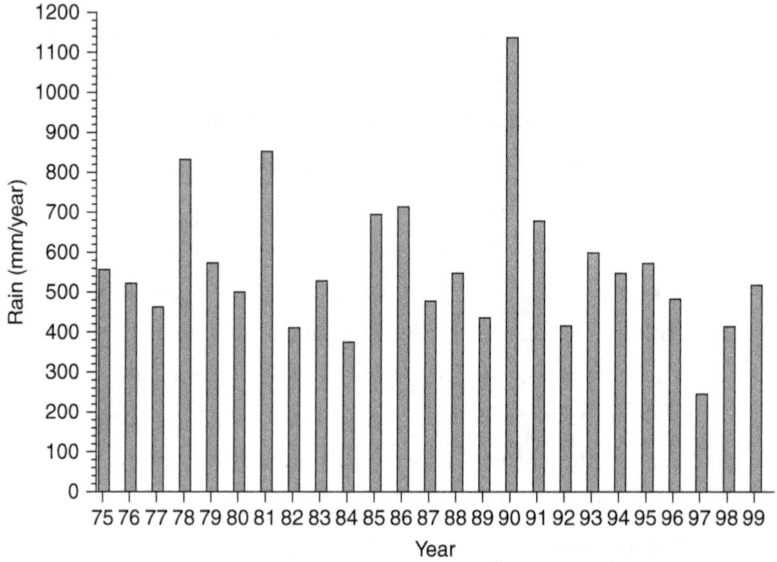


Fig. 9.4 Comparison between the annual amount of rainfall (*above*) and the discharge of a perch spring (*below*, p. 211) (after Peleg et al.).

> [M]oderate to extreme droughts lasting only relatively short durations may have led to abandonment of the springs as water resources and as focal sites of agricultural production (livestock, and irrigated orchards and fields) . . . hydrological parameters that are important for the village livelihood are sensitive to the climatic changes due to the amplification and reduction effects in discharge of springs.

The drought that hit the Judean Hills and the hinterland of Jerusalem between 2007 and 2011 left the region with more than 300 mm a year, enough to cultivate grain and therefore to prevent hunger. The total amount of precipitation between 2004 and 2011 was of less than one standard deviation below the long-term mean average (see Table 9.1).[23] But the consequences were no less than disastrous. Many of the perched springs in the Jerusalem Mountains

[23] Source: Rainfall Seasons at Jerusalem www.o2ws.com/station.php?section=RainSeasons.php&lang=1

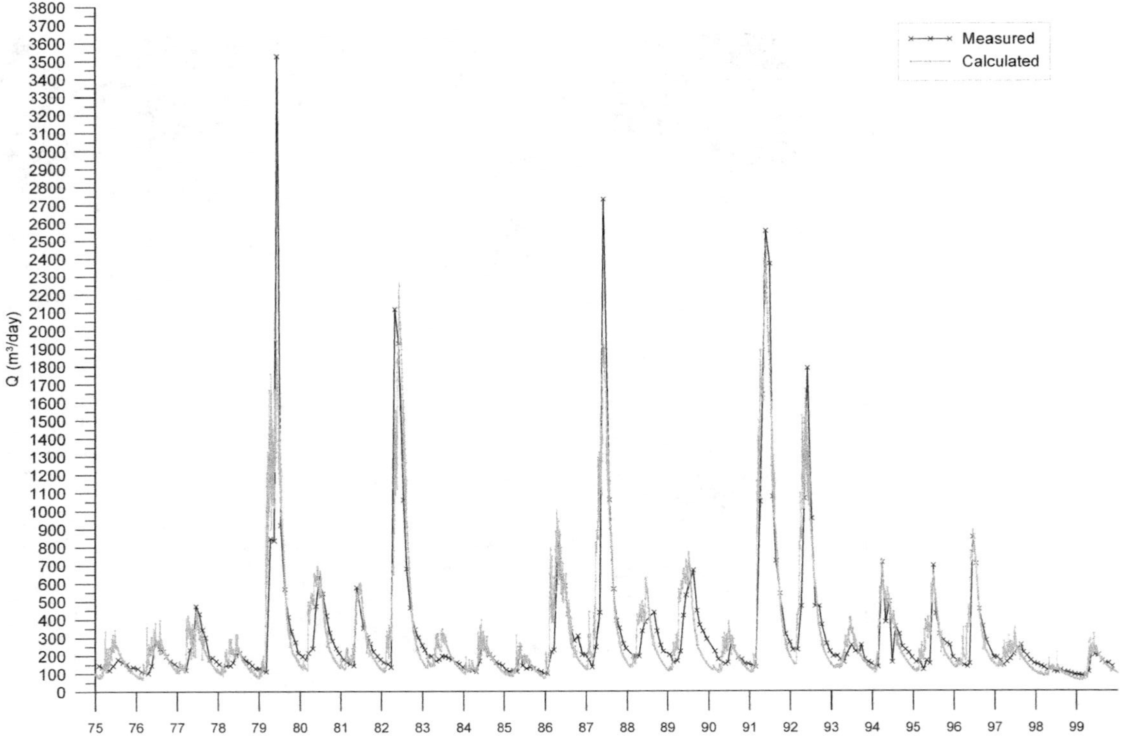

Measured
Calculated
Q (m³/day)
3800
3700
3600
3500
3400
3300
3200
3100
3000
2900
2800
2700
2600
2500
2400
2300
2200
2100
2000
1900
1800
1700
1600
1500
1400
1300
1200
1100
1000
900
800
700
600
500
400
300
200
100
0
75
76
77
78
79
80
81
82
83
84
85
86
87
88
89
90
91
92
93
94
95
96
97
98
99


Fig. 9.4 (cont.)

Table 9.1 *Rainfall in Jerusalem, 2004–2011*

| | | |
|---|---|---|
| 2004–5 | 586 mm | 105.7% |
| 2005–6 | 499.3 mm | 90% |
| 2006–7 | 532.7 mm | 96.1% |
| 2007–8 | 347 mm | 62.6% |
| 2008–9 | 337 mm | 60.8% |
| 2009–10 | 429.6 mm | 77.5% |
| 2010–11 | 324.7 mm | 58.6% |
| 2004–11 | 3056.3 mm | 78.8% |

Fig. 9.5 The drying up of a mountain spring: *above*, 2004; *left*, 2011.

Fig. 9.5 (cont.)

area dried out. An intensive field survey conducted in May 2011, when, under normal conditions, all the springs are supposed to flow, showed that only 18 out of 37 perched springs were still flowing, 17 were totally or almost totally dry and 2 were flowing at half normal capacity (see Figure 9.6).[24]

The drying-out of permanent sources of water for more than two years could easily lead to the desertion of villages that depend on irrigation, to a parallel decline of the number of villages and to a sudden increase in food prices. The drought of 2007–11 clearly shows that four or five consecutive years of

[24] Azriel Yehezkeel, 'The influence of long term drought on springs in the Judean Hills', unpublished seminar paper under the supervision of Amos Frumkin; Yehezkeel Azriel, *A guide to the springs in the Judean mountains* (Jerusalem: privately published, 2004; 2nd and rev. edn, 2008).

insufficient rain can lead to the desertion of villages and to the decline of cities depending on the transportation of water from perched springs.

It is impossible to assess the amount of rainfall during medieval droughts, but it is clear that the drought of the mid eleventh century led not only to the deterioration in the standard of living in the cities (that depended to a great extent on the excess of water), but also to the desertion of villages that lost their agricultural *raison d'être*. The desertion of the villages led to a further price rise and to hunger, which augmented the vicious circle of the famine.

Occasions of springs that dried up and ceased to flow, leading to the desertion of villages, are mentioned between the mid tenth and the early twelfth centuries. According to Matthew of Edessa, for example, the disastrous drought that hit the Jazira during the 340s/950s 'stayed in that country for seven years ... Many villages and regions became uninhabited, and nothing else has been built [in them] to the present day'.[25] Following the severe drought in the same region in 438/1047–8, Michael the Syrian reports, 'the springs dried up, and many places without rivers and fountains were deserted'.[26] Bar Hebraeus refers to the agricultural hinterland in Baghdad of the late 1050s, while noting 'Agriculture came to an end.'[27] The fact that both the Abbot Daniel and William of Tyre were not aware of the existence of springs in the environs of

[25] Matthew of Edessa, *Armenia and the Crusades, tenth to twelfth centuries: the chronicle of Matthew of Edessa*, trans. Ara E. Dostourian (Lanham, MD: University Press of America, 1993), 1.1, p. 19.

[26] *Chronique de Michel le Syrien*, ed. Jean-Baptiste Chabot, 5 vols. (Paris, 1899–1924, reprinted Brussels, 1963), vol. III, pp. 640–1.

[27] Bar Hebraeus (Abū al-Faraj), *The chronography*, translated from the Syriac by Ernest A. Wallis Budge, 2 vols. (Oxford University Press, 1932), vol. I, p. 208.

Jerusalem could therefore be accurate and reflect a reality of the drying-out of these sources.[28]

The lingering droughts resulted in the desertion of many villages, even in the Galilee. Gil points to the abundance of Jewish Palestinian locative bynames originating from villages and the rural areas of the north in letters that were written during the 1050s and the 1060s. The bynames are indicative of people coming from Gush Halav, from Dalton, Iʿbillin, Tiberias, ʿAmqa and Kafr Manda as well as from Acre, Caesarea and Haifa. Toponymic bynames are usually regarded as evidence of social and geographical mobility, but Gil suggests that these names point to the abundance of refugees and to the desertion of many of the Jewish villages in the Galilee sometime between the end of the tenth and the beginning of the twelfth centuries. Gil believes that the Turcomans and the Crusaders were responsible for the desertion, 'inflicting the final blows on these communities', but the evidence he brings is based on letters written well before the arrival of the Seljuks and the Crusaders. Gil himself asserts that 'Jewish communities in these localities were *gradually wiped out during the Fatimid wars in Palestine*' that ended many years before the arrival of the Turcomans.[29]

Desertion was not limited to small urban centres and villages in Palestine but is directly attested in the documents and the archaeology of bigger centres as well. The city of Tiberias, located on the shores of the Sea of Galilee, attained its zenith and greatest dimensions during the early eleventh century,[30] but was decimated several decades later. During the early eleventh century the

[28] Daniel, *Vie et pèlerinage*, ed. Khitrovo, pp. 25–6; *Willelmi Tyrensis Archiepiscopi Chronicon*, 8.4, pp. 388–90.

[29] Moshe Gil, *A history of Palestine, 634–1099* ( Cambridge University Press, 1992), pp. 216–17, emphasis the present author.

[30] For an extensive overview of these excavations, see Gideon Avni, '"From Polis to Madina" revisited – urban change in Byzantine and early Islamic Palestine', *Journal of the Royal Asiatic Society* (forthcoming). See Yizhar Hirschfeld and Katherine Galor, 'New excavations in Roman, Byzantine, and early Islamic Tiberias', in *Religion, Ethnicity, and*

city extended for two miles from north to south, contained a congregational mosque and was surrounded by a wall.[31] Large-scale excavations conducted in the last two decades exposed a well-planned network of residential quarters containing large buildings, wide arteries and even bridges connecting the newly built quarters with the city core.[32] The residential quarters were abandoned abruptly between the late 1050s and the late 1070s, leaving behind vestiges which were no more than pale shadows of the city's glorious past. At least part of the population deserted the city in a hurry, probably because they aspired to return to it in the future. A hoard of a rich atelier – more than a thousand tools, including bronze vessels, lampstands and candlesticks, oil lamps, tableware and kitchenware, bowls, goblets, cups, buckets, cooking pots, frying pans – was deposited during the 1070s, attesting to a rich artisan or merchant who had to leave his native place and property without knowing that he was not going to return.[33]

A letter written by the leper community of Tiberias contains a rare testimony to the real hunger that prevailed in the city in 1030,

*Identity in Ancient Galilee*, ed. Jürgen Zangenberg, Harold W. Attridge and Dale B. Martin (Tübingen: Mohr Siebeck, 2007), pp. 207–30.

31 Katya Cytrin-Silverman, 'The Ummayad mosque at Tiberias', *Muquarnas* 26 (2010), 37–62; Muqaddasi, *Ahsan al-Taqāsīm*, p. 161; Muqaddasi, *The best divisions for knowledge of the regions* [*Aḥsan al-taqāsīm fī maʿrifat al-aqālīm*], trans. Basil A. Collins (Reading: Garnet, 2001), p. 137.

32 These rescue excavations were conducted in 2008. For a preliminary notice, see Moshe Hartal, 'Hammat Tiberias (south), preliminary report', *Excavations and Surveys in Israel* 121 (2009), www.Hadashot-esi.org.il

33 For an astonishing hoard of bronze vessels hidden in three storage jars, see Yizhar Hirschfeld and Oren Gutfeld, *Tiberias: excavations in the House of the Bronzes, final report*, vol. I, *Architecture, stratigraphy and small finds*, Qedem 48 (Hebrew University of Jerusalem Press, 2008); Yizhar Hirschfeld and Oren Gutfeld, 'Tiberias – the "House of the Bronze" and associated remains', *New Encyclopedia of Archaeological Excavations in the Holy Land* 5, supplementary volume (Jerusalem: Israel Exploration Society, 2008), 2053–4. For one of the residential quarters, see Moshe Hartal, 'Tiberias', *Excavations and Surveys in Israel* 120 (2008), www.Hadashot-esi.org.il

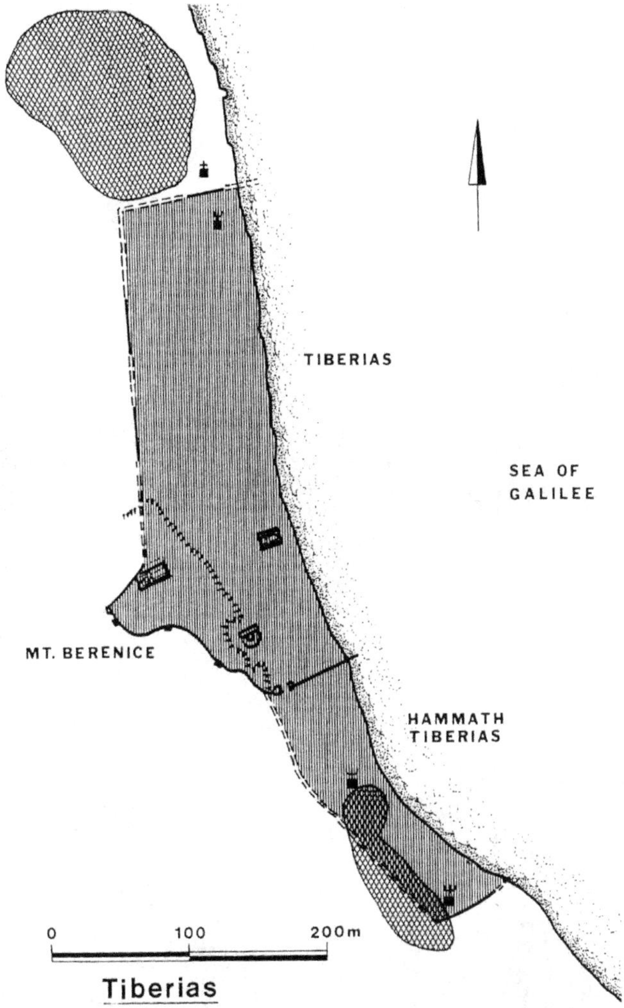


Fig. 9.6 Plan of eleventh-century Tiberias. Note the dimensions of the Byzantine city (centre) and newly built Muslim suburbs (to the north and south of the city).

and to other effects that usually accompany such a famine: the land of Israel, it is said, was destroyed and cities were deserted by their inhabitants.[34] In another undated eleventh-century letter written by

[34] Gil, *Palestine* vol. II, p. 468 (no. 262, lines 12–14).

Fig. 9.7 A hoard from eleventh-century Tiberias.

Fig. 9.8 A metal hoard from Caesarea Maritima (mid eleventh century).

the son of a widow from Tiberias (on behalf of the mother) to her brother who was contemplating settling in Palestine, the woman describes Tiberias as being cheaper than Ramla, although the price of bread quoted is still one dirham a ratl – a very high price for bread at the time, indicating severe scarcity of the commodity.[35]

Caesarea Maritima is another example of a city that flourished during the ninth and tenth centuries but which declined abruptly during the second half of the eleventh century. Caesarea was probably the biggest city in Byzantine Palestine that declined in importance after the establishment of Muslim Ramla as the new capital of Filastin (formerly the Byzantine province of Palaestina Prima). During the ninth century, however, an entirely new urban layout was established in Caesarea, consisting of well-planned *insulae* and a grid pattern of streets. This residential quarter was expanded and the houses were enlarged and improved during the tenth century, and the public realm was ameliorated as well. Streets were repaved, new cisterns were dug and new pipes were laid. A strong wall was constructed during the first half of the eleventh century, delineating a much smaller area than that of the Byzantine city. This wall continued to be in use during the twelfth and thirteenth centuries, and was recently excavated in the core of the Crusader city wall. It is perhaps not superfluous to assume that it was conceived, together with the new city wall of Jerusalem, during the period of Fatimid prosperity between the early 1030s and the late 1040s.

The abrupt decline of Caesarea occurred during the same troubled years of the mid eleventh century. A hoard that was excavated testifies to the same fate of wealthy artisans and the necessity of merchants to desert their city in haste, intending to

[35] Gil, *Palestine* vol. II, pp. 450–2 (no. 247, lines 16–19); Joseph Braslavski (Braslavi), *Studies in our country, its past and remains* (Tel Aviv: Hakibbutz Hameuchad, 1954), pp. 45–6 (Hebrew).

return later to continue making their living by using the tools they left behind. They took all their money but did not take their tools because transport of such precious property was too risky along the disordered and troubled roads.

The Jewish community of Caesarea was still flourishing and thriving during the mid 1020s when a letter found in the Cairo Geniza was directed to the 'entire holy community living in the fortress of Ḥaṣor (Caesarea)'.[36] However, it deteriorated gradually until the end of the century when the whole community became miserable and 'drowned in sorrows due to poverty and constant fear'. 'Our souls are in fear and trembling from too many rumors', wrote the community's leader, who wished to move elsewhere, to the Nagid of Egypt, complaining about the local residents who 'are good for nothing' and about the local qadi, who 'detains and forces the community'.[37]

The fact that the Jewish community in Caesarea declined during the 1050s is hinted at in a Geniza letter written in 1060 by the Maghribi merchant Jacob b. Salmān al-Ḥarīrī to Nahrai b. Nissim in Fustat. Jacob informs his addressee that he was planning to do business in Ramla but that his ship, which was destined for Jaffa, was wrecked near Caesarea, forcing him to abandon it and to remain in the city for a while. However, he was unable to find a proper place to stay and was forced to remain in the synagogue for five days.[38] There is no doubt that the city, which during the 1020s was a successful commercial centre, had deteriorated considerably.

36 Gil, *History of Palestine*, p. 218.

37 Moshe Gil, *Be-malkhut Yishma'el bi-tequfat ha-ge'onim* [*In the kingdom of Ishmael*], Texts from the Cairo Geniza, 4 vols. ( Tel Aviv University Press, Bialik Institute, Ministry of Defense, 1997), vol. III, p. 460 (no. 48, line 7); ibid., vol. III, p. 507.

38 Gil, *History*, p. 218.

Ramla is the last Palestinian centre that will be mentioned here.[39] It was founded in 716 by the Ummayad caliph Sulayman Ibn ʿAbd al-Malik and became the capital of the province of Jund Filastin. It flourished during the eighth and the ninth centuries and became one of the principal cities in Palestine. It continued to develop until the eleventh century, spreading over a vast area. There were at least three synagogues in the city and the Jewish community there was bigger and more powerful than the community of Jerusalem.

Al-Muqaddasī describes Ramla thus in AD 985:

> A delightful and well built city. The water is good to drink and flows freely; fruits are abundant, and of every possible kind. It is situated in the midst of fertile rural areas, splendid cities, holy places, and pleasant villages. Trade here is profitable, and the means of livelihood easy. There is not in Islam a more splendid mosque than that here, no more delicious or excellent than its white bread. No lands more favoured, not any fruits more delicious! It is situated in a productive countryside, with walled towns and pleasant suburbs. It possesses elegant hostelries and pleasant baths; superb food and condiments in abundance; spacious houses, fine mosques, and broad streets . . . Its fields yield without irrigation . . . The city is a mile square, and its houses are of finely quarried stone and baked brick . . . The chief mosque is in the market, more magnificent, more elegant than the mosque of Damascus. It is called 'the White', and in all Islām there is found no larger miḥrab than that here, and after the pulpit in Jerusalem there is no more beautiful pulpit than the one there; it also possesses a splendid minaret.[40]

Al-Muqaddasī was, however, well aware of the difficulties during the summer, when the aqueduct did not supply the city with enough water:

[39] For a recent summary of the excavations, see Gideon Avni, '"The most beautiful of cities": Ramla during the early Islamic period: an archaeological survey', *Qadmoniot* 41.135 (2008), 2–10 (Hebrew).

[40] Al-Muqaddasī, *Best divisions*, pp. 150–1.

in summer . . . no water flows nor is there anything green; the soil is not moist, nor is there snow . . . The wells are deep and salty, and the rain-water is held in closed cisterns; hence the poor go thirsty, and strangers are helpless and at a loss what to do. In the baths a fee must be paid so that the attendants will turn the water wheels.

No less than a hundred and fifty archaeological excavations have been conducted in Ramla since 1990, some of them vast and intensive and most of them very limited. The archaeologists have revealed residential and industrial quarters as well as public buildings. Water was stored in underground cisterns and pools nourished by a ramified system of channels and an aqueduct that in rainy winters supplied the city with water brought from Tell Gezer (Mont Gisard of the Crusaders). Most of the residential quarters were deserted and ceased to exist during the second half of the eleventh century. The city wall has not been uncovered to date, but according to the present calculations the built part of the city covered an area of 3 x 2.5 km.

This magnificent city continued to expand until the early eleventh century, when it reached its peak and declined abruptly. The sharp decline of one of the jewels of the early Muslim period occurred, like the sharp declines of Tiberias, Caesarea Maritima, Jerusalem and many other cities of the Levant, sometime between the late 1020s and the late 1060s. Historians (including Mamluk chroniclers) and archaeologists tend to ascribe the decline, or the destruction of the city, to the two earthquakes of 1033 and 1068.

Evidence of the dearth that prevailed in Ramla and of the forays and conquests of the city by nomads between the late 1020s and the beginning of the 1030s (at exactly the same time when a real hunger is recorded in Tiberias) is quite abundant.[41] Letters from the Geniza

[41] See chapter 3, pp. 38–9.

testify to the desertion of the hunger-stricken Jewish community from Ramla, to the incessant attacks by the Bedouins and even to starvation – as rare an occurrence in Ramla as it was in Tiberias.[42]

The community of Ramla recovered in the years of restoration and renovation that characterized the early 1030s. Later evidence testifies to the existence of a considerable Jewish community that dwelt there during the late 1030s.[43] A letter written in February 1039 by Nathan b. Abraham mentions that approximately four hundred people gathered in the main hall of the synagogue of Ramla on Purim (with more in the entrance hall), among them about two hundred Karaites.[44]

Unlike the dearth of the late 1020s, we have no direct evidence about life in Ramla during the famine of the 1050s or during the great Egyptian calamity of the late 1060s. The only evidence for the fate of Ramla during these two turbulent events is that of al-Maqrīzī, who attests to the anarchy that prevailed in Ramla and asserts that the unpaid Turkish regiment in al-Mustanṣir's army invaded Ramla in 460/1067. The invasion took place, according to al-Maqrīzī, in the month of Muḥarrām (November), two years after the beginning of the most severe famine of the century and about four years before the invasion of the Seljuks, and six months before the earthquake that allegedly led to the destruction of Ramla.[45] In Ramla, as elsewhere, we tend to overestimate the importance of political events and natural disasters for the fate of cities. Prosperous historic cities are usually not abandoned because of an earthquake.

[42] Gil, *Palestine*, vol. II, pp. 83–4 (no. 49); ibid., vol. II, pp. 85–7 (no. 50); ibid., vol. II, p. 164 (no. 89, lines 11–12); ibid., vol. II, p. 167 (no. 90, line 17).

[43] See chapter 3. [44] Gil, *Palestine*, vol. I, p. 174 and vol. II, p. 314 (no. 183, line 12).

[45] Al-Maqrīzī, *Itti'āẓ al-ḥunafā'*, ed. Jamāl al-Dīn al-Shayyāl and Muḥammad Ḥilmī Muḥammad Aḥmad, 3 vols. (Cairo, 1967–73), vol. II, p. 275.

More often they decline and are deserted because of a collapse of the economy or due to a deterioration of the standard of living. Catastrophic political events or singular natural disasters can seal the fate of declining cities. This, in my opinion, is what happened in the case of Ramla, which was the biggest city in the country during the early eleventh century and declined for the same reasons that led to the decline of the other cities in the country – extended droughts, dearth that occasionally deteriorated into periods of hunger, attacks of nomads and the collapse of public order. The earthquake hit the city in 1068, when it was too weak to withstand the calamity and recover, and the Seljuk conquest that followed the period of hunger probably contributed to the city's comparative recovery.

## CITIES IN THE WESTERN AND EASTERN MEDITERRANEAN: AN ATTEMPT AT A SUMMARY

The cities in the eastern Mediterranean began to evolve differently to those in the western Mediterranean during the seventh century AD. Notwithstanding the obvious regional differences and despite the exceptions, we can deduce that almost all the cities in the western Mediterranean and in western Europe declined and some of them even ceased to exist as significant commercial, demographic, administrative, artistic or intellectual centres between the seventh and the tenth centuries AD. The decline of some of these cities can be attributed to the attacks of nomads; others were deserted because of their failure to withstand the calamities of the fifth and sixth centuries. The reason for the decline of other cities is not yet known.

The long period of stagnation, however, that started during the sixth and ended during the late tenth centuries corresponds to the period which Henri Pirenne referred to as a period of silence indicative of the decline.

The evolution of the cities of the eastern Mediterranean at this time was different. Many declined during the sixth century (simultaneously with the decline of the cities in the entire Mediterranean basin) for no clear political or economic reason, but the decline was not complete and was followed, in many cases, by periods of prosperity. The results of recent archaeological excavations clearly show that this decline was not continuous and that many of these cities succeeded, after an initial period of decline, to recover and attract thriving commercial and intellectual communities. Many successfully regained their position as cultural, political and economic centres.

The period between the sixth and the tenth centuries in the eastern Mediterranean was not only one of continuity. Many urban centres were established during the same period, and some – such as Fustat, Baghdad and Qayrawan – prospered as flourishing megalopoli reaching unprecedented cultural and economic peaks and attracting literate and wealthy communities. At the same time, the urban culture was declining in the West, giving way to the establishment of a rural and monastic landscape.

The very period that Henri Pirenne defined, according to his *argumentum ex silentio* type of explanation, as a decline of the Classical cities was also the period of urban intellectual and artistic achievements in the East.

The seesaw effect was reversed in the mid tenth century. While western Europe was enjoying a warm and rainy period that led to a dramatic increase in the population, the recovery of the economy and the establishment of many urban centres, the eastern Mediterranean was affected by repeated cold spells, by famines and pestilences and by subsequent collapse. The dearth diminished the ability of bureaucracies to govern and increased the temptation of hunger-stricken nomads, unpaid deserting soldiers and marauders to attack and pillage existing cities and villages. The lingering droughts caused springs to dry up and cities to be deserted. The decline of the tenth and eleventh centuries, therefore, affected not only the urban centres but their hinterlands as well.

The sharp decline is discerned in all scales of urban centres: in a giant Roman-Byzantine megalopolis such as Constantinople, in the important commercial centres of Iran such as Nishapur, in Muslim capital cities such as Baghdad in Iraq and Fustat in Egypt, in Muslim provincial centres like Ramla in Palestine and Qayrawan in north Africa, and even in all the Byzantine provincial towns of Palestine, as the excavations in Jerusalem, Caesarea Maritima and Tiberias attest.

The decline of the cities of the eastern Mediterranean was unprecedented, affecting almost the entire region. Cities of the northern Levantine coast, situated away from the 'drought line', and cities like Damascus depending on rich perennial aquiphers, suffered less than the cities situated closer to the 'drought line' and those depending on rain-water and perched springs only, but most did not succeed in evading partial or even total collapse; indeed, very few cities succeeded in avoiding this fate.

Climatic events are ephemeral events. When the cold is abated, when the rain returns, then the famine and the dearth are forgotten. But the collapse of both the cities and the countryside of the eastern Mediterranean was irreversible. Baghdad and some of the cities of Iran managed to recover, at least partially, within a generation or two. Qayrawan was destroyed for ever, sharing its gloomy fate with Fustat, which was also abandoned, to be replaced by neighbouring Cairo. Jerusalem only regained part of its glory during the Mamluk period and Constantinople did so only during the Ottoman period.

The cities of many regions in southern and western Europe declined during the High Middle Ages, but a theory assuming a similar decline in the eastern or southern Mediterranean area is certainly not correct. Urban centres in the east recovered from the calamities of the sixth century and many of them continued to exist, and even to flourish, during later centuries, acquiring strength, fame and wealth. New types of cities were established while other cities that had existed during the Classical period continued to develop their economies and societies.

The seesaw of development between the eastern and the western Mediterranean was renewed during the tenth century. The West enjoyed a lengthy warm and rainy period, accompanied by abundant yields and an unprecedented increase in the population. The amelioration of the natural conditions was accompanied by technical innovations that helped the West to return to its previous leading positions. The eastern Mediterranean suffered, at exactly the same time, from one of the worst climatic disasters in the region's recorded history. The influence on urban history is evident. Scores of cities were decimated and many that had successfully recovered from the calamities of the sixth century underwent catastrophic decline, together with the villages that supplied them.

CHAPTER TEN

# Food crises and accelerated Islamization

The conversion of the populations of the eastern and southern Mediterranean to Islam was a major transformation that affected almost every conceivable characteristic of the region and altered its future forever. The advance of Islam implied a total disruption of social connections, family habits, tastes in fine arts, architecture and music; diets, land use, spatial distribution of power, languages, daily routines, and so on. The pace of these transformations, however, their stages, regional differentiations and the motives of the converts, are still highly debated.

In the first fifty years of the twentieth century there was a consensus among Islamists that the conversion to Islam was a comparatively fast process, whose main phases were completed within a few generations of the conquest.[1] The reservations raised during the second half of the century by Gaston Wiet (in his later

[1] The number of publications on the process of Islamization is immense. See, among many, Richard J. H. Gottheil, 'Dhimmis and Moslems in Egypt', in *Old Testament and Semitic studies in memory of William Rainey Harper*, ed. Robert F. Harper, Francis Brown and George F. Moore (University of Chicago Press, 1908), pp. 353–87; Thomas W. Arnold, *The preaching of Islam*, 3rd edn (London: Luzac, 1935), pp. 9–10, 81–2; Arthur S. Tritton, *The caliphs and their non-Muslim subjects* (London and Oxford: H. Milford and Oxford University Press, 1930); Arthur S. Tritton, 'Islam and the protected religions', *Journal of the Royal Asiatic Society* (1931), 311–38; Abraham N. Poliak 'L'Arabisation de l'orient sémitiques', *Revue des Études Islamiques* 12 (1938), 35–63; Antoine Fattal, *Le Statut légal des non-musulmans en pays d'Islam* (Beirut: Imp. Catholique, 1958); Gaston Wiet, *L'Égypte arabe de la conquête arabe à la conquête ottomane: 642–1517 de l'ère chrétienne* (Paris: Plon, 1937).

publications), Moshe Perlmann, Daniel Dennet, Marshall Hodgson and many others led to the modification of this scholarly consensus and to the creation of a new one. It is now commonly assumed that the process was gradual and slow, rather than sudden and fast, and that it occurred later than was previously assumed.[2] Therefore, many recent publications tend to follow Richard Bulliet's assumption that Islamization became irreversible and engulfed the majority of the population during the second half of the tenth century and the beginning of the eleventh century.[3] Recent works on the Islamization of Egypt suggest that the mass conversion of the Copts did not precede the Fatimid period, and even that there was no mass conversion of Copts to Islam before the thirteenth century.[4]

2 Gaston Wiet, 'Ḳibṭ', *Encyclopedia of Islam*, 2nd edn, ed. Peri J. Bearman,Thierry Bianquis, Clifford E. Bosworth, Emeri van Donzel and Wolfhart P. Heinrichs (Leiden: E. J. Brill, 2010), vol. II, pp. 990–1003. Dennett shows that exemption from paying the poll tax could not be a sufficient reason for earlier conversion; see Daniel C. Dennett, *Conversion and poll tax in early Islam* (Cambridge, MA: Harvard University Press, 1950). Moshe Perlmann, 'Notes on anti-Christian propaganda in the Mamluk empire', *Bulletin of the School of Oriental and African Studies* 10 (1942), 843–61. Marshall G. S. Hodgson, The venture of Islam, *vol. I,* The classical age of Islam (University of Chicago Press, 1974), pp. 301–5. See also Michael Brett, 'The spread of Islam in Egypt and North Africa', in *Northern Africa: Islam and modernization*, ed. Michael Brett (London: Frank Cass, 1973), pp. 1–12.

3 Richard W. Bulliet, *Conversion to Islam in the medieval period: an essay in quantitative history* (Cambridge, MA: Harvard University Press, 1979), pp. 44, 50–1; Ira Lapidus, 'The conversion of Egypt to Islam', *Israel Oriental Studies* 2 (1972), 256–7; Ira Lapidus, *A history of Islamic societies* (Cambridge University Press, 1988), pp. 142–6; Richard N. Frye, 'Comparative observations on conversion to Islam in Iran and Central Asia', *Jerusalem Studies in Arabic and Islam* 4 (1984), 86; Jonathan M. Bloom, 'The mosque of the Qarafa in Cairo', *Muqarnas* 4 (1987), 7–20; Michael G. Morony, 'The age of conversions: a reassessment', in *Conversion and continuity: indigenous Christian communities in Islamic lands, eighth to eighteenth centuries*, ed. Michael Gervers and Ramzi J. Bikhazi (Toronto: Pontifical Institute of Mediaeval Studies, 1990), pp. 135–50; Nehemiah Levtzion (ed.), *Conversion to Islam* (New York: Holmes & Meier, 1979).

4 See John Iskander, 'Islamization in medieval Egypt: the Copto-Arabic 'Apocalypse of Samuel' as a source for the social and religious history of medieval Copts', *Medieval Encounters* 4 (1998), 219–27; Tamer el-Leithy, 'Coptic culture and conversion in medieval Cairo, AD 1293–1524', unpublished PhD dissertation, Princeton University, 2004.

I single out Bulliet's theory from those of the rest of the scholars who modified the scholarly consensus, mainly because Bulliet was the first to abandon traditional methodologies and introduce new, statistical ones in their stead. Scholars of the previous generation assumed that the same methodologies which were valid for the reconstruction of historical events could be applied for the reconstruction of sociological and cultural processes of the *longue durée*. Many looked for direct testimonies, statements and even proofs for mass conversion, although direct testimonies that do not rely on statistical data are usually not accurate. Bulliet avoided reliance on scanty and often biased references, incidental testimonies scattered throughout the written narratives, and legal and religious commentaries.

Bulliet suggested an alternative statistical methodology based on the first appearances of one of four typical Muslim names in the lineages of important Islamic figures. He rightly assumed that the bearers of names such as Muḥammad or ʿAlī were already Islamized and that the first appearance of typical Islamic names in a lineage is clear evidence for the presence of Muslims in it – and therefore for the beginning of Islamization in a certain family lineage. He concluded, therefore, that the Muslims had attained a solid majority in the population during the late tenth and early eleventh centuries.

Reliance on medieval biographical encyclopedias that contain an enormous amount of data but are restricted to Muslim personalities alone, and the basing of the pace of Islamization on a sample of names that appear in lineages of leading *Islamic* figures only, led Bulliet to come to circular conclusions and to limit the validity of his hypothesis in regard to the entire population. Statistically valid results should have been obtained from sources that depict the situation in other communities as well.

Nevertheless, despite this and other statistical flaws, Bulliet's approach is still more firmly founded than that of his predecessors, and in any event it is probably impossible to obtain better results or to produce better narrations of the decline of Christianity (or of any other religion) in the eastern Mediterranean during the first five hundred years of Islam. It is certainly difficult to better date the period in which the followers of Islam gained a solid majority in the population, and it is even more difficult to explain differentiation in the spatial distribution of that religion in the region.

Nevertheless, scholarly interest in conversion has shifted since the late 1970s, as more studies devoted themselves to analysis of the process of Islamization (or Christianization) rather than to the process of *conversion of religion*. The term *Islamization* is often used to discern the means by which a culture or an entire ethnic group gradually adapts its habits to suit Muslim (or Christian if 'Christianization' is the case) habits, whereas the process of *conversion* refers to the personal and radical transformation of the faith of an individual.[5] Many of the studies that deal with the Christianization (or Islamization) of societies examine partial topics such as the Islamization of sacred spaces, the Christianization of the calendar, death, kingship, family, and so on.[6] Unlike personal conversions, which are usually finite, ending at a very specific

[5] William G. Kilbride, 'Why I feel cheated by the term "Christianisation"', *Archaeological Review from Cambridge* 17.2 (2001), 1–17; Richard A. Fletcher, *The conversion of Europe: from paganism to Christianity 371–AD 1386* (London: HarperCollins, 1997); Przemysław Urbanczyk, 'Christianisation of early medieval societies', in *Conversion and Christianity in the North Sea world*, ed. Barbara E. Crawford (St Andrews: Committee for Dark Age Studies, 1998), pp. 129–33.

[6] Joseph H. Lynch, *Christianizing kinship: ritual sponsorship in Anglo-Saxon England* (Ithaca, NY: Cornell University Press, 1998); Frederick S. Paxton, *Christianizing death: the creation of a ritual process in early Europe* (Ithaca, NY: Cornell University Press, 1990).

moment,[7] conversions of groups and Islamizations are diachronic and open-ended and their completion often takes more than one generation. Islamizations evolve constantly, implying structural transformations of cultures, economies and societies; Islamization is therefore a process of the *longue durée* that can be halted temporarily, reversed, perpetuated or intensified, and the exact point in time at which it terminates is often debated.[8]

A common intuitive tendency is to refer to the process of Islamization (or Christianization) as a process that involves both an ethnic group and the region in which it takes place. Many studies go one step further, omitting the reference to ethnic group and referring only to the region, as if the region is the body that undergoes conversion and not the ethnic group, or an infinite number of individuals living in it are converted. Examples are numerous, but it seems that 'Islamization of Egypt' is deemed to be as correct as 'Islamization of the Copts' and that 'Christianization of Ireland' is considered as relevant as the conversion of the Irish people.

Reference to the region stems, perhaps, from the fact that the geographical setting is considered to be a factor that remains

[7] For the development of the more traditional approach regarding Christianization as an accumulation of an infinite number of personal conversions, see William James, *The varieties of religious experience: a study in human nature, being the Gifford Lectures on natural religion delivered at Edinburgh in 1901–1902* (Cambridge, MA: Harvard University Press, 1985), pp. 157–209; Arthur Darby Nock, *Conversion* (Oxford: Clarendon Press, 1933), p. 7. See also Edwin Diller Starbuck, *The psychology of religion: an empirical study of the growth of religious consciousness*, 3rd edn (London: Walter Scott Publishing Co. and New York: Charles Scribner's Sons, 1911); Alfred C. Underwood, *Conversion: Christian and non-Christian: A comparative and psychological study* (London: Allen & Unwin, 1925); Steven T. Katz, 'Language, epistemology and mysticism', *Mysticism and philosophical analysis*, ed. Steven T. Katz (Oxford University Press, 1978), pp. 22–35.

[8] Jacques Le Goff, La Civilisation de l'Occident médiéval, *Collection Les Grandes Civilisations 3* (Paris: Éditions Arthaud, 1964); Ludo J. R. Milis, 'Introduction: the pagan Middle Ages – a contradiction in terms?', in *The pagan Middle Ages*, ed. Ludo J. R. Milis, trans. Tanis Guest (Woodbridge, Suffolk and Rochester, NY: Boydell Press, 1998), pp. 1–12.

comparatively stable throughout, such a diachronic process that takes generations to be accomplished. Regions, however, are not rigid platforms on which conversional processes are taking place. They are spatially transformed to accommodate the cultural transformations: new mosques, new churches, new synagogues and new religious schools or ritual baths are constructed as the transformation proceeds; conspicuous geographical and urban points are altered to emphasize the success of one group at the expense of the other and to symbolize the decline of the culture that prevailed in the same landscape in the past.

Islamization is usually referred to as a psychological or a cultural process, but the ascensions and declines of ethnic and cultural groups are also the result of demographic processes.

Demography is an important factor in the advance of religious transformation. In many cases the transformation of a certain region that undergoes religious change is achieved without personal conversions being involved. Emigration of inhabitants belonging to one religious group out of a certain region or the immigration of another group into it can lead to the 'conversion' of a region. Even differential birth rates and differences in the age of marriage can lead to such a result. Similar processes occur in contemporaneous landscapes throughout the world. Regions that attract immigrants are constantly being transformed and the change in demography is manifested in additional changes in centres as important to Christianity as Bethlehem and Nazareth, which were 'Islamized' during the second half of the twentieth century as the result of the outbound emigration of Christians and the immigration of Muslims (who also benefit from a higher birth rate). No personal conversion of religion of any of the Christians who lived in these centres is recorded, and if such personal conversions exist, their numbers are negligible. The landscapes of Nazareth and Bethlehem have been 'converted' without a single actual and personal conversion from one religion to the other.

We can safely assume that similar demographic mechanisms affected ancient landscapes as well, and that such processes can explain diversities between one region and another. We can also assume that such demographic processes were not linear, that they slowed down during periods of prosperity and were considerably accelerated during periods of dearth.

The descriptions of the crisis of the eleventh century are dotted with testimonies of such demographic processes that affected the religious status quo, leading to the comparative weakening of the Christians and strengthening of the Muslims. Inter-religious strife, persecutions, forced conversion and intentional destruction of prayer-places were intensified during the lingering crisis of the eleventh century, and some of them appear for the first time as official and widespread phenomena during the crisis. It is true that the most important demographic processes, such as the emigration of elites, economic collapse of communities and the desertion of agricultural and urban centres, affected the entire population and not only one group or another, but their effect on the minorities was more devastating.

The reinstallation of abolished episcopal sees and the reconstruction of ruined monasteries and churches needed the cooperation and participation of central governments, whereas the rebuilding of mosques and madrasas enjoyed an a priori consent of any Muslim government. Even the willingness of the Fatimids, who were prepared to allow the partial repair of the churches which were ruined during the reign of al-Ḥākim, disappeared during the later eleventh century, and many institutions that were abandoned and deserted remained so forever.

Therefore, if the common assertion that Islam attained a majority in the entire population during the late tenth and the early eleventh centuries is correct, then that very majority was probably augmented due to demographic processes and inter-religion events during the latter half of the same century. The crisis of the eleventh century in the eastern Mediterranean resulted also in the strengthening of Islam and in the weakening of Christianity throughout the region.

## OUTBOUND EMIGRATIONS

Emigration is probably the most effective factor in processes of 'demographic conversion' of landscapes. The Jews and Zoroastrians who began deserting Baghdad after the cold spell of 332–4/943–6,[9] when conditions in Baghdad became difficult to bear – when the residents were reduced to eating dogs and devouring human flesh and when looting became widespread – signalled a tendency that finally led to the desertion of Baghdad as a leading Jewish intellectual centre during the mid 1030s.[10] The desertion of entire dioceses by their Christian inhabitants is attested by Sāwīrūs Ibn al-Muqaffaʿ, who clearly associates the terrible famine that prevailed in the Nile Valley during the 960s with the decline of some of the episcopal sees in the same region:

[9] Eliyahu Ashtor, 'Un Mouvement migratoire au haut Moyen Âge: migrations de l'Irak vers les pays Méditerranéens', *Annales: Histoire, Sciences Sociales* 27 (1972), 185–214; Muḥammad Ibn Yaḥyā al-Ṣūlī, *Akhbār al-Rāḍī billāh wa'l-Muttaqī billāh: Histoire de la dynastie abbaside de 322 à 333/934 à 944*, trans. Marius Canard, 2 vols. (Algiers, 1946–50), p. 251. This event was a part of an extended period of drought that lasted from 330/941–2 to 334/945–6.

[10] Marius Canard, 'Baghdād au IVe siècle de l'Hégire (Xe siècle de l'ère chrétienne)', *Arabica* 9 (1962), 282–3.

The famine did not cease until the end of seven successive years, and it was great in all of Egypt, so that the land was depopulated ... and the hunger ... prevailed. ... *A number of the Episcopal sees* were abandoned ... joining the populated sees which were neighboring to them.[11]

A differential tax burden and special taxes imposed on minorities during periods of dearth and bankruptcy is another mechanism that can lead to the desertion or to mass conversion, and certainly to the decline of weakened communities. Scholars who wrote during the first half of the twentieth century assumed, as a matter of fact, that even the regular taxes (the poll tax *jizya* and the land tax *kharāj*) that were imposed only on dhimmis (Christians and Jews) were enough to lead many to convert. This notion, however, is not as popular as it was fifty years ago, and very few scholars still believe that the attempt to avoid land and poll taxes led masses of people to convert to Islam. The temptation to impose additional taxes on politically weak (and often economically rich) minorities augments during periods of dearth and when governments find it more difficult to cover their increasing financial debts and the financial pressure leads masses of people to emigrate. The crises of the eleventh century provided enough occasions for repeated attempts to levy additional taxes upon congregational minorities.

The association between an increased burden of taxes and outbound immigration was made by the head of the Academy of Jerusalem during the late 1020s while he was warning the Fatimid

[11] Sāwīrūs Ibn al-Muqaffaʿ, *History of the patriarchs of the Egyptian Church: known as the history of the Holy Church*, vol. II, part 2, *Khaël III – Shenouti II (AD 880–1066)*, trans. and annotation Aziz Suryal Atiya, Yassa ʿAbd al-Masīḥ and Oswald H. E. Burmester, Publications de la Société d'Archéologie Copte, 3–5, 11–5, Textes et Documents (Cairo: Société d'Archéologie Copte, 1948–59), pp. 134–45; emphasis the present author.

governor of the city that increased taxes would lead to the desertion of 'half of the population'.[12]

The differential decline of religious minorities is attested by Bar Hebraeus when estimating the number of Christians who survived the famine of the late 1060s in the city of Tinnis. Bar Hebraeus does not specify if the reason for the decline in numbers was the conversion of the Christian population, the death of members of the community because of the famine and the pestilence, or because of their emigration, but he asserts that only a small part of the pre-famine Christian population remained in the city: 'In . . . Tannis (the Biblical Zoan), a short time before the famine there were counted three thousand men who [paid] the poll tax (jyziya), and during the time of the famine fewer than one hundred souls were found in it.'[13]

The connection between famines, outbound migrations, desertion of agricultural provinces by their Christian inhabitants and invasions of the Turks is further attested by Matthew of Edessa. While relating the famine that prevailed in Asia Minor in 1079–80, he describes domino effects and a mass migration from the Christian regions:

At the beginning of the year 1079–80 a severe famine occurred throughout all the lands of the venerators of the Cross, lands which are located on this side of the Mediterranean Sea . . . The cultivation of the land was interrupted, there was a shortage of food, the cultivators and laborers decreased due to the sword and enslavement and so famine spread throughout the whole land . . . *Many areas became depopulated; the Oriental [Armenian] nation began to decline, and the country of the Romans became desolate*; neither

[12] Moshe Gil, *Palestine during the first Muslim period*, 3 vols. (Tel Aviv University Press, 1983), vol. II, pp. 63 (no. 37) (Hebrew).

[13] Bar Hebraeus (Abū al-Faraj), *The chronography*, translated from the Syriac by Ernest A. Wallis Budge, 2 vols. (Oxford University Press, 1932), p. 246.

food nor security for the individual was to be found anywhere except in Edessa and its confines.[14]

The scale of the desertion of Christians from southeastern Anatolia can be gathered from this description of Matthew of Edessa:

Security of life did not exist in Antioch ... Cilicia ... Marash, and in ... their surrounding areas. For all the peoples rose up en masse and came to these regions in countless droves, tens of thousands deluging the various areas. Because of the tremendous number of these peoples, the whole land was covered as if by hordes of locusts ... very important and illustrious personages ... roamed about begging [for food]; indeed our eyes witnessed all this. Because of the famine and the vagabonds there was a great amount of mortality throughout the whole land and it was virtually impossible to bury all those who had died. The land was filled with their corpses, and to such an extent that the animals and birds grew tired of feeding on them ... the land stank ...

*All this was the beginning of the destruction of the Oriental and Greek peoples*; for because of our sins, we were punished by God, the righteous judge ...[15]

Attaleiates observes a similar phenomenon that occurred in western Anatolia when large numbers of people fled inland and to Constantinople itself.[16] Similar desertions were observed in many other parts of Asia Minor.[17]

## INBOUND IMMIGRATION

Inbound immigration to the region was limited to nomadic tribes who agreed, during their quest for warmer refuge, to be converted

[14] Matthew of Edessa, *Armenia and the Crusades, tenth to twelfth centuries: the chronicle of Matthew of Edessa*, trans. Ara E. Dostourian (Lanham, MD: University Press of America, 1993), 2.72, p. 143; emphasis the present author.

[15] Ibid., 2.73, pp. 143–4; emphasis the present author.

[16] Michael Attaleiates, *Historia*, ed. Immanuel Bekker, Corpus Scriptorum Historiae Byzantinae 36 (Bonn: Weber, 1853), pp. 211, 267–8.

[17] Speros Vryonis, Jr, *The decline of medieval Hellenism in Asia Minor and the process of Islamization from the eleventh through the fifteenth century* (Berkeley: University of California Press, 1971), pp. 169–70.

in order to be admitted by Islamic authorities as legitimate dwellers of the region. Says Bar Hebraeus:

The Amir Sāljuk . . . went forth from the land of Turan . . . to the land of Iran . . . under the pretence that they were shepherds. And when they saw that Persia was flourishing with Islam, they took counsel together and said, 'If we do not enter the Faith of the people of the country in which we desire [to live] and make a pact with them (or conform to their customs), no man will cleave to us, and we shall be a small and solitary people.' And they . . . sent to the city of Zandak, which . . . was in the neighbourhood of the desert in which they were pasturing, and they asked the governor there for a learned man who would teach them how to worship God. And the governor with great gladness sent to them . . . an old man, together with gifts and presents, and he taught them.[18]

Another tribe, which included altogether ten thousand tents and which used to raid Islamic territories in the regions of Balasghun and Kashgar, was converted to Islam in 1043. Ibn al-Athīr, who relates this event, describes the converts as pastoralists who slaughtereed twenty thousand head of sheep during their first feast of sacrifice. After their conversion, they were scattered throughout the lands, each district absorbing a thousand tents.[19]

Another attempt of mass Islamization of nomads is recorded during the cold spell of 1045–7, with nomads arriving from lands as remote as Tibet. They did not convert to Islam, but 'remained friendly'.[20] We can safely assume that similar events occurred elsewhere.

[18] Bar Hebraeus, *Chronography*, p. 218.

[19] ʿIzz al-Dīn Abū al-Ḥasan ʿAlī Ibn al-Athīr, *al-Kāmil fī al-taʾrīkh*, ed. Carl J. Tornberg, 13 vols. (Leiden: E. J. Brill, 1862–71; reprinted Beirut: Dār Ṣāder, Dār Beyrouth, 1965–7), vol. IX, p. 520; for an English translation, see *The chronicle of Ibn al-Athīr for the crusading period from al-Kāmil fī'l-taʾrīkh*, trans. Donald S. Richards, 3 vols. (Aldershot: Ashgate, Variorum, 2006–8), vol. I, p. 56.

[20] Ibid., vol. IX, p. 535; English translation, vol. I, p. 62.

## FORCED CONVERSION AND DESECRATION OF SACRED PLACES

'Apart from the days of al-Ḥākim', says Moshe Gil, 'we have no explicit evidence of mass conversion of Christians to Islam [during the early Muslim period]'.[21] Milka Levy-Rubin points to an attempt that occurred in Samaria during the hunger of the 840s, but she agrees that such attempts were rare and that Islamic laws that clearly forbade forced conversion were generally kept in the eastern Mediterranean.[22]

And indeed, the religious frenzy of al-Ḥākim, his decision to destroy churches and synagogues and to enforce Islamization throughout his realm,[23] was presented by many as reflecting his insanity, although it actually highlights a turning point in the history of conversion to Islam. The possible connection between the hunger that prevailed in Egypt and his decision to destroy the Church of the Holy Sepulchre and other churches in Egypt has been suggested in previous chapters.[24] Al-Ḥākim's concurrent decision to compel the Jews and the Christians either to embrace Islam or to leave his realm for the Byzantine lands was certainly unprecedented. Many did convert and returned to their original faiths only after the end of the persecutions,

[21] Moshe Gil, *A history of Palestine, 634–1099* (Cambridge University Press, 1992), p. 221.

[22] Milka Levy-Rubin, 'New evidence relating to the process of Islamization in Palestine in the early Muslim period – the case of Samaria', *Journal of the Economic and Social History of the Orient* 43.3 (2000), 257–76. For the prohibition of forced conversion, see Fattal, *Statut légal.*

[23] Aḥmad Ibn ʿAlī al-Maqrīzī, *Ittiʿāẓ al-ḥunafāʾ bi-akhbār al-aʾimma al-fāṭimiyyīn al-khulafāʾ*, ed. Jamāl al-Dīn al-Shayyāl and Muḥammad Ḥilmī Muḥammad Aḥmad, 3 vols. (Cairo, 1967–73), vol. II, p. 75.

[24] Chapter 3, pp. 33–5.

but many others 'have left behind their creed and dropped their religion'.[25]

The decrees were revoked during al-Ḥākim's own lifetime. The *Synaxaire arabe jacobite* maintains that the persecutions lasted for only seven years (or for eight years and a month in another passage). The Caliph himself permitted the reconstruction of most of the destroyed churches and synagogues.[26]

The destruction of the Church of the Holy Sepulchre was not the first attempt to conspire against it. An early attempt to pillage the church and set it on fire is recorded in AD 842, one of the earlier rounds of cold spells (see Chapter 3 above) that hit the Jazira in the first half of the ninth century. The cold spell, which was accompanied by a drought in the Levant, was described by Michael the Syrian: 'Seeds did not germinate until April, when it rained'.[27] A plague that followed spread for two years throughout the Jazira, Syria, Palestine and the coast, leading to the desertion of many villages and fields.[28] A rebellion of thirty thousand 'starved and naked people' that broke out in Palestine under the leadership of a certain Tamīm Abū Ḥarb, led to the pillaging, killing and spreading of destruction everywhere. Tamīm succeeded in taking Jerusalem and started destroying mosques and churches while threatening to

25 According to Ibn al-Athīr, *Kāmil*, vol. IX, p. 209. Maqrīzī, *Mawāʿiẓ*, vol. II, p. 496, and Bar Hebraeus *Chronography*, vol. I, p. 184 speak about thousands of churches that were destroyed in the Fatimid kingdom at that time. See also *Histoire de Yaḥyā Ibn Saʿīd d'Antioche*, facsimile 2, *Patrologia Orientalis* 23.3 (Turnhout: Brepols, 1924), p. 511; Gil, *History of Palestine*, pp. 376–7.

26 Gil, *History of Palestine*, pp. 377–8; for the letter see Moshe Gil, *Palestine*, vol. II, no. 26. According to *Le Synaxaire arabe jacobite (rédaction copte)*, texte arabe publié, traduit et annoté par René Basset, *Patrologia Orientalis* 1.3 (Turnhout: Brepols, 1904), p. 560.

27 *Chronique de Michel le Syrien*, ed. Jean-Baptiste Chabot, 5 vols. (Paris, 1899–1924; reprinted Brussels, 1963), vol. III, p. 109 and vol. IV, p. 542.

28 Ibid., vol. III, pp. 109–10 and vol. IV, p. 543.

set the Church of the Holy Sepulchre on fire. Finally, he was bribed by the Patriarch to vacate the city.[29]

Several years later, during a (probably local) famine that occurred in the second half of the 840s, the food shortage and rising prices led to the mass conversion of the inhabitants, who attempted to be exempted from the *jizya*. Levy-Rubin, who edited the text, translates part of it as follows:

> [Then] there came a great rise in prices and three *uqqāt* of flour were sold for a *dīnār*. Many people were compelled to take charity because of the pains in their stomach and the hunger. How many left their faith as a result of the terrible rise in prices and because they were exhausted by the *jizya*! Many sons and families who left the faith, were lost. [But] God in his mercy watched over him who endured patiently, and comforted him with satiety and well-being.[30]

The last attempt to conspire against the Church of the Holy Sepulchre occurred during the hunger of 1056, following the inability of the impoverished Byzantine Empire to supply Egypt with grain. The furious Fatimid caliph ordered the expulsion of three thousand Christians from Jerusalem, the locking of the Church of the Holy Sepulchre and the looting of all its treasures.[31]

Four of the five recorded attempts to harm the Church of the Holy Sepulchre occurred, therefore, during periods of extreme

[29] Ibid., vol. III, p. 103 and vol. IV, pp. 541–2; Gil, *History of Palestine*, p. 296; Bar Hebraeus, *Chronography*, p. 139.

[30] Levy-Rubin, 'New evidence', p. 266.

[31] See Gil, *History of Palestine*, p. 380, Abbas Hamdānī, 'Byzantine–Fatimid relations before the Battle of Manzikert', *Byzantine Studies* 3 (1974), 169–79; Wolfgang Felix, *Byzanz und die islamische Welt im frühen 11. Jarhundert: Geschichte der politischen Beziehungen von 1001 bis 1055*, Byzantina Vindobonensia 14 (Vienna: Verlag der Österreichischen Akademie der Wissenschaften, 1981), pp. 80–1. The acts were explained as a reaction to the Byzantine decision to stop the invocation of the names of the Fatimid caliphs during Friday services in the mosque of Constantinople.

dearth and hunger. This concurrence cannot be incidental and characterizes the behaviour of the Seljuks too.

The hunger in Egypt during the mid 1050s was also accompanied by the desecration of monasteries and by attacks on Christian property. Sāwīrūs b. al-Muqaffaʿ describes cruel attacks on Christian communities in Upper Egypt, including the systematic destruction of Christian farmhouses and monasteries and the massacre of monks.[32]

Anti-Christian persecutions also characterize the behaviour of the Seljuks towards Christian minorities since the conversion of Tughril to Islam, or since his decision – taken most probably in 1048 – to adhere to the Caliph's demand and avoid harming Muslims in return for legitimacy, and certainly since the conquest of Baghdad in 1055. Tughril attempted to direct the destructive energies of his men towards Christian rather than Muslim targets. The differential destruction of Christian targets is manifested during the cold spell of 1056–8 in the Seljuk raid on Melitene (Malatya). After the killing, enslaving of citizens and looting of property,[33] the Seljuks also destroyed the Monastery of Bar Gagai, which they encountered in the vicinity of the city, to such an extent that it 'was never inhabited again'.[34] Later they raided the Muslim city of Sanjar, but this was because this city did not accept their authority during the civil war. The temptation was probably too big to avoid.[35]

[32] Sāwīrūs, *History* (Cairo), vol. II, part 3, pp. 314–15.

[33] Matthew of Edessa, *Armenia and the Crusades*, 2.11, p. 94; Bar Hebraeus, *Chronography*, p. 212; *Anonymi auctoris chronicon ad AC 1234 pertinens, II*, translated by Albert Abouna with an introduction and notes by Jean M. Fiey, *Corpus Scriptorum Christianorum Orientalium*, 354 (Scriptores Syri, 154) (Louvain: Secrétariat du Corpus SCO, 1974), 2.33 (p. 234). Bar Hebraeus relates other descriptions of these events: 'Joseph the monk . . . wrote three discourses on the event, and Mar John the son of Shoshan composed four discourses on the destruction of Melitene' (*Chronography*, p. 213).

[34] Bar Hebraeus, *Chronography*, p. 213.

[35] Ibid., p. 210; Ibn al-Athīr, *Kāmil*, vol. IX, p. 630–1; English translation, p. 112. Ibn al-Jawzī, *Mirʾat al-zamān*, the years 1056–86, pp. 22–3 do not refer to the destruction of the mosque.

During the 1060s, while the Seljuks were diverting their energies to state-building in Baghdad, they continued their destructive raids on Christian communities, marked by mass murder and the pillaging and destruction of churches. In 1062–3 they attacked Armenian territories '[like] bloodthirsty wolves . . . [filling] the vast plain . . . with blood, captives, and merciless slaughter – something we are not able to relate',[36] and in 1064–5 they 'subject[ed] [Armenia] to the sword and enslavement, killing many Christians that no one is able to relate . . . this disaster to the Christian faithful'.[37] Finally they captured the capital, Ani,

> a city that previously contained 1,001 churches . . . They massacred the believers heaping their bodies like heaps of stones, fetching the big cross from the dome of the cathedral and using it later as a threshold of their mosque . . . for them to trample.[38]

Another testimony for the selective demographic effects of Turkish raids on the Armenian minority is provided by Matthew of Edessa in 1066–7:

> A Persian emir . . . collected troops and desolated many regions, bloodily massacring the Christian faithful . . . The emir marched forth with a very great number of troops and wintered at the foot of the Black Mountains. There was a tremendous amount of bloodshed and slaughter in the whole region, and many of the holy monks were subjected to the edge of the sword and to being burned . . . *Many monasteries and villages were burned to the ground, and their traces are still evident today*. Thus the Black Mountains and the entire region from one end to the other were covered with blood of monks, priests, men and women, aged and young. This is the sort of calamitous destruction which the wicked and vicious beast Afshin brought upon the faithful.[39]
>
> In this same year . . . Gümüshtigin . . . came forth from the sultan's court . . . he went against the Christians . . . causing rivers of their blood to

[36] Matthew of Edessa, *Armenia and the Crusades*, 2.15, p. 97. [37] Ibid., 2.20, p. 101.
[38] Ibid., 2.21, p. 102. [39] Ibid., 2.46, p. 125; emphasis the present author.

flow . . . devastating the district of T'lkhum and mercilessly slaughtering those who had escaped the previous invasions . . . The Turks burned everything in sight. Wielding the sword and inflicting deadly wounds, they caused the slaughter of all the distinguished men of the district of Ḥiṣn Mānṣūr and they led into captivity noble ladies together with their attractive sons and daughters.[40]

It is clear, therefore, that if one is looking for incidents big enough to influence the demography, one should look for them in the Christian sources and not in the Muslim narratives, which usually avoid mentioning them.

The Seljuks' trail of destruction did not stop in Asia Minor until the end of the climatic crisis during the mid 1080s. Other nomadic tribes of Turkish origin, who invaded Asia Minor at the same time, were not behaving any better.

The thirteenth-century epic poem *Danishmendnameh*, for example, details the mythical history of al-Malik al-Ghāzī (the warrior for the sake of Islam) Danishmend, who was the leader of tribes that were later referred to as the Banū Danishmend and which spread destruction in Anatolia and the Jazira between 1086 and 1104. The poem contains a significant number of references to forced and violent conversion, probably attesting to the fact that such behaviour was not considered rare and certainly not unthinkable. Al-Malik Danishmend, the hero of the poem, is thus presented: 'I am al-Ghāzī Danishmend, the destroyer of churches and of towers.'[41] Elsewhere the epos relates the simultaneous conversion of five thousand people to Islam and the mass murder of five thousand

40 Ibid., 2.47, pp. 125–6. For the destruction of the city of Manzikert by Alp Arslān prior to the battle and as a result of insults directed years earlier to Tughril Beg, see 2.56, p. 130; for the month-long unsuccessful siege on Edessa and the destruction of its hinterland, see 2.56, pp. 131–2.

41 *La Geste de Melik Danishmend Gazi – étude critique du Danishmendname*, ed. and trans. Irenen Melikoff (Paris: Bibliothèque Archéologique, 1960), p. 270.

others. One of the stories of conversion is the forced Islamization of Sisiya Comana near Malatya. Al-Ghāzī swore to convert the citizens and fulfilled his oath. The new Muslims did not adhere to their new faith, and al-Ghāzī forced them, even by flogging, to pray five times a day and refrain from drinking wine. The forced Islamization evaporated with the arrival of a Christian army. The new Muslims deserted their new faith, killed the governor, destroyed mosques and converted them into monasteries. The fate of the city of Yankoniya Euchaita in northern Anatolia was similar, and the inhabitants of another city, Mankuriya Gangra to the north of Ankara, were forced to desert their city. Similar testimonies are scattered throughout this epic poem, and despite the difficulty of relying on such a source, it seems that forced conversions were a quite common phenomenon at the time.[42]

The destruction of churches, monasteries and sacred places and the widespread cases of forced conversion had begun during the hunger that prevailed in Egypt in 1004–9, and were led by an insane Egyptian caliph. His insanity was used as an excuse for his diversion from the norm. The wave of destruction of churches and monasteries led by the Seljuks and the Banū Danishmend, during the 1060s and 1070s, was probably perceived as additional evidence of their adherence to Islam and did not reduce their legitimacy as rulers.

The wave of destruction and pillage of Christian cities and communities, accompanied by repeated attempts at forced conversion and mass murder, initiated a wave of millenarian prophecies. One is brought by Matthew of Edessa, describing the rise and fall of the Seljuks. Matthew begins his prophecy with the events that occurred in 1036–7 while the Seljuks were gaining strength. He compares the severity of the events to the crucifixion of Christ:

[42] Ibid., pp. 204–5, 257, 270, 275–80, 284, 287, 367, 380, 381, 384, 414–15, 421.

[In 1036–7] the sun darkened with a frightful and horrible appearance. For, as it became dark at the crucifixion of Christ . . . the sun's light was hidden and darkness clothed it. The mountains and all the rocks, shaken, trembled; the vast large Mediterranean Sea, moving back and forth, billowed, and all mankind mourned and wept, horror-struck with fear as if dead.

The frightful omens led the Armenian king and the Patriarch to send for a holy man named John for religious interpretation. The holy man prophesied about the Jazira in the following decades and about the fate of the 'Christian nations' who were going to be the only nations to suffer from famine and from the invasion of the Seljuks:

Henceforth there will take place invasions by the infidels, the abominable forces of the Turks, the accursed sons of Ham, against the Christian nations; and the whole land will be consumed by the sword. All the nations of the Christian faithful will suffer through famine and enslavement. *Many regions will become uninhabited.* The power of the saints will be removed from the land *and many churches will be destroyed to their foundations* . . . and the land will be ravaged by the sword and enslavement for sixty years. Then the valiant nation called the Franks will rise up; with a great number of troops they will capture the holy city of Jerusalem . . .

Matthew describes the expected end of the reign of the Turks as the end of the famine and drought:

The offspring of men and beasts will multiply, and the springs will gush forth with water. The fields will produce more than before. From then on famine will come upon the country of the Persians for many years, to such an extent that people will attack and devour one another. Out of fear of the might of the Roman emperor many Persian chiefs will leave their towns and regions and, without warring, flee to the other side of the Pyramus River.[43]

The rapid decline of congregational minorities during the eleventh century was therefore not only the result of an insane ruler

[43] Matthew of Edessa, *Armenia and the Crusades*, 1.64, pp. 56–60, emphasis the present author.

(al-Ḥākim) or regular taxes; it was also the result of long and lingering periods of dearth that were followed by mass migration, by death and by the rise of new political elites (the Seljuks or the Banū Danishmend) that ignored, at least temporarily and during the crisis only, the norms that protected these minorities. The famine, together with the destruction of minorities, appears as a matter of fact in all the descriptions of the decline of the Christians or the Jews in this part of the world.

When the crisis came to an end and the authorities returned to their normative behaviour it was more difficult for the minorities to fully recover. The decline of Christianity in Asia Minor, Mesopotamia, the Jazira, the Levant and in Egypt continued as before, but started anew from a lower level than in any previous era.

CHAPTER ELEVEN

# Reflections

## CLIMATIC CRISES AND THE *LONGUE DURÉE*

Attempts to explain cultural and societal declines in terms of climatic disasters are often discarded as deterministic. Historians prefer long-term social, economic or cultural processes or even short-term political events – such as conquests, the rise of new dynasties or the takeover of cities and countries by their rivals – as valid interpretations for declines. Even unique disasters like earthquakes and outbursts of volcanoes are considered legitimate explanations for the decline and decay of cultures, unlike climate, hunger and lingering periods of dearth. The protagonists of the resilience theory take this tendency one step further, extending the alleged effects of the processes of the *longue durée* across civilizations and maintaining that even the most destructive events of decline and collapse were no more than temporary fluctuations in the long-term developments of cultures.

The cultural and societal results of the crisis of the eleventh century emphasize the relevance of climate in historical reasoning and bring nature back to the front of the stage of historical discussions. Climate changes trigger famines, and lingering famines are usually beyond the ability of human beings to withstand. Civilizations are altered and transformed by calamities, although they usually succeed in finding, when the crisis is over, ways to reconstruct new stable societal structures and a new equilibrium that resemble, to a certain degree, the pre-calamity social order. Differences between pre- and post-calamity cultures, however, are often discerned. Many pre-calamity cities continued to exist, but in a diminished and sometimes even totally different form and location. The spatial and demographic divisions of the population between the ethnic and the congregational minorities, such as the Christians, Muslims and Jews, were considerably altered. Agricultural methods that were developed in the east during centuries of comparative abundance continued to be employed, but entire agricultural provinces were abandoned. Islam continued to prevail, but even the basic structure of Islamic education was no longer the same.

The statement that a calamity can be the reason for a change is probably obvious. There is no reason to assume that natural disasters are not as important and influential in the development of civilizations as wars, political manipulations or the whims of this or that leader. The calamity of the eleventh century, which struck some of the most established civilizations of the eastern Mediterranean, clearly shows that no pre-modern society was immune to climatic disasters, and that many had to undergo very fast – and often very cruel – transformations in order to survive such events.

Climatic disasters are ephemeral occurrences, and when they come to an end they are often forgotten: new generations are born, new bureaucracies are established and new intellectual elites are created. But the transformations themselves are not ephemeral and cannot be explained only within the context of the processes of the *longue durée*. Behaviours are modified, new actors are introduced, powerful kings are weakened and villains become saints.

It is probably more accurate to refer to the climatic collapse itself not as an event but rather as a process whose details should be studied very carefully. Both the climatic conditions and the responses of the affected civilizations to them develop over space and time. Droughts and food crises are not continuous, nor is their severity dependent on the ability of the administrations to accumulate surpluses and to distribute them efficiently. The severity of a famine depends on the severity of previous events almost as much as it is dependent on the severity of the current event.

Administrators usually prepare themselves only for scenarios, which they have encountered in the past. However, the droughts of biblical dimensions were not recorded for at least a millennium, and cold spells that lingered for decades were not recorded since the fifth century. The bureaucracies of the eastern Mediterranean were not prepared for the length and severity of the famine, and therefore they collapsed.

## THE REGIONAL AND THE GLOBAL

The collapse of the eastern Mediterranean was a regional event. The region is certainly vast and important enough to justify a volume dedicated to such a happening, but the result of this collapse is probably only part of a wider occurrence. Other regions, and certainly the regions that border on the eastern Mediterranean, were also affected by climatic changes. The insufficient rises in the Nile Valley, for example, were undoubtedly the results of droughts in eastern Africa that probably affected the Ethiopian civilization of the time as well. The lingering cold spells that prevailed around the Dnieper Basin and along the Caspian Sea were probably also felt in Rus and in the steppes as well. It is even possible to assume that the beginning of the Islamic invasion to the Indian subcontinent during the reign of Maḥmūd of Ghaznī was partially affected by the same deteriorated climatic conditions that led to Maḥmūd's own defeat in his struggle against the swelling wave of dislocated nomads, and if it did, then the climatic disaster of the eleventh century accelerated the Islamization of the Indian subcontinent as much as it affected the Islamization of other regions in the eastern subcontinent.

The climatic change of the eleventh century, however, affected regions in at least two diametrically opposing directions. The region of western Europe, for example, underwent a climatic change at the same time, but it was a change for the better and the region benefitted from a period of unprecedented warmth, mildness and growth that is known today as the Medieval Warm Period (MWP) or the Medieval Optimum.

Scientists dealing with climate change, who were also the first to refer to this very period as the MWP, calculated a considerable warming of the global climate that brought the global mean temperature of the eleventh century almost to the mean degree of the global temperature that was calculated for the late 1980s. Many of these studies dealing with the reconstruction of the Medieval Warm, however, attempt to ameliorate previous results and to determine if the mid-eleventh-century mean global temperature was actually as warm as it was during the last decade of the twentieth century, or if it was slightly lower. The scientific agenda is therefore directed to the reconstruction of *global* warm events in the past in order to better understand the reason for the present climate change and to be prepared for, or to avoid, *future* changes that might harm the world if the change is indeed anthropogenic. Questions about the relevance of the change to the local and to the regional are usually answered by horrible scenarios, depicting disastrous catastrophes that will virtually destroy important parts of the world if the change continues as it did during the last decades of the twentieth century. It is true that the millenarian prophecies will materialize only if the change is indeed anthropogenic, and if the pollution that assumably led to the change continues.

But concentration on the global rather than the regional and the local is not the only way to study such a change, and the millenarian prophecies ('the future flooding of Manhattan') do not refer to all the possible effects of such a global warming. The medieval warming, for instance was most probably not anthropogenic, and it affected humanity in at least two different directions: western Europe prospered, while the eastern Mediterranean declined. Mild winters were the lot of the west, leading to better yields, an increased population, a thriving economy and even to an intellectual and cultural renaissance, whereas the east was affected by severe cold spells, droughts, hunger and pestilence and suffered from a decrease in population and declining economies and cultures.

If the reason for these diametrically opposing trends is indeed the same – a global warming – then what was the actual effect of the eleventh-century warming on medieval societies? Did it lead to their decline or to their prosperity? How can we calculate and assess cultural changes? And if one can learn anything from past experience, what will be the real effect of global warming on mankind in the future? Are we going to prosper from the change as did western Europe during the eleventh century, or to suffer like the eastern Mediterranean? Are we going to collapse, as many intellectuals and scientists convincingly preach, or to change towards a yet unknown end?

I do not know the answer; I can only lament the limited participation of trained historians in the world climatic discourse that has been exciting the entire globe, politically, economically and culturally since the 1950s when the idea of an imminent global change was first broached. The discourse is led and conducted within the scientific community with a very limited participation of historians, despite the obvious historical questions it raises.

Earth and climate scientists cannot measure past phenomena instrumentally, and they depend therefore on indirect signals reflecting past events. The annual growth of tree rings is a reliable 'proxy' reflecting past events of freeze or drought, and the annual change in the width of these rings is the measured 'signal'.

Rocks, glaciers, ruined buildings, dead coral reefs, sediments of the Dead Sea and even the isotopic composition of certain chemical compounds are a few among the scores of 'proxies' whose signals are measured all over the world. But even the accumulation of all the measured signals is not sufficient for an appropriate reconstruction of regional past events. Proxies are usually too scarce and poorly distributed, and the measured dating is usually too vague to be relevant for the reconstruction of human cultures and past landscapes. They are, however, very valuable statistically for the calculation of the average global temperatures and hence the preference of scientists who depend on measuring signals for the global over the regional and the local.

If historical evidence is available, it is usually better dated and is usually interpreted within the framework of its culture and region, which implies a higher degree of regionalism in historical studies and a preference for the local over the global. The diametrically opposed effects of the same climate change in the two neighbouring regions of western Europe and the eastern Mediterranean probably reveal the difficulty of using a global yardstick to assess the change and of implying the low resolution of proxies in the reconstruction of past civilizations. The trained historians that do participate in the discourse, however, contribute their own data or check their own evidence vis-à-vis calculations. But the discourse is still directed by global questions, not regional ones.

The reduced participation of trained historians in leading of climatic (and other scientific) discourses is a matter of another important discussion. It is probably the result of many processes that reduced their/our relevance in the discourses that excite the entire (real) world. Is it because of our denial of natural reasoning of historical and cultural events? Is it the overwhelming success of the critical trend that led many historians to draw away from empirical data and scientific reasoning?

It is probably not too late to go back to Jean-Jacques Rousseau, who was the first to notice, in his correspondence with Voltaire about the cultural meaning of the earthquake of Lisbon (1755), that disasters are social constructs, that they are defined according to the existing cultural norms, and that their importance depends on the identity of the affected societies and regions. He says: 'You might have wished . . . that the quake had occurred in the middle of a wilderness rather than in Lisbon . . . But we do not speak of them, because they do not cause any harm to the Gentlemen of the cities, the only men of whom we take account.'[1]

I do understand the desire to find a satisfactory scientific explanation for climatic disasters. I was trained as a scientist and one of my most cited articles deals with earthquakes, and therefore I was also tempted to find 'a viable scientific solution' for the medieval disaster. But I fully understand the limits of such an approach. The attempt to connect 'scientific signals' and to find a 'scientific explanation' for all the measured data led scientists in the past to miss the main point and look for the average 'global change', which is probably less important than the 'regional change' in our case. Regional testimonies have not yet been reconstructed: How did the Medieval Warm affect eleventh-century China? Did it thrive or decline? And what do we know about the Indian subcontinent? The

[1] *The collected writings of Rousseau*, ed. Roger D. Masters and Christopher Kelly, 3 vols. (Hanover: University Press of New England, 1990), vol. III, p. 110.

archives and archaeology of the East probably contain as accurate and as meaningful data as the signals that are currently measured in tree rings or icebergs. In the present volume I suggest that the climatic collapse of the East was the result of concurrent disasters that occurred in three usually independent climatic zones: in eastern Africa, in the Mediterranean, and in central Asia (probably the barometric 'Siberian High'). When historical data is properly understood, and when new regions (China, India?) are included in the model, it will probably be easier to develop a model of this rare occurrence and extend it to a better understanding of the cultural effects of climatic change.

## THE FATE OF CLASSICAL HERITAGE

Centres where Classical heritage was taught and developed shifted geographically. When they ceased to exist in one place they continued to flourish elsewhere, moving from Greece to Rome, from Carthage to Hippo, and from the western Mediterranean to the eastern Mediterranean. In the tenth and early eleventh centuries culture flourished in the eastern Mediterranean: in Constantinople, Fustat, Baghdad, Damascus and Isfahan. After the collapse of the centres of the East, during the mid eleventh century, they moved even further, to the Iberian Peninsula. Classical heritage was resilient to the decline of geographical centres of Classical Antiquity in the West and continued to flourish in the eastern Mediterranean: in thriving cities that continued to expand and outgrow their predecessors when contemporaneous cities were vanishing in the West; in the schools in which law and grammar, arts and letters were taught in Constantinople, centuries after similar schools and libraries ceased to exist in the West; in the libraries and schools of Damascus, Rayy and Baghdad, where an entire corpus of Greek philosophy, science and medicine was preserved and taught.

For medieval historians, the Roman Empire did not come to an end in the fifth century but rather continued to exist as the Holy Roman Empire straight through to their own time. For them, the *Imperium Romanum* still existed although the rule over it had been transferred from the Romans to the Byzantines and then to the Holy Roman Empire. The *Imperium* was conceived as an idea and an ideal that can be transformed and altered. It was a process rather than a geographical entity.

The division of the course of history into two sharply defined periods, before and after the 'decline' of Rome, began only in the Renaissance, following the decline of the Byzantines, the Holy Roman Empire and Classical Antiquity itself. It was during the Renaissance that the division line was set either at the adoption of Christianity as a state religion in the fourth century AD, when the Roman Empire began to be ruled by the 'Barbarian' emperors, or even earlier with the transformation from republic to empire.

Petrarch identified the locus of Rome with the legacy of its culture, ideas and ideals and with the representation of Classical Antiquity itself. Applying all to Rome alone, he asked: 'What else, then, is all history, if not the praise of Rome?'

The culprits were to change later, but the *culpa* remained the same. Scholars sought the reason for the 'decline' – or even the 'fall' or the 'collapse' – of Rome, identifying the decline of the city with the decline of its civilization. Until the beginning of the twentieth century, it was either the Church or the Barbarians who were blamed. Henri Pirenne rehabilitated both, suggesting a new actor to bear the guilt: the Muslims, who conquered the southern Mediterranean, truncating it from the north. But Pirenne's thesis was as Eurocentric as those of his predecessors and still attempted to explain the decline of the *Imperium* as the reason for the decline of Classical Antiquity.

The collapse, or even discontinuity, of Classical heritage, if there was any, did not occur in the sixth century. Peter Brown has clearly shown that the period between the third and eighth centuries AD can be interpreted not as a decadence of the Roman 'golden age' and Classical civilization as depicted by the Renaissance-Gibbonesque school, nor as an obscure period as Pirenne depicted it, but as a period of immense cultural innovation. Classical heritage did not collapse during the crisis of the eastern Mediterranean in 1055, and it was almost immediately replaced by the thriving new culture of Sunni Islam in Baghdad and by the creation of new intellectual centres in the Iberian Peninsula. Civilizations are more resilient than their physical manifestations in this or that region. Classical heritage continued wandering around the Mediterranean, adopting different appearances and reaching new summits in different locations. The constant stream of human greatness continued to flow. It was not dependent on one locus only, be it Rome or Baghdad, Seville or Florence. But many characteristics of Classical heritage were lost on the way. Rome as a centre declined during the crisis of the fifth century; Constantinople declined for many centuries and returned to its previous greatness only during the sixteenth century. Classical cities in the eastern Mediterranean lost their importance, eastern Christianity declined and the victory of Islam was established during the mid eleventh century.

## EAST AND WEST

The number of modern historical schools that study the history of the eastern Mediterranean of the eleventh century corresponds to the number of civilizations that flourished there at the time. There is a modern historical school for each language, and each is confined by the geographical extent of each of these civilizations. Byzantinists are trained to read Greek (or Latin) but not Arabic; Orientalists are trained to read Arabic, Coptic, Armenian, Syriac or Persian and their interest in what happened beyond 'their' linguistic or ethnic territory is occasional and partial.

Most contemporaneous western sources, on the other hand, were written in Latin and do not suffer from the linguistic division that determines the history of the East. Western European historians can read, and therefore are usually more interested in, documents whose provenances are the various regions of Latin-speaking Europe. They are less interested, however, in what happened in the East in the same period.

The fact that the crisis of the eleventh century was documented in so many sources and was written in so many languages is probably one of the reasons for its being ignored until now. The only way to understand the scope of the events and to comprehend their real magnitude and effects is by the simultaneous reading of many sources written in many languages and deciphering a puzzle that is played on vast regional dimensions.

Such a solution, however, is opposed to the way we teach students, opposed to the very definition of professionalism and excellence in historical studies. One has to wait until he receives tenure to dare think about material that is clearly beyond his philological reach, and usually by then it is already too late. It seems to me, although I cannot prove it, that disasters of this magnitude were very rare occurrences, affecting the eastern Mediterranean once in a millennium on average. A very similar event, which is still unexplained, was the societal collapse of the Late Bronze. The comparative study of such events entails creation of bigger teams than the team of a single person who created this volume. But there were smaller and less effective regional events that occurred between the bigger ones, affecting one of the regions and not entire continents. Collapses due to climatic reasons are short-term and ephemeral events. They can be effective for a decade and disappear thereafter, undocumented, leaving structural changes behind. It is not easy to single them out, and one should look for proxies in addition to the usually scarce historical data. Above, I pointed to the 'historical proxies' of climatic crises – sudden outbursts of nomads and violent behaviour of peaceful pastoralists on the sedentary lands, abrupt price-rises, lingering periods of freeze and of hunger, and lingering pestilences. These are all historical 'proxies' that should be thoroughly examined on the way to the reconstruction of history and culture in their more accurate natural setting.

# Index

CPSIA information can be obtained
at www.ICGtesting.com
Printed in the USA
LVHW050113290623
751002LV00005B/100

9 781107 688735